Sarah Smith

AVALON WORKING

AVALON WORKING

a landscape grimoire

Mark Nemglan

SCARLET IMPRINT · MMXXIV

The time is approaching when the Quest shall be renewed, and in a form that reflects present needs.

– Gareth Knight, *Merlin and the Grail Tradition*

Our knowledge becomes tangled in its thickets;
Our words lose their power.
Not steel, nor speech, nor blood
Can undo the fastness
Of the Old Magick
That girdles this Island
And lies upon it like a dawn mist.

Published by Scarlet Imprint. Edited by Peter Grey; designed and typeset by Alkistis Dimech; set in Haultin and Garda Nova III; cover concept, illustrations and photographs (except where indicated) by Mark Nemglan. The hardback and paperback were printed and bound in the United Kingdom by Gomer Press; the fine editions were bound by Ludlow Bookbinders.

ISBN 978-1-912316-91-5 (cloth) / ISBN 978-1-912316-88-5 (paper)

BM BOX 77777, LONDON WC1N 3XX
SCARLETIMPRINT.COM

contents

EXORDIUM xi

On Celtic and Other Traditions xiii
On Brythonic xiv
On the Avalonian Powers xiv
On the Magick of Avalon xv
On Dowsing xvi
On Sex and Gender xvi
On the Scope of this Work xvii
On Drug Consumption xix
On the Duration of the Quest xx

LIBER PRINCIPIA

I THE SUPERFICIES OF THE HOLY ISLAND 5

Summarium 7
limina 8 *the templum* 10 *the names of the holy island* 11 *the red spring and the white spring* 12 *the oaken path* 13 *the abbey and the hides* 13
Glastonbury, Avalon and New Age Eschatology 14

II THE NUMEN OF THE HOLY ISLAND 23

The Red and the White 23
The Springs and the Serpents 32
Intermissio: Sacred Directionality 35
The Gates of the Sun 41
Sky Lore 46
The Avalonian Otherworld 51
The Draoidhean 58

De Sororitas Avalonis 64
The Graal 67
The Vesica Piscis 71
Sovereignty and the Sacral Cycle 72
The Arthurian Archetypes 77
the artifex 79 *the servitor* 84
Intermissio: Magicko-Religious Continuity 87

III THE QUATERNITIES OF THE HOLY ISLAND 91

The Sorcerous Geographies 91
The Four Initiatory Queens 93
The Lineaments of the Ennead 94
the dark queen 98 *the pale queen* 99
the aureate queen 100 *the roseate queen* 101
The Four Graals of the Holy Island 102
The Four Bodies of the Quest 103

LIBER MYSTERIA

I THE OUTER PRECINCTS 111

Summarium 111
Intermissio: The Umbra Animae 114
Theoria 118
Parousia 122
Cultivating the Oculi Magicka 123
The Numen of the Outer Precincts 124
Acquiring Spirit Allies 128

II THE INNER PRECINCTS 133

Acquiring the Sacramentalia 133
The Sacrament of the Waters 135
The Sacra Via of the Oaken Path 137
The Rites of Adjuration 140

III THE TEMPLE AND THE ADYTUM 145

The Rites of Lustration 145
The Ophidian Rite 149
The Epiphanic Rites 154
Intermissio: Divinity and Duality 160
The Stations of the Sun 166
day 167 *sunset and dusk* 169 *night* 170 *dawn and sunrise* 173

IV THE GREAT QUEST 175

Consecration of the Graal Hypostasis 175
The First Station 177
Intermissio: The Sol Niger 182
The Second Station 185
The Third Station 189
The Fourth Station 194
The Great Synaxis 197
Post Sacra 205
frìth 206 *solstitial rites* 206 *imbas* 207 *discessus* 209

POSTSCRIBO 213

IN ELYSIUM

The Outer Precincts 220
The Inner Precincts 228
The Templum and the Adytum 252
The Avalonian Counterculture 264

Selected bibliography & further reading 269
Index 277

exordium

Glastonbury is a palimpsest, a verdant register whereon recensions of its mysteries have been inscribed for millennia. The wise acknowledge it as a living vessel; a blessed theandry; a convocation of myths, powers and sacred geographies. Since the Neolithic it has perhaps been revered as such: a ritual landscape, a stellar observatory and a place of otherness wherein profane feet were forbidden to tread. Once enclosed by estuarine waters on three sides and separated from the world-at-large by an apotropaic linear earthwork to the east, the source of the Holy Island's abiding sanctity is the congressum of three natural landscape features: the great terraced hill of the Tor, and two freshwater springs, one red and one white, which rise at its base. The vicissitudes of time have not weakened the island's renown. Rather, it has accreted myths, legends and folklore even while its denizens and pilgrims have waxed and waned. Its living traditions, nurtured and upheld by Glastonbury's adorants, are located at the tenebrous threshold of fact and belief. It is a place perhaps unique in the western world: a crucible of myth where the unfolding entelechy of its spiritous denizens is actively supported by a community of practitioners and pilgrims, co-creating reality through acts of becoming, drawing the unseen into the world of manifestation.

Its thousands of pilgrims and visitors attend, or are called to, the Holy Island for untold reasons: peace; healing; its mythic and folkloric allurements; its numinosity and pastoral *eudaimonia*. Many experience sensations of ecstasy, immanence, the growing awareness of an undefined presence, personal revelation, or a heightened aesthesis. Some are compelled to remain.

A few undergo an initiation of sorts; an unveiling or something approaching a profound spiritual crisis, journeying through a metaphorical Chapel Perilous often modestly referred to as the Glastonbury Experience. It can manifest as severe personal trauma, a sundering; disharmony and dissipation leading to spiritual breakdown and a total reconstitution of the self.[1]

There is no doubt that the Holy Island is a locus and fountainhead of extraordinary magickal power. It saturates the land and coagulates the very air. Yet the power is autotelic and veiled; its intent manifests in ways subtle and profound, but always exerting an influence on things within its purview. This presiding power is broadly identified as the Magna Mater, also colloquially known as the Angel of Avalon (an appropriate epithet given the mystery of Earth-as-angel in esoteric tradition.)[2] The Angel is a tutelary aspect of mighty Gaia who, as Protectrix of the Holy Island, is wont to castigate those whose praxis is misaligned with her own motives, or effect dramatic change on those she deems in need of transformation. There are also other powers at work.

To the magician this place is a realm of wonder and possibility, and also of risk: any magickal ambition must be undertaken respectfully, in conformity with the Island's greater will. Therefore, to bring about trust and concord, the postulant must first undergo an initiatory cycle whilst physically located upon the Holy Island. Its arcana can only be revealed *a posteriori*, as the process of initiation is one of personal transformation, a concrescence of self and the Avalonian powers.

This codex is subtitled 'a landscape grimoire' for one reason; the arcana of Glastonbury are rooted in the land, reified in its soil. The Holy Island is a book to be read and, in its reading, its phenomena are revealed as manifestations of concealed numen rooted in our oldest myths. The island entire is an embodied recension of mythic truths from the earliest epochs, its very purpose being a means to directly apprehend divinity. Thus, the goal of this text is two-fold: to elucidate the sorcerous landscape of the Holy Island through a specific magickal grammar, thereby unveiling its Inner Mysteries to the diligent practitioner; and to rehabilitate the Holy Island as Albion's preeminent magickal locus, a vessel of power where the *ichor* of the gods may be tasted, and the dutiful catechumen anointed with their gnosis.

1 See Taylor (2010) for a personal account of the call to Glastonbury.

2 Devereux, 94–5, 104.

¶ ON CELTIC AND OTHER TRADITIONS

Celtic culture is unquestionably at the heart of the Avalonian current, and as the wellspring of Arthurian lore, provides its richest set of precursors. Its associations with Brigid, the wheel of the year, Druidry and Celtic Christianity, have also become prominent aspects of Glastonbury's numinous character, along with veneration of the divine feminine – a trait commonly advanced as being consonant with Celtic religion. Furthermore, possessed of a pantheistic, animistic and metempsychotic worldview, Celtic myth recounts a vibrant and profound symbiosis between the phenomenal and unseen worlds, all of which yield fertile ground for praxis, and underpin the initiatory circuit of the Great Quest.

Yet the Avalonian current is not wholly Celtic. Rather it is multiple threads of sorcerous idioms; an eternal conjunction, fermentation and distillation of ideas. Alchemy plays an additionally significant role due to Merlin's status as the father of British hermeticism and the founder of Druidism. According to legend, alchemy both originated in Glastonbury and was a continuation of the religion of the Druids. The fundamental Avalonian motifs of polarised red and white powers can, on one hand, describe the spagyric conflict between red sulphur and white mercury. Yet they also reference the red and white cruets of Joseph of Arimathea and the red and white springs rising at the foot of the Tor. Glastonbury's preeminent status as the wellspring of British alchemy is confirmed in the activities of Abbot Dunstan and a subsequent discovery of what may have been the *ultima materia* by John Dee's scryer, Edward Kelley, within the grounds of the abbey. The consanguinity of lore relating to the *lapis exilis* and the Holy Graal is widely acknowledged.

Geomancy is a further thread, not least in relation to the ophidian telluric currents passing through the Holy Island. Egyptian tradition is another, along with Atlantis; its geographies and twin religions of ophiolatry and heliolatry are echoed in the sorcerous landscapes of Avalon. Others include Rosicrucianism and Theosophy; Thelema is yet another, along with aspects of esoteric Christianity. Therefore, one ambition of this work is to resolve these otherwise disparate threads and fashion a new braid of interweaving *terma*.

¶ ON BRYTHONIC

The magickal use of barbarous names is well-attested. Words with seemingly no meaning, when spoken in ritual, enable the interlocutor to modify understanding beyond the noetic and epistemic. Pure sound and rhythm devoid of normal comprehension stimulate intuition and imagination, and endows barbarous names with magickal power.

The work contained herein employs Brythonic in a similar context. As a language it is essentially moribund, a long-dead ancestor to Celtic offshoots such as Welsh, Cornish and Breton, and is understood only in fragmentary ways, though attempted reconstructions are ongoing. Yet in magickal terms, there is power in a forgotten, archaic language when it is spoken. When put to use it differs from ordinary, everyday speech by dissociating the speaker from normal conventions. Instead it forms a vinculum to a particular time, place or current, and arouses the attention of specific deities. As Crowley observed, 'The most potent conjurations are those in an ancient and perhaps forgotten language.'[3] Given that Celtic traditions form a significant part of the Avalonian current, spoken Brythonic is an appropriate tool for calling the spiritual atavisms of the Holy Island. The catechumen need not understand the meaning of the words spoken in order for their potency to reverberate throughout the realms. Focussing instead on the inherent strangeness of the words when formed and vocalised, on their special rhythmic qualities, is key; as such, they may be delivered in the traditional vibratory register.

However, the reconstructed phrases documented in this work do have meaning relevant to their context; the words will be comprehended by the powers to whom they are addressed, and their effects will be felt.

¶ ON THE AVALONIAN POWERS

One objective of this work is to revive a concept rooted in antiquity: that initiation into the Mysteries occurs at specific geographic locations; places of sanctuary or mythic import. Glastonbury is already a renowned focus of pilgrimage. Yet it is as much a centre of initiation as Samothrace, Eleusis, Thebes, Lemnos or Andania once were. This text aims to elucidate why this is the case,

3 Crowley & Skinner, 68.

and provide a sequence of initiatory rituals homothetic to the Island's divine telos.

The presiding deities of the Holy Island are the ennead – the nine-who-are-one. They are recensions of antediluvian powers associated with creation, healing, prophesy and fertility. From their first primordial emergence, this sorority has evolved in concert with humanity, even while their fundamental nature has remained undiminished. The numinous qualities of the Holy Island can be largely attributed to this ongoing exchange between spirit, nature and man, which has ebbed and flowed according to the vicissitudes of time. A putative highpoint in this chain of theandry is the era of Celtic culture. Yet the modern resurgence from the early twentieth century onwards is notable.

The sapient reader will acknowledge the aeonial nature of these deities. In conformity with certain traditions, only the titles of certain of the ennead are provided. Their true names may be revealed in time to the fortunate devotee.

¶ ON THE MAGICK OF AVALON

The author can attest to the potency and efficacy of magick enacted on the Holy Island. When done in tandem with an acknowledgement of its sanctity, even minor acts yield tangible outcomes, which is unquestionably a consequence of its status as a wellspring of deity, a nexus of power, a terrestrial otherworld, and a place of mythopoetic emergence.

That Glastonbury is a haunted island, populous with spirits, is evinced by certain responses to the magician's directed will. The land's embodied sentience, an uncanny but persistent presence swiftly acknowledged by the receptive catechumen, will react in ways surprising but unequivocal, and not always benign. Its government, by a spiritous hierarchy wherein the Magna Mater is sovereign, is eternally watchful for extraneous, unfamiliar forces that may threaten its homeostasis. For in truth the Goddess does not merely oversee the Island, she is the Island; not transcendent but wholly immanent. To provide one example, on a cool September evening when mist began to gather around the precincts of the Tor, a fully manifested but phantasmal horse, formed from the pale brume, emerged unbidden and approached the author before quickly fading into the twilight.

When acting in conformity, the Island rewards directness, purity of intent and sincerity above verbosity. The magick of Avalon is atavistic, not refined.

It is broadly intuitive, unstructured, creative, libertarian, ecstatic and equitable. It does not distinguish between ceremonial or folk magick; paganism or witchcraft; Wicca or shamanism, which are false distinctions. It is not sacerdotal, having no need of any form of mediating priesthood. This is reflected in the lineaments of the rites and ceremonies contained herein, which conform to the dictum 'simple magick in powerful places.'

¶ ON DOWSING

Dowsing appears to be an under-utilised divinatory tool in contemporary occultism, yet its application and efficacy are undeniable. Unlike other prognosticatory methods, dowsing provides a binary response to questions, requires little knowledge or prior experience and, with some practice, quickly gives rise to a reliable level of competency. Further, it attunes the operant to the 'spirit of place' and to the subtle etheric and terrestrial energies of the land. The geomantic nature of the initiatory cycle therefore benefits from a working knowledge of dowsing, and its virtues are strongly commended to the pilgrim.

¶ ON SEX AND GENDER

Cosmogonic myths frequently describe the bifurcating and sexing of divinity into two polarised powers. Through their union, the cosmos is birthed. Magick explores the manipulation of those polarised powers across manifold mythologies, cosmologies and modalities, in which further binary, but not necessarily sexed, division takes place. However, issues arise when this semiosis of opposites is bent out of shape, and false inferences are made. Take for example this syllogism: if the physical world is female (Gaia, Terra Mater) and the physical world is evil (as espoused in the fallen world doctrine), then all females are evil. These and other flaws of binary thinking, especially in the context of a magicko-mythical semiotic framework, are discussed later.

In relation to the Avalonian current, which is concerned with the union of opposites, certain powers and deities are necessarily sexed (examples include the Michael and Mary ley lines and the red and white springs.) Terms such as 'mother' and 'father' are also employed, in order to remain consonant with the ancestry and traditions from which they derive, and to maintain the complex interwoven correspondences. One reason for the Avalonian current emerging from a broadly Celtic tradition is the supposed Celtic bias towards matrifocal theologies, which provides an antidote to established patriarchal systems of orthodoxy. Whether fictive or not, the position has become canonical in pagan belief. In 1898 Dr John Goodchild authored *The Light of the West*, a treatise on the matrifocal nature of Celtic society and its original veneration of a Great Goddess. He proposed that the sacred feminine was central to Celtic theology, overseen by an euhemerised Mórrígan in the role of cult leader. Monica Sjöö and Barbara Mor similarly argued that Celtic society inherited the legacy of Neolithic matriarchal theologies, including a deity who may or may not be cognate with Robert Graves's White Goddess, or even the Mother Goddess of Wicca. Evidence suggests that Celtic culture afforded women greater freedoms than some contemporary equivalents. While the office of monarch or chieftan was often male, the pseudo-historical figures of Boudica and Cartimandua, and various high-status burials, suggest this was not exclusively the case. History and myth attest to the existence of female Druids who, by extension, fulfilled the role of healer, priestess, advisor, leader and augur.

The initiatory cycle contained herein requires the catechumen to assume the role of solar hypostasis. Although this relates to traditions of sacral rule, it also alludes to certain aspects of shamanic practice. Furthermore, not all monarchs were male, not all sovereignty goddesses are female, and not all mythologies sexed the sun as a masculine power. By the same token, the cycle's initiatory rites are not gender dependent. They do not involve sexual acts and are wholly accessible to all. Indeed, dualities are not immutable principles but complementary forces that transmute into one another. The power of mutability, of the threshold, the intersection and the nonconformist or mercurial state, is fundamental to the Great Quest. The body of the initiand is acknowledged as a retinue of co-located beings existing literally and figuratively, simultaneously between and beyond individual biology and anatomy.

¶ ON THE SCOPE OF THIS WORK

The mythopoetic process at work upon the Isle of Avalon is evidence of its status as a magickal verendum, and the corpus of research, insight and recorded practice concerning Avalonian phenomena is vast. The focus of this work is specifically the Holy Island and the Tor Temple, the latter being the preeminent locus of power and sanctity. Consequently, certain aspects of the Holy Island's arcana must be precluded – primarily those concerned with large-scale landscape modification and geomantic engineering – although this should not be interpreted as a dismissal of them. Three features of the Avalonian landscape beyond this book's ambit include:

- The Glastonbury Zodiac, the gigantic subastral wheel, 30 miles in circumference, writ upon the landscape to the southwest of Glastonbury, has stimulated the imagination since Katherine Maltwood's unveiling of the Temple of the Stars. Countless denizens have traversed its houses in pilgrimage or quest, or identified myriad correspondences, symbols, alignments and orientations to confirm its veracity. Yet its very existence has proven divisive, not least because the Somerset Levels upon which it is located were flooded at the time of its supposed creation in the third century BCE. Nevertheless, the odds of its existence being a result of chance patterns has been estimated at 149,000,000 to one against.[4] Others have observed that the zodiacal constellations fit over their earthly counterparts, and its figures have been designed in proportion to each other. Those with an interest in the subject are encouraged to research further, and consider its relationship to the Holy Island and other aspects of the surrounding landscapes.

- Since Frederick Bligh Bond first employed unorthodox techniques such as channeling, geomancy and gematria to discern the secrets of Glastonbury Abbey, its mysteries have been ceaselessly researched and studied. Geomancers such as John Michell and Nigel Pennick have documented its significant alignments, orientations, metrology, and sacred geometry. Michell in particular has proposed a perennial philosophy at work behind the proportions of St Mary's chapel, wherein the renowned wattle church was located, such that a common cosmological pattern can be applied to other far earlier sites including Stonehenge. Regardless of the powers at work behind its construction, or the esoteric knowledge employed by its builders, the abbey remains a later addition to the Holy Island's ritual landscape, which has forever shown fealty to a singular temple free of artifice and in harmony with the land: the Holy Hill of the Tor.

4 Roberts (1992), 21.

- The Tor labyrinth as proposed by Geoffrey Russell is a ceremonial labyrinth in the classical Cretan style, conforming to the seven levels of visible terracing and describing an ascending, winding route towards the Tor's summit. Reckoned to be coeval with the terraces' creation – potentially during the Neolithic – one purpose of the labyrinth is thought to be ceremonial or ritual, to evoke or invoke the spiralling telluric powers beneath the Holy Hill, and to come into harmony with its morphic aura. The noumenon of the Tor labyrinth is debated, yet it has become largely accepted as canon. Its exclusion from this work is simply a matter of pragmatism; traversing the labyrinth takes several hours and is not a prerequisite for the Great Quest. However, the pilgrim should feel free to wander the Tor's terraces in pursuit of labyrinthine wisdom.

¶ ON DRUG CONSUMPTION

Given that one goal of magick is the attainment of transpersonal states of consciousness, its propinquity with drug use is unsurprising. The history of the occult is the history of applied drug use – primarily, although not exclusively, entheogens – to provoke exstasis and theandry in the operant; to tear the veil asunder and apprehend realms and entities beyond the mundane; to transcend the fleshy sensorium; to acquire gnosis and, through experimentation, confirm their veridical nature. It spans the technologies of otherworldly ingress developed by the earliest shamans, to the ecstatic warrior rituals of the *úlfhéðnar*; from the flight to the witches' sabbat, to the initiatory rites of Eleusis and Dionysus; from the Vedic *soma* of the gods to consumption of the 'red flesh' of the fly agaric by Irish Celtic poets to achieve visionary inspiration. Crowley advocated consumption of certain drugs prior to magickal ceremonies because they assisted access to mystical experiences and induced reproducible moments of revelation. Yet he was unable to evade their obvious risks; for much of the latter half of his life, drugs haunted and enslaved him.[5]

Given Glastonbury's status as both an otherworldly refugium and countercultural mecca, drug consumption is intimately intertwined with its *natura loci*. For better or worse, it has become rooted in aspects of the alternative community's cultural ideology. However, because of the Holy Island's inherent

5 See Partridge.

numinosity, their effects will vary from anticipated norms when consumed upon it; some will be suppressed, others heightened. Certain of its spiritous denizens will tolerate the intoxicated pilgrim; others will regard them as an abomination. Therefore, care should be taken with any eliding of drug use with the Great Quest's praxis. They should not interfere with the required level of ascesis or ability to perform rituals in a disciplined, attuned manner. Nor should they profane the Avalonian *prohairesis*; at all times, the pilgrim must respect the sanctity of the Island. Therefore, it is recommended that consumption be restricted to acts of wayfaring, or when at repose in nature. Minimally processed native plants and fungi are preferable, along with those assisting in the attainment of meditative or transcendent states. While useful for securing brief moments of revelation, they should not become an option of first resort. Neither should the subtly psychedelic Avalonian atmosphere be ignored or underestimated.

¶ ON THE DURATION OF THE QUEST

The Great Quest is a physical circumambulation of the Holy Island's eldritch geographies. It is also a visionary descent into, and return from, the psychic soil of Avalon; an engagement with its invisible, otherworldly and chthonic domains. It is an alchemical drama where the *opus alchymicum* is acted out upon the *prima materia* of the self. It is a directed exploration of the Avalonian aetiology, whose mythic symbols are fundamental to any mystical apprehension of this place. And it is a means to enter into communion with the spiritual intelligences who preside over the Holy Island, who actively seek to bring the dedicated catechumen into the precincts of Magistery.

The duration of a single initiatory circuit is dependent on the one who undertakes it. It has been completed in a single intensive week; it could be conducted over a year, interpolating its ritual activities with the waxing and waning of the seasons, the passage of the Sun across the ecliptic and its chief Gates, and the transit of other ouranian bodies. Yet the cycle should be oft repeated, to renew and deepen the bonds and covenants made. Although its effects are immediate and profound, in truth the Great Quest is a perennial undertaking of initiatory circuits, each drawing the catechumen closer to an apprehension of the Holy Island's mysteries, embodied in the Graal.

LIBER PRINCIPIA

Mystery stirs this domain of quiet liberty.
And I understand that the Island has her own proud purpose.
She does not bend to any thing
Except Time and Tide
And her own private devotions.

The Land enchants itself
With its own choirs.
The Oak listens;
The Ash listens.

Here is the myth that led to this:
That the King and the Land were one.

Here is its legacy,
Preserved in our souls' nameless yearning.

the superficies of the holy island

As a place of emergence, Glastonbury's mythopoeia is forever evolving and coming into being. The founding of its abbey perhaps formally established this mythopoetic process. In the early twelfth century, William of Malmesbury authored its history and alluded to its great antiquity, implying its foundation by the disciples of Christ (this later evolved into the legend of Joseph of Arimathea establishing England's first church on the site of the abbey in approximately 63 CE.) In 1191 the purported discovery of a tomb containing two skeletons and a lead cross bearing the legend *hic jacet sepultus inclitus rex Arturius in insula Avalonia* ('here lies interred the famous King Arthur on the Isle of Avalon') initiated an enduring association of Glastonbury with Arthurian legend, even though the tomb's authenticity can be dismissed as a cynical ruse to attract pilgrims and revenue. Nevertheless, the associations persisted and evolved, and further embellishments were promulgated by medieval historians such as Geoffrey of Monmouth, who wove Glastonbury more deeply into Arthurian tradition. These alligations continued into the 1500s, drawing the attentions of sorcerer, astrologer and alchemist John Dee and his scryer Edward Kelley. Throughout the sixteenth and seventeenth century the renowned Glastonbury Thorn became a locus of conflict between two opposing camps: those of the Protestant reformation and the popular folk beliefs of the general public, contesting the very notions of sacralised landscapes, relics and supernatural agency.

In the early twentieth century Glastonbury entered a Golden Age. The writer and feminist Alice Mary Buckton purchased Chalice Well. Dion Fortune, occultist, Theosophist and founder of the Fraternity of the Inner Light, discerned through visionary means the profoundly atavistic powers at work upon the Holy Island. There, she received the text for her seminal work *The Cosmic Doctrine*, and engaged in ongoing magickal congress with powers in the vicinity of the Tor. Coeval with Fortune's praxis another occultist, Katherine Maltwood, unveiled the details of a gigantic terrestrial zodiac – the so-called Temple of the Stars – embedded in the landscape surrounding Glastonbury. The archaeologist Frederick Bligh Bond employed psychic techniques to guide his excavations of the abbey, leading to an assertion that its dimensions were based on sophisticated gematria. And the novelist John Cowper Powys published *A Glastonbury Romance*, which brought Avalonian themes into the wider public purview.

By the 1960s and 70s, and following the establishment of the renowned festival of performing arts at nearby Pilton, Glastonbury became a focal-point for the nascent New Age movement, attracting a riotous countercultural mix of hippies, mystics, activists, spirituals, freaks, drop-outs, environmentalists, acid casualties, travellers and occultists, all pursuing their own highly individualised spiritual quests but homothetically drawn to the Holy Island's uncanny anthroposophy. Alison Collyer founded Greenlands Farm (now Paddington Farm)[1] in the nearby hamlet of Wick, which became a sanctuary for numerous pilgrims. Meanwhile, the notable esotericist and earth mysteries proponent John Michell successfully wove the many braids of Avalonian lore into a coherent whole, further securing Glastonbury's status.

By the 1980s Glastonbury was suffering economic decline through the collapse of traditional farming and craft practices, and of local industry. In parallel, a convoy of New Age travellers known as the Rainbow Village – evictees from the proposed cruise missile site at Molesworth, Cambridgeshire, and survivors of the infamous Battle of the Beanfield – descended on Greenlands Farm and set up an informal camp. The Village's occupants were ultimately expelled, but a number remained in the town and settled cheek-by-jowl with preexisting members of earlier utopian generations, and established Somerset families. These uneasy alliances coalesced around an evolving Glastonbury community in support of their heterodox lifestyles. And as the Glastonbury Festival grew in scale and reputation, many residents of the town began to rely upon it for regular, seasonal employment.

1 See Taylor (2010), 53; and Garrard (1986).

As early as the 1970s, certain commentators were critiquing Glastonbury's new hierarchies for peddling fake spirituality, where the 'eternal dream' of Avalon was being betrayed, packaged, monopolised and sold.[2] Today, it exists at a crossroads. On one path, the Holy Island remains an omphalos for myriad practitioners, seekers and free thinkers; from tarot readers and healers, disciples of every form of eastern spirituality and New Age religion, to Wiccans, Druids, traditional witches, pagans, heathens, Goddess devotees and ceremonial magicians. On the other, Glastonbury's living heritage and tradition is wantonly commercialised and exploited such that it risks becoming a crass parody of its true self. Its insular subculture of self-styled Glastonians or Glastafarians reflect this dichotomy; some are sincere and devoted in their spirituality, while others embody the worst aspects of New Age culture, commoditising and trivialising the sacred. Even though the Holy Island will always prevail as a sacred unicum, let this creeping apostasy serve as a warning: capitalism is a wily foe, dressed in sheep's clothing but inwardly a ravenous and pitiless wolf.

¶ SUMMARIUM

The Holy Island, known in this era as Glastonbury, has not always been an island in recent geological time. It was instead a peninsula, linked to higher ground by an isthmus to the east. However, from the west Glastonbury would have appeared as an island, with water on three sides. Modern day rhynes (drainage ditches) bring some respite from flooding, but historically marine inundations at high tide encroached from the Bristol Channel to the shores of Glastonbury. Running north-south, a much wider River Brue would have further contributed to flooding of the surrounding marshy wetlands.

Despite, or because of, the presence of the mighty Tor and a number of freshwater springs, the island is notable for its lack of prehistoric settlement. Mesolithic flint tools have been excavated near Chalice Well, and finds from the Tor include flint from the Upper Paleolithic, along with a Neolithic polished axe of greenish stone. But otherwise there is little evidence of human occupation compared to the surrounding area. The places where settlements did gain a foothold lie further west, towards the islands of Meare and Westhay.

2 Roberts (1992), 12.

Here, Neolithic wooden trackways crossed the Levels, linking those wetland islands to the higher ground of a larger peninsula, which reached as far as modern-day Puriton. These wooden tracks included the well-known Sweet Track.

In the Iron Age, two lake villages were established at Meare and to the west of Glastonbury. The latter settlement, located in swampland, was likely permanently settled until the first century BCE and housed roughly one hundred people.

limina

The paucity of early settlement evidence at Glastonbury may be explained by the existence of *Pontis Vallum* or Ponter's Ball, a 1000 metre-long bank and ditch earthwork up to 10m wide and 3.5 metres high, running approximately north-south across a neck of higher ground, the only land-based route onto the Glastonbury peninsula. Based on pottery finds it may date to the Iron Age, although this is inconclusive.[3] The bank lies to the west of the ditch, suggesting a defensive structure. But an absence of any indicative archaeology, and the lack of any substantial community to the west, renders this pointless. It may therefore have functioned as a symbolic boundary, demarcating the threshold of the Holy Island; a temenos or *cordon sanitaire* defending against unwanted and potentially dangerous physical and spiritual incursions from beyond its borders.

There is further evidence to support Glastonbury's status as a place of ancient sanctity. Excavations at Chalice Well in 1961 revealed flints and Roman pottery, and the stump of a Roman-era yew tree (radiocarbon-dated to around 300 CE), implying magicko-religious significance; a grove of yews still grows by a Roman temple site at Pagan's Hill, to the north of Mendip. And upon the Tor, excavations of a fifth to seventh century settlement revealed Mediterranean amphorae, animal bones, a bronze mask fashioned in an elongated Celtic style, and two human inhumations oriented north-south; their sex has not been determined, but they were both aged under twenty. It has been proposed that this settlement could be of a Celtic Christian or pagan religious

3 Ratz & Watts, 30.

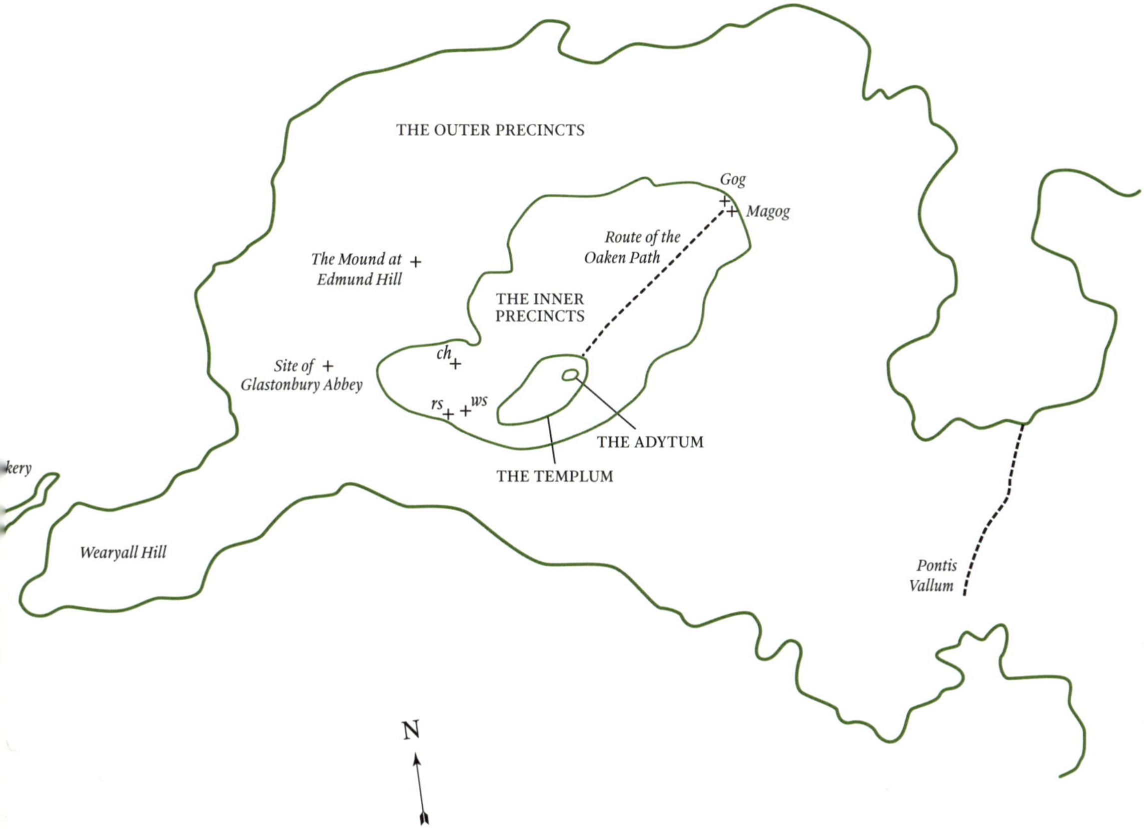

ch Chalice Well
rs Red Spring
ws White Spring

figure 1 The Outer and Inner Precincts of the Holy Island.

type, possibly a Romano-British hilltop shrine.[4] The area around Glastonbury remained under the control of British tribes until the mid-sixth century CE. And despite the official conversion of Rome to Christianity under Emperor Constantine in 313 CE, the new imperial religion made only limited inroads into Albion. This is inferred from apparent ongoing pagan mortuary practices throughout the period, the evidence of persistent paganism in material culture, and the likelihood that Britain escaped the decree of Emperor Theodosius in 391 CE banning the practice of paganism. In reality, Britain was likely a patchwork of heterogeneous traditions, beliefs and practices, many of a highly localised nature.

the templum

The Tor itself is one of the most prominent hills in the area, visible for up to 25 miles in any direction and rising to a height of over 150 metres. Yet it is one of four hills upon the Holy Island, the others being: Wearyall and Chalice Hill to the west, and Edmund or Windmill Hill to the northwest.

Aside from the ruined tower of the church of St Michael, the most prominent feature of the Tor is its terracing, consisting of seven visible tiers. Of the more mundane explanations for this phenomenon, one proposes the terraces are evidence of natural erosion across alternating layers of stone and clay; another that they are medieval plough platforms known as strip lynchets (although a drawing of the Tor from 1670 depicts agriculture occurring only on the lower slopes of the Tor, where orchards exist today.) A further theory, put forward by Geoffrey Russell in the 1960s, suggests the terraces describe a three-dimensional maze, based on the classical Cretan labyrinth, or the *caerdroia* – the Welsh turf maze. A theory deemed feasible by Historic England proposes the initial natural erosion of the hill led to further deliberate modification, beginning in the Neolithic period.

An egg-shaped Tor burr, formed by the natural erosion of sandstone, is located to the south of the hill; another can be found within the grounds of Glastonbury Abbey (likely at one point removed from the Tor), leading to speculation that these were employed as *omphaloi*, cult-stones marking the centre-point or navel of a sacred landscape. At one time they were plentiful

4 Ibid., 71–78.

and used in building construction.[5]

The Tor and its surrounding precincts conform to the topographies of Druidic sanctuaries and Celtic cult centres. There is further congruence with the arrangement of so-called shamanic and ritual or ceremonial landscapes, legendary earthly paradises and otherworldy geographies; particularly those incorporating a central sanctuary atop a hill or mountain. One example curiously analogous to the Tor complex is the contested megalithic site at Gunung Padang in Western Java, Indonesia.[6] The site covers a hill in a series of man-made earthen terraces bordered by retaining walls of basalt. The holy hill is associated with a Javanese sovereignty goddess who, in myth, is linked to the star Vega. Circa 11–13,000 BCE, Vega occupied the position of the pole star, around which the cosmos rotates, thus elevating the goddess to a primeval stellar deity, and establishing Gunung Padang as an omphalos and axis mundi.[7] Notably, at least one chamber is thought to be located below the hill's central axis. And an ancient spring at its base is positioned 360 ft from its peak – an elevation comparable to the rising points of Glastonbury's red and white springs in relation to the Tor's summit.

the names of the holy island

Of Glastonbury's many names, Avalon provides the clearest link to its otherwordly status. In his twelfth century *Historia regum Britanniae*, Geoffrey of Monmouth applies the term *Insula Avallonis* and later *Insula pomorum*, the isle of fruit trees. He describes this fortunate isle as a place where 'nine sisters rule by a pleasing set of laws.' Later, Thomas Malory declared these nine sisters to be sorcerers, 'ladies who know all the magic in the world.' It is they who forged the sword Excalibur and escorted the mortally wounded Arthur to Avalon, his final resting place, to tend his body. An alternative etymology of Avalon combines the Brittonic world *aβall* meaning 'apple tree' with *onn* meaning 'stone,' suggesting a perception of Glastonbury as an axis mundi or omphalos.[8]

5 Bond (1914), 64–73.

6 See Natawidjaja for details of the original research. See Sulistyowati for the controversies surrounding the site.

7 Observations made by Andrew Collins as part of the lecture, 'Gunung Padang and Lost Cultures from the Last Ice Age.'

8 Bond (1914), 64–73.

Glastonbury's earliest name, according to William of Malmesbury, is the Gaelic or British *Ynys Witrin. Ynys* means 'island' and *Witrin*, equated with the Latin *vitreus*, means 'glass.' Gerald of Wales declared that the Welsh name for Glastonbury is *Ynys Afallach*, which means the Island of Apples and may be derived from the Irish *Emhain Abhlach*, an island paradise in Irish myth. The Middle Welsh poem the *Book of Taliesin* refers to several otherworldly fortresses including *Caer Wydyr*, the glass castle, which is reminiscent of the Island of Glass. *Caer Ochren* is another, which translates as the castle of the 'angular or shelving sides' and recalls the stepped terraces of the Tor. Glastonbury's Saxon name was *Glæstyngabyrig* or *Glestingaburg*. The *Glestinga* element is likely derived from an Irish personal name, although a variant Glastingebury is derived from the epithet 'Island of Glass.' The twelfth century *Life of Gildas* by Caradoc of Llancarfan refers to Glastonbury as Glastonia and the Summer Country; the domain of King Melwas who, according to legend, abducted Queen Guinevere, wife of Arthur.

the red spring and the white spring

At least seven natural freshwater springs of various magnitude surround the Tor. Five have been capped or diminished unto cessation. Its two remaining, most vigorous and venerated, rise at the foot of the Holy Hill to the west. The Red Spring is a chalybeate spring and famously yields some 19 to 25,000 gallons of water per day at a consistent temperature of 11 degrees. It is often claimed that the waters have never failed, even in drought. In common with many wells and springs, the water is mildly radioactive. High levels of iron oxide impart a reddish hue, leading some commentators to suggest that its source is an iron-rich area of the Mendip Hills. Others have reasonably concluded it originates in an aquifer within the Tor, fed by rainwater, the lower part of which is saturated with iron. The Red Spring is understood as feminine, its red hue representing menstrual blood.

The White Spring is masculine, its calcium-rich waters representative of seminal fluid. It rises a few metres further south, fed by a shallower aquifer within the Tor, situated above the iron-rich layer, and is therefore more responsive to fluctuations in rainfall. In turn its rate of flow varies from 4,500 to over 70,000 gallons of water per day. Prior to the erection of a pump house in 1872, the spring emerged from a cave system beneath the Tor and flowed through a series of lime-encrusted dropping-wells. The top of the Tor aquifer is thought to lie around 30m below the hill's summit, to a depth of roughly 100 metres.[9]

the oaken path

To the northeast of the Tor lie Gog and Magog, the last male and female vestiges of a grove of ancient oaks. These 'Avalon Oaks' are believed to have originally formed a ceremonial avenue from the modern hamlet of Wick, following the contours of Stone Down Hill, towards the Tor. The oaks were cut down in 1906 to make way for a farm. One tree measured over three metres in diameter, with a circumference of more than ten metres. Its seasonal growth rings suggested an age of at least 1,000 years. Of the two extant oaks, only Magog remains alive.

the abbey and the hides

Glastonbury Abbey is reputedly the site of England's first church, the Vetusta Ecclesia, and, according to legend, was established by Joseph of Arimathea in approximately 63 CE. After the last of Joseph's companions died, the wattle church became wild and overgrown until it was restored by the missionaries Phaganus and Deruvianus, dispatched from Rome by Pope Eleutherius in 166 CE. The site was further preserved by Celtic monks who established a monastery around the old church. St Patrick reputedly arrived at Glastonbury in the fifth century and organised the hermit-monks, followed by St David and St Brigit. King Ine of Wessex refounded and rebuilt the monastery, which grew in prestige under abbot Dunstan from c.940 CE. Although unlikely to be the burial-place of Arthur and Guinevere, a claim largely debunked, more probable internments include the saints Patrick, Dunstan and, temporarily, Aidan and Paulanus.

The abbey's landholdings included the so-called Twelve Hides. A hide was much like an Anglo-Saxon hundred, an area of land large enough to sustain a single household. The Twelve Hides were islands, now visible as small hills

9 See Mann and Glasson (2010).

rising from the relatively flat terrain of the Levels. The fourteenth century *Chronica* of John of Glastonbury suggests that the Twelve Hides were identified as the location of the hermitages of the twelve disciples of the apostles St Phillip and St James, who have been credited with the construction of the first church at Glastonbury. In support of this, the tenth century Charter of King Edgar suggests that each of these twelve 'holy islands' possessed a chapel. Of the Twelve Hides, the principal holdings included the islands of Beckery, Godney, Martinsey, Andersey, Westhay, Meare and Panborough. These seven islands were elevated to a special status, each exempted from normal jurisdiction. Along with the Holy Island itself, the charter names them as 'Bekaria quae parva Hibernia dicitur, Godenia, Marteneseia, Ferramere, Padenaberga, et Andredeseia.' The eldritch significance of these islands, as asserted by John Michell, is revealed in their sacred geography.[10] Their configuration approximates the constellation of Ursa Major, or Arthur's Wain. This stellar landscape describes a form of geomancy, at once honouring the celestial correspondences with the once-and-future king, while drawing down his blessings to fructify and enchant the land.

Beckery, to the northwest of Wearyall Hill, was one of the daughter-houses of the abbey and included a small Anglo-Saxon monastery. Traditions from the twelfth century record a visit to the monastery by St Brigid in 488 CE, and an oratory dedicated to Mary Magdalene. A thirteenth century reference to Beckery notes that repairs were made to the chapel in honour of St Brigid, which may have been rededicated following her visit. A hole in the southern part of the building, if passed through, was thought to grant absolution from sin. The monastery has been associated with the Chapel Perilous of Arthurian tradition.

¶ GLASTONBURY, AVALON & NEW AGE ESCHATOLOGY

By virtue of its uniquely luminary afflatus, Glastonbury has drawn to its bosom those for who the spiritual and metaphysical are preeminent concerns. Through the influx of like-minded groups and individuals, in the last half-century in particular, the town has become inextricably associated with the rise of alternative, non-mainstream, spirit-led lifestyles. This broad cultural ideology, a development of the countercultural 1960s, is widely termed the

10 Michell (1990), 9–18.

New Age movement, being rooted in the prophetic belief of an imminent or unfolding new age. Predicated on a stellar shift in zodiacal constellations, or an orthogenetic apocalypse presaging an evolution of consciousness, its global consequences are assumed to include a dismantling of incumbent political, religious and socio-economic systems otherwise perceived as unenlightened at best or, at worst, antagonistic to the human spirit. Whether the threshold has yet been crossed is dependent on the beliefs of its adherents, given that the New Age may refer to: the Age of Aquarius, the Aeon of Horus, the Omega Point of 1984, the Harmonic Convergence of 1987, the 2012 phenomenon, or another event yet to pass, such as the awakening and return of King Arthur. Regardless, these eschatological preoccupations are central to the Avalonian dialectic and to the town's identity, which is entwined with the fulfilment of a national and global destiny.

In conformity with general definitions of the New Age movement, Glastonbury's alternative communities have been characterised as comprising a bricolage of spiritualism, self-development, holistic medicine, alternative therapies and environmentalism, all marshalled in the pursuit of ultimately liberating the higher, inner self. Because of this admixture, the community has developed its own rules and modes of behaviour existing apart from, and sometimes in opposition to, the pre-existing cultures of mainstream society.[11] For example, unorthodox attitudes to personal wellness, coupled with the practice of holistic medicine and alternative therapies, and a mistrust of 'big pharma', have yielded fault lines in the community, particularly in relation to programmes of mass vaccination.[12]

Glastonbury's high crime-rate cannot be ignored. For complex reasons, in part at least related to its countercultural and individualist lifestyles, in 2023 Glastonbury enjoyed the dubious status of the most dangerous small town in Somerset, being 67% more dangerous than the county's average. Violence and sexual offences were the most common crimes.[13]

An anthropological study of the Glastonbury community, conducted in the 1990s, observed certain demic tropes, despite its cultural and ethnic diversity, and heterogenous nature. As might be expected, a rejection of capitalism

11 This is an attempted synopsis of Prince's anthropological study, which is highly recommended. Some sentences may include verbatim excerpts from the source text.

12 See https://normalforglastonbury.uk/nearly-normal-in-glastonbury/

13 See https://crimerate.co.uk/somerset/glastonbury

and consumerism is commonplace. This distrust of conventional society and mainstream economic life has resulted in a more informal economy characterised by a lack of commercialisation and objectives beyond mere utility or profit. However, in recent years, entrepreneurialism coupled with so-called prosperity consciousness, and the rise of monied middle class incomers, has shifted this position.[14]

Spirituality is of utmost importance, along with the freedom to forge a lifestyle in which spiritual beliefs are reflected in all parts of life. Green consciousness is part of the spiritual communitas, being aligned with broadly pre-Christian, alternative Christian, indigenous, pagan, Wiccan, animistic or shamanistic worldviews. In particular, Celtic spirituality is celebrated through its associations with Brigid, Arthurian and Graal mythology, seasonal rites expressed in the eight-fold wheel of the year, Druidry and Celtic Christianity, certain sacred geographies, and a set of alleged matrifocal theologies. An overt veneration of the divine feminine is a related component, forming a direct response to what is perceived as a male-dominated orthodox and institutionalised spiritual hierarchy. Indeed, Avalon itself is often described in terms of a female identity, whether colloquially or in relation to the presiding spirit of place: the Goddess. The town is additionally regarded as the spiritual omphalos of Britain, itself a sacred enclosure since antiquity; an *insula sacra* of the west and the 'Egypt of the Occident.'[15]

An individualist ethos places emphasis upon the self and self-responsibility. The health of the whole person is a primary consideration, and health is associated with spiritual attunement. This is a fundamental insight into the Avalonian mindset, given that the immediate locale is widely regarded as sacred, mythologically resonant, initiatory, and a nexus of healing. The Holy Island is a place where veils are thin and beneficent energies are manifested, concentrated and made accessible. Thus, as a locus of vivifying power, Glastonbury is understood to work in concert with the individual to develop the wellbeing of the self as part of its spiritual evolution. As Jung and his cohorts have noted, a community connected to a mythic life-story enjoys psychological wellbeing; through a shared language of mythic symbolism, life is endowed with meaning, thereby leavening the existential predicaments of the individual.[16]

14 See also Garrard (2014) for a history of Glastonbury's alternative communities.

15 Spence, 17.

16 Jung (1964), part 2.

One extreme conclusion of self-determining holism manifested in Glastonbury is the strain of New Age practice concerned with the attainment of physical immortality. Its localised variant posits a complex geomythology rooted in Avalonian philosophy. According to writer Robert Coon, the telluric currents identified as the Michael and Mary ley lines, which pass through the town, are segments of a greater energy path encircling the earth, formed by a female rainbow serpent and a male winged feathered serpent. in 1984, at Easter sunrise, 'the descent of the Solar Logos into the body of the earth upon the summit of Glastonbury Tor' signaled an Omega Point, an orthogenetic alchemy prompting a revolutionary stirring of humanity in general, and a revival of Albion's true spirit in particular. Glastonbury is the British locus of this revelation, the global heart chakra within a planetary system of energy lines and terrestrial meridians. This fountainhead of *potentia* is cognate with the Graal and the philosopher's stone which, according to tradition, imparts immortality to those who attain it. A lineage of immortal ascended beings including Enoch, Melchizedek and Merlin act as Graal guardians and gatekeepers of its secrets. In practical terms, the attainment of physical immortality is a function of spiritual discipline, practice and enlightened engagement with the Glastonbury landscape.[17] Physical health is determined by spiritual health which, in turn, is granted via congress with the beneficent energies of the Holy Island. Thus, in Avalonian terms, death is not an inevitability; rather, it is a personal choice directed by gnosis and self-control.

Specifically in relation to Glastonbury, a further consequence of this personal, national and global awakening is the establishment of a New Jerusalem on Earth; a terrestrial paradise reflecting the heavenly order.[18] Although espoused by John Michell, Robert Coon, Anthony Roberts and others, the concept may date to as early as the sixteenth century. William Blake co-opted the idea into his personal mythology and gave it voice in his prophetic works. Its nineteenth century apogee took the form of British Israelism, an ideology proposing a direct genetic and linguistic link between the peoples of Britain and the Tribes of Israel. Some British-Israelists claimed that 'Israelites and Druids all adored the same God,'[19] even suggesting an etymological link be-

17 See all listed works by Coon.
18 See Roberts in particular.
19 See Cottrell-Boyce.

tween the Brittonic deity Esus and Iesu / Jesus.[20] Others argued that Jesus was a Druid missionary, having learned the secrets of Druidry during a boyhood visit to Britain. Thereafter, his mission was to supplant the Jewish priesthood of Aaron with the priesthood of Melchizedek, an ascended master of Atlantis and Graal-guardian.[21] Glastonbury became a notional centre for this belief system as a result of its persistent legends concerning Joseph of Arimathea: his arrival at Glastonbury with the boy Jesus and his subsequent return, years later, with two cruets containing the blood and sweat of the crucified Christ, whereafter he established Britain's first seat of Christianity – the wattle church – in 63 CE at the site of the present Glastonbury Abbey. In the 1930s, Wellesley Tudor Pole and Dion Fortune argued for the restoration of Glastonbury as the centre of a British spiritual renewal framed in terms of a New Jerusalem. Thus, this small market town has become uniquely positioned at the centre of the so-called Matter of Britain. It possesses a sense of mythic proportion, a forward momentum that, perversely, requires a retrospective understanding in order to divine its unfolding destiny.

A third and final strand of Avalonian cosmology relates to a form of occult perennialism, or the theory that the world's corpus of esoteric wisdom derives from a single source. That radix is identified as Atlantis.[22] Plato's incomplete recounting of the rise and fall of Atlantis has been elaborated over the centuries and shaped into a tale of powerful, immortal mages who, through their overweening ambition, inadvertently (or intentionally) brought Qlippothic entities into the world and, in so doing, ushered in the end of a Golden Age. The consequences of this were an existential fall from grace for humankind, and the annihilation of the Atlantean continent. The island was submerged – an act retold in the world's flood myths – and the surviving Atlantean diaspora carried their secret doctrine first to Egypt, thence to all ancient civilisations and, eventually, Britain. Dion Fortune presents Merlin as a civilising hero, an immortal mage of Atlantis and master of the Mysteries who tutored the Druids in the secrets of the Primordial Tradition[23] (a position not dissimilar to occult scholar Lewis Spence, who proposed that Druidry was derived from the

20 Williams and Morganwg, 221.

21 Greer, 6.

22 See Michell (2013).

23 Fortune, Lumley Brown, Knight, 15, 96–99.

practices of an Egyptian cult of the dead.)[24] Avalon became a locus of Druidic-Atlantean geomantic wisdom, in part because it recalled the geographies of the Atlantean continent's central island: a sacred mountain surmounted by a sun temple, functioning as an axis mundi for the surrounding polity. Plato's *Critias* describes Atlantis thus:

> Bordering on the sea and extending through the center of the whole island there was a plain … and near the plain … stood a mountain that was low on all sides … And Poseidon himself set in order with ease … the central island, bringing up from beneath the earth two springs of waters, the one flowing warm from its source, the other cold.

The parallels with Glastonbury are clear. This arrangement was part of a more profound twelve-tribe scheme, where geopolitical divisions corresponded to the zodiac and the twelve months of the year. Atlantis provided the prototype for this plan, one that concealed the promise of a return to an harmonious Golden Age.

The two root-religions of Atlantis – serpent and solar veneration – are exemplified in the aeonic Draco-Pendragon and Ursa-Arthur currents, and are reified in the crucible of Avalon through the convergence of serpentine earth-energies and the sun temple of the Tor. Thus, the entire arcana of Avalon, from its great terrestrial zodiac to the sacred geometry of St Mary's chapel within Glastonbury Abbey, can be said to spring from the deep magick of 'Atlantean' tradition.[25] Furthermore, its lost Golden Age can be regained through an 'invocation of paradise'; a process of deliberate, directed enchantment exemplified in John Michell's assertion that a Druidic perpetual choir at Glastonbury – one of ten centred on the hamlet of Whiteleaved Oak in Herefordshire – literally en-chanted the land and maintained cosmic harmony through the chromatic correspondences of its unfailing music.[26] This complex interweaving of Atlantean mythology, geomancy, Druidism, Arthurian legend and New Age utopianism is successfully summarised by author and esotericist Anthony Roberts:

24 See Spence, chapter 1.
25 See Michell (2008).
26 Michell (1990), 108.

> In the esoteric system of 'spiritual harmonics' that sings through all history, there sounds the constant hope for history's future. The magic disciplines were brought to fruition once before in the long ages past, and this is what the story of Atlantis is really all about. When the rule of universality was the guiding light, all the living entities of the earth, those human and non-human, were joined together in an ecological and religious equality that was physically satisfying and spiritually ennobling. In the transcendental imagery of Golden Age Atlantis lies the essence of Total Freedom.[27]

Some may regard these theories and beliefs as preposterous, deluded, outdated or dangerous. Indeed, it has been argued that John Michell's brand of 'radical traditionalism' reveals latent fascist sympathies.[28] Others may believe they constitute inalienable truths. Either way, they are presented here without prejudice for background and context, and to elucidate the mythopoetic fabric of Avalon's long-standing esoteric traditions. It is also important to re-emphasise the profoundly countercultural, iconoclastic and revolutionary nature of Glastonbury's alternative communities, which impart an unmistakable energy to the town and are fundamental to its status as an ever-evolving geomythical cynosure.

In the context of this grimoire, certain of the motifs explored above are of particular interest. But the plenary aspect of Glastonbury's rich mythology lies in its phenomenological and participatory nature. Ritual interaction with the Holy Island's landscape yields a tangible connection to its legendarium. For example, Maltwood argued that the stories of the Graal Romances in fact took place within the Glastonbury Zodiac, reflecting movements through each zodiacal house as part of the turning of the seasonal wheel.[29] Thus, those stories can be re-enacted by anyone who chooses to undertake a ritual journey through the locality, fulfilling the maxim *quod est superius est sicut quod inferius*[30] and bringing the heavens and Earth into cosmic harmony.

27 Roberts (1977), 113.

28 See Hale. It is a position this author wholly disagrees with.

29 Bowman, 335.

30 That which is above is like to that which is below, and that which is below is like to that which is above.

Glastonbury is a legominism, a topography in which occult secrets and universal truths are encoded. The actions of the individual within its precincts have meaning and consequence, being both probative and initiatory. They simultaneously evolve the whole self while contributing to a greater goal: the fulfilment of Avalon's destiny which, to many, is the land's restoration to a prelapsian, Edenic state. This transcendent individualism can be understood as a modern Graal Quest, or a summoning of the Celtic spirit; an harmonious method for becoming attuned to the Avalonian current. Its cosmology grants agency to the individual, inviting active participation in the great cycles of ever-living myth.

the numen of the holy island

THE RED AND THE WHITE

Because of the serpent's enduring association with immortality, wisdom, healing, fertility and renewal, ophiolatry is one of humankind's oldest religious practices.[1] In Atlantean tradition it is one of two root-religions, the other being heliolatry.

The earliest ur-myths are concerned with the world emerging from the primordial waters as a hill or egg, and a colossal snake creating the earthly landscape through its movements. The Orphic symbol of an egg encircled by a serpent is an illustration of ophidian power; as a result of its constricting influence, the cosmic serpent cracks the egg and releases its *potentia* into the universe, giving rise to life. Two serpents intertwined around a staff are emblematic of the union of the upper and lower realms via the world pillar or axis mundi. Its earliest representation is in association with the Mesopotamian fertility and underworld god Ningišzida, which also recalls the two-thousand-year-old depictions of Fuxi and Nuwa, the Chinese Sky Father and Earth Mother, entwined as snakes in a double helix. References to kundalini physiology are also apposite; Ob and Od, the intertwining snakes of the Hermetic caduceus are the two opposing vital energies held in equilibrium, their union embodied in the orb crowning the staff, representing the Supreme Essence.

1 See Deane for an early but thorough examination of ophiolatry.

These two polarised ophidian deities play a significant role in the mythopoesis of the Holy Island.

The Tor is a nexus for myriad earthly alignments and telluric currents. Example 'ley alignments' include: Dod Lane, a pre-Christian road of the dead connecting Glastonbury Abbey with Stonedown Lane, which is oriented to the equinoxes; the Rose Line, connecting Glastonbury with Rosslyn Chapel and the Findhorn Community; and the Cardiff Castle-Tara-Camelot line. The abbey forms a further alignment with Chalice Hill and the Tor.[2] Mightiest of Albion's alignments is the three-hundred-mile St Michael line, oriented to the Beltane / Lammas sunrise / sunset, which connects St Michael's Mount in Cornwall with St Michael's Church at Hopton, on the East Anglian coast. First mapped by John Michell in the late 1960s, it approximately follows the path of the prehistoric Icknield Way and Ridgeway.

In the 1950s the artist, mystic, occultist and writer Ithell Colquhoun identified foci of telluric currents as 'Fountains of Hecate,' a reference to both the role of Hecate-as-world-soul in the Chaldean Oracles and the belief that witches congregated at places of potent subterranean energies. Glastonbury Tor was considered one such place of numinous power, which were typically identified by the presence of prehistoric monuments located within sacred landscapes.[3] Colquhoun's esoteric milieu was especially interested in centres of so-called Michael-force, sites associated with the Archangel St Michael. The occultist and author Kenneth Grant postulated a worldwide complex of divine centres, which reflected in macrocosm the seven major chakras of the human subtle body. He described Glastonbury as the centre of the western mystery tradition and an occult powerhouse. On this basis, the Holy Island is one of two cult centres corresponding to the Anahata chakra located in the chest, the Tipareth-centre.[4] Similarly, Robert Coon has asserted that Glastonbury represents the global heart chakra within a greater pattern of two interweaving energy paths encircling the earth, drawing parallels with the great world-serpents Ouroboros and Jörmungandr.

2 See Mann (2004).

3 See Colquhoun. Two related essays of note are https://www.spikeisland.org.uk/fountains-of-hecate-an-essay-by-amy-hale/ and http://www.artcornwall.org/features/Amy_Hale/Ithell_Colquhouns_Magic.htm

4 Grant, 76–79.

Michell claimed to have painted an early mural of the Michael line in Glastonbury 'depicting a pair of differently coloured serpents, positive and negative' intertwined along its spine.[5] Yet the notion that the St Michael line was not simply a series of alignments, but also a vector of telluric energy, was not explored fully until the 1980s when the entire line was dowsed, revealing two currents, one masculine and one feminine, meandering in an ophidian path across the landscape, weaving in and out of one another.[6] The solar 'Michael' line touches the top of the highest hills and mounds; the earth-bound 'Mary' line follows the curves of the land, rivers and wells, snaking through and around valleys. This conception reflects the *Lung Mai* or Dragon Meridians of Chinese geomancy, where the masculine Mountain Dragon veins follow ridges and spurs, and the feminine, underground Water Dragon veins pass through low-lying ground. The *Lung Mai* are the earth's circulatory system: millions of subterranean veins, arteries and capillaries that transport *qi* – the etheric vitalising energy – across the natural realms.

Avalon's sorcerous topographies are reflected in certain mythological relationships between serpents, directionality and the solar path. The serpent deities known as *Nāga* are otherworldly creatures dwelling in rivers, lakes and caves. They are allied to the Buddhist Heavenly King of the West, Virūpākṣa. In Egyptian myth, the liminal eastern and western Sun Gates are guarded by serpents. The foundation myth of Chinese folk religion tells of the god Fuxi and the goddess Nuwa, siblings and lovers, who dwelled in the region of the Kunlun mountains. They were sole survivors of a flood and were tasked with repopulating the earth. As such, they can be understood as progenitors, the earliest ancestors of humankind. Fuxi is associated with the sky and the Sun, Nuwa with the Earth and the Moon. They are frequently depicted as human-headed snakes, intertwined in a double-helix, symbolic of their union. Their ophidian marriage gave rise to four sons: Qing Gan, Zhu Sidan, Bai Daran and Mo Gan, who governed the four directions and four seasons. As a result of this beneficial ordering of nature, the vitalising qi energy, polarised according to the dualistic principles of yin and yang, began circulating between the mountains and hills, the seas and rivers.

Another parallel can be found in the traditions of Haitian Vodou. Danballa, a chief spirit of the *loa*, is a sky-father and progenitor of humankind. Portrayed

5 Mackay, 37.

6 See Broadhurst & Miller.

as a giant white serpent, he represents the creative principle through his forming and fertilising of the land. His wife, Ayida-Weddo, is also a serpent. Typically associated with the rainbow and the colours green and blue, she may additionally manifest to her devotees as a wholly red, or red and yellow snake. She dwells both in the sky and in springs, pools and rivers. Their union, reflected in the sacraments of blood and semen, is expressed as an ophidian double helix, or as a serpent coiled around the world-egg. The conjunction of the serpent and egg is a primal crossroads of exchange, a gestation which sires and sustains all life.

Dragon or serpent legends (the two terms were interchangeable in medieval texts) can be interpreted as figurative encounters with real telluric forces. One apposite example concerns the Celtic warlord Vortigern, who attempted to build a castle upon the hill of Dinas Emrys. A boy advised him that, beneath the hill, two dragons – one red and one white – lay sleeping in a subterranean lake. When construction began, the dragons were roused and began to fight, causing devastation. In some traditions the boy is a young Myrddin, or Merlin. A reservoir beneath a hill wherein red and white 'dragons' reside echoes the Tor's geology, where aquifers within the hill feed the red and white springs. Myrddin's role also recalls the function of Chinese geomancers, who determined the most propitious location for a structure. When the Dragon Meridians are disturbed, the consequences are severe. An example of this can be found in the Welsh tale *Lludd and Llefelys*, where the same red and white dragons cause trauma across the land. As a result of their violence 'all the animals and trees and the earth and the waters, were left barren.' This dire geopathy is a result of diseased Dragon Meridians; their disunity gives rise to a wasteland.

The Michael line is so-named due to the preponderance of sites upon its route dedicated to the archangel. Yet the association is problematic inasmuch as St Michael is typically associated with dragon-slaying, where the dragon is the embodiment of evil in biblical eschatology. Yet, as outlined above, in other contexts the dragon or serpent is the vital force of Nature, symbolic of initiation, wisdom and renewal. This tension has been partially resolved by the suggestion that a tradition of seasonal 'dragon-slaying' occurred at Beltane in the form of bonfires located at node-points along the line.[7] However, St Michael's influence in cleansing the land of negative influences, as Colquhoun and others have proposed, is redolent of the Christianisation of pagan sites, as

7 Broadhurst & Miller, 57.

instructed by Pope Gregory to the Catholic mission to Britain in 597 CE:

> The shrines of idols amongst that people [the English] should be destroyed as little as possible, but that the idols themselves that are inside them should be destroyed. Let blessed water be made and sprinkled in these shrines, let altars be constructed and relics placed there: since if the shrines are well built it is necessary that they should be converted from the worship of demons to the service of the true God, so that as long as that people do not see their very shrines being destroyed they may put out error from their hearts and in knowledge and adoration of the true God they may gather at their accustomed places more readily.[8]

For Jung, the symbolism of dragon-slaying relates to the 'battle for deliverance from the mother' – the emergence of self-consciousness and ego.[9] By extension, the same symbolism can describe subordination of the Draconian terra-vulvic impulse, marking the ending of the Aeon of Isis.

To overcome this incompatibility and disharmony, the Michael and Mary lines are understood as the non-denominational White Serpent and Red Serpent, terms which articulate their fundamentally ophidian nature. Together, these two powers express the unity of opposites within the living macrocosm of the earth entire. The Red Serpent gives material form to the solar power of the White Serpent who, in turn, infuses the Magna Mater, the Earth Mother – her soils, caves, wells and rivers – with warmth. This is in conformity with numerous myths where, in particular, serpent goddesses such as Chalchiuhtlicue, Ayida-Weddo, Wadjet, Eingana, Mami Wata and Mamlambo are associated with wetland areas, lakes and rivers. The ophidian dance of the White Serpent and Red Serpent is a sacred union, a *hieros gamos*. Together they generate and manifest life. The red snake is the river of menstrual ancestral blood which flows from the primordial well of life; the white snake is the hierophantic phallus and semen, the divine, animating breath of the godhead. These are the twin aspects of ophidian power: the Logos and the Sophia, the Priest and Priestess, Frater Mysterium and Soror Mystica.

8 Oxford Reference online: 'Pope Gregory's Letter'; https://www.oxfordreference.com/display/10.1093/oi/authority.20110803100337215

9 Jung (2014 ed) chapter 6.

Uniquely, at Glastonbury the Red Serpent flows into the Holy Island from the northwest, passes through the Red Spring, then the Tor, and exits towards the southeast. The White Serpent flows from the southwest, passes through the White Spring and the Tor, and departs towards the northeast. Upon the Tor, the braids of telluric energy ascend through its terraces and meet at the summit, where the feminine current receives the masculine current. Even though their potencies and routes vary according to time and tide, the significance of this persistent ophidian congress is clear: it represents the conjoining of polarities, the alchemical marriage, the *lapis exilis* or philosopher's stone, which is synonymous with the charged Graal.

The relationship between white and red dragons or serpents can be further understood in alchemical terms, as an hermetic drama between white mercury and red sulphur, the two opposing fundamental substances that give rise to the quintessence. The fifteenth century alchemist Bernard of Treviso makes the association between red and white dragons and alchemical processes explicit. His allegory tells of:

> An old fort or castle, wherein dwelt two Dragons, the one red and heavy of body, without wings, and the other white, with wings. And they came together and embraced each other in the heat of the Sun ... and they sported together until the united dragons lost themselves and were converted ...[10]

Fuxi, the Chinese ophidian progenitor of humankind, is said to have 'looked upward and contemplated the images in the heavens, and looked downward and contemplated the occurrences on earth.' Thus, alchemy is defined as the astrology of the lower world; one half of the two Artes that, together, unite the celestial and the chthonic. Its geomantic roots reveal that the alchemical Great Work is concerned with the hidden chthonic powers within the earth, combined with the effects of heavenly forces upon them. Via this pursuit of opposites, alchemy becomes a means of personal and worldly transfiguration; unification of the self giving rise to an harmonious and enlightened whole.

10 The full text of the Allegory of the Fountain is available at https://www.alchemywebsite.com/bernard_allegory.html. A similar allegory can be found in *The Book of Lambspring* by Nicolas Barnaud Delphinas where two birds – one red and one white – fight each other; one bird is subsequently transformed into the Phoenix.

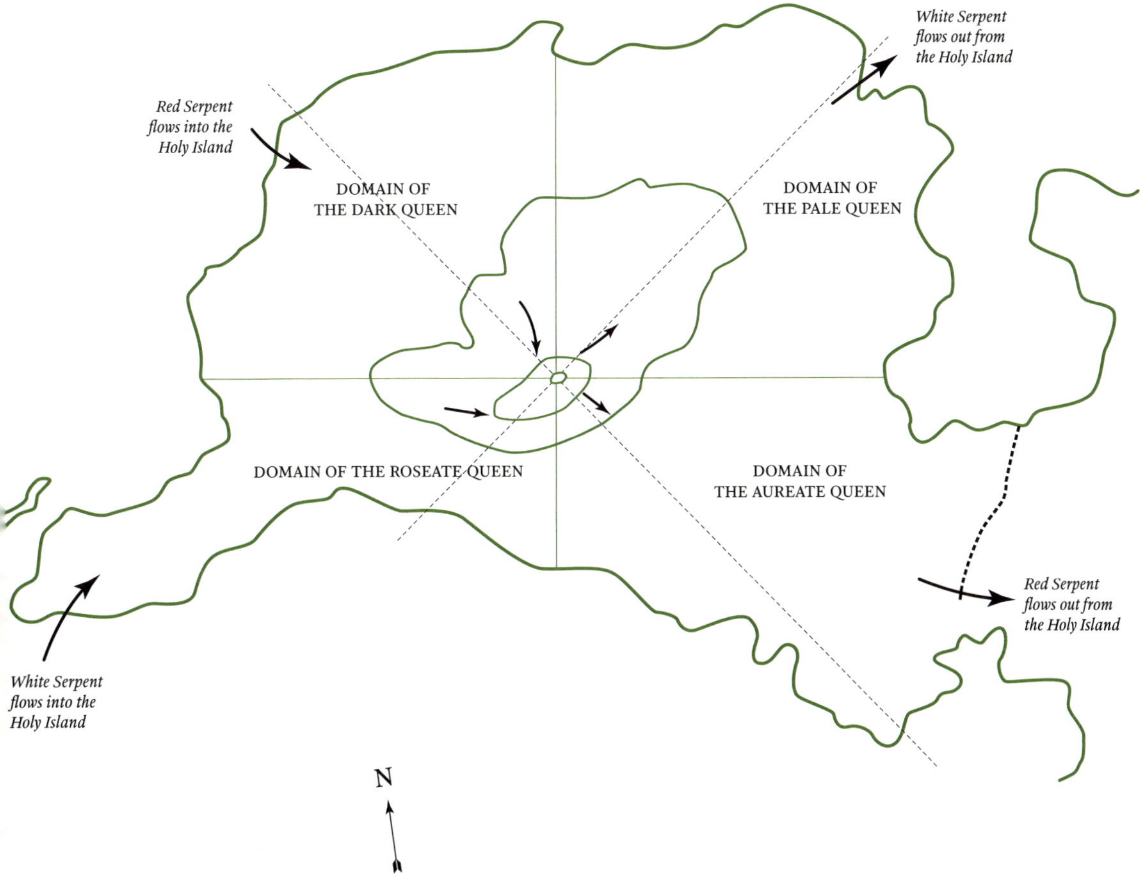

figure 2 The paths of the Red Serpent and the White Serpent.

This arcanum is reflected in the symbolism of St Joseph's heraldic shield, designed by Abbot Richard Bere (1493–1524), and found as a stained glass window at St John's Church, Glastonbury. It depicts heavenly dew descending onto the red and white cruets of Joseph of Arimathea, which flank a cross of green thorn. The cruets represent the alchemical distillations of white mercury and red sulphur; the green cross is the flourishing of Nature via attainment of the *prima materia*, the water of creation or heavenly dew, which is synonymous with the *lapis exilis*, the unity of opposites. That Glastonbury is the locus of this alchemical *conjunctio* is confirmed in the prophesy of the sixth century CE bard Melkin, who declared that 'neither water nor heavenly dew will be lacking for the inhabitants of the Holy Isle.'[11]

This alchemical union of celestial and chthonic has an additional aeonic aspect. The Tor, being an axis mundi, is the point at which the Holy island receives the ascending energies of the underworld and the descending celestial energies, channeled through the North Star, which forms the tip of the world pillar's axis. In this aeon the North Star is Polaris in Ursa Minor and, thus, its in-flowing virtues are Arthurian in nature; that is, epitomising the Aeon of Osiris, being concerned with the veneration of a dying-and-rising masculine solar deity. It is also schismatic, the Arthurian solar-phallic current being estranged from its feminine terra-vulvic opposite – a condition reflected in the Graal legendarium. The previous Aeon of Isis was defined by veneration of a cosmo-vulvic primordial Great Goddess, from whom all things emanate. Thus, one of her subastral aspects is the Magna Mater, the Earth Mother. Amongst the stars she was enthroned in the constellation of Draco, when Thuban fulfilled the role of the North Star, the axis mundi. Draconian rather than Ursine energies descended the world-pillar and ensorcelled the Holy Island, giving rise to the Red and White Serpents. In mythic time, the aeon was governed by the Pendragon, the Draconian monarch who presided over a period prior to the schism described in the *Elucidation* of Arthurian lore.[12]

More recondite aspects of Arthuriana also relate to red and white powers. The *Estoire del Saint Graal*, part of the thirteenth century CE literary cycle

11 Hughes, 16.

12 The *Elucidation* is an anonymously authored prologue to Chrétien de Troyes's *Perceval*, dating from the thirteenth century at the earliest. It describes the rape of certain maidens of the wells by King Amangon, an act precipitating the wasting of the land. Its allegorical import is clear, and this is discussed later is some detail.

known as the Lancelot-Grail cycle or Vulgate Cycle, includes encounters with various enchanted boats. One such vessel was owned by King Solomon, within which were three wooden spindles supporting a bed. The spindles were from a tree grown from the Edenic tree of life, a cutting of which was taken from Paradise by Eve. The tree miraculously changed colour, from green to white to red; the spindles were fashioned from a wood of each colour. In modern faerie lore, the red and white spindles refer to the bloodlines of human and faerie, both races being consanguineous. The former is the red human blood of the earth; the latter the luminous white faerie blood of the star Sirius.[13] The green spindle represents the living mystery of the human-faerie dynamic, the possibility of reconciliation and reunification. Again, this is echoed in the symbolism of the stained glass at St John's Church. The story of the spindles speaks to the restoration of a covenant between humankind and the otherworld, a union broken by King Amangon's schism, as described in the text of the *Elucidation*.

A related model can be found in the tradition of the red and white roses, where both are nourished by opposing otherworldly rivers: the red rose by the White River of Tears and the white rose by the Red River of Blood. The roses are representative of polarised micro- and macrocosmic energies.[14] In Celtic myth, red in combination with white are colours indicating the presence of the otherworld;[15] for example, the red-eared, white hunting dogs of Arawn and the white, red-eared cows of the *sídh*, from the Irish *Book of the Dun Cow*. It is also notable that Plato describes the buildings of Atlantis being constructed from red and white (and also black) stone.

Red feminine and white masculine energies are present in the microcosm of the subtle body. In certain traditions, red and white essences emerge from a fiery, indestructible drop within the chest – the spark of divinity – following conception. The white drop – the sperm of the father – ascends to the crown, while the red drop – the ovum of the mother – descends to the navel. The white drop gives rise to the creation of bone and brain tissue, the red drop to blood, muscle and viscera. It is also associated with the earth. Both are esoteric doors of conception. As part of the metempsychotic cycle, a consciousness seeking rebirth as a male will identify with the white drop of the father. A

13 See Berg.
14 See Stewart.
15 Heinz, 48.

female consciousness will identify with the fertile red drop of the mother. The white drop is more potent in males, the red drop more potent in females; thus, the male-female tantric union becomes a means of achieving the *coincidentia oppositorum* in the body.

Polarised red and white creative powers are described in the protological Second Book of Enoch, part of the biblical Pseudepigrapha. Within the context of a fascinating and unconventional creation story, God summons a luminous creature known as Adoil, ordering him to become the foundation of created things. Bearing a belly of primordial white light, creation is birthed from him, even as his own body is destroyed as a result. In this sense he can be understood as the 'mother' of creation. God then summons a second being known as Archas, Arkhas or Arukhas. His role as a mediator and demiurgic being is similar to Adoil, yet he contains darkness rather than light, and is described as heavy and red. The 'lower things' of creation issue from him which, it may be argued, are chthonic in nature.

A final example of the red and white motif can be found in the twin crown or *pschent* of the Egyptian king. Symbolising the union of Upper and Lower Egypt under his rule, the crown was comprised of a tall, white skittle-shaped crown, and a shorter red crown in the form of a coiled serpent. Following the sacral rites of Heb Sed, the double-crowned king emerged from a symbolic death, descent to the underworld, and rebirth to assert his sovereignty over the mortal and spiritual realms.

¶ THE SPRINGS AND THE SERPENTS

The Red and White Serpents must be considered in relation to the Red and White Springs, which flow from a two-tiered aquifer beneath the Tor. Geomancy has revealed the aquifer to reflect the seven-tiered external structure of the hill. It is said to generate two major currents, male and female, which follow a spiral path upwards and downwards, in and out.[16] This is a function of the in-flowing currents of the Red and White Serpents passing through the Tor, their swirling sheaves of telluric energy fructifying the waters of their respective springs. In turn, the spring waters are infused with, and reify, the virtues of their corresponding serpent currents.

16 See Mann (2004) for a thorough exposition of the Tor's energies.

The potency of waters drawn from natural springs is well attested. The Sanctuary of Asclepius at Epidaurus, the renowned centre for 'dream incubation' in the Classical world, is located close to mineral springs, which were used in rites of ablution and healing. At Delphi, priests, postulants and the Pythia herself bathed in the cleansing waters of the Castalian Spring before engaging in oracular activities. And at Aquae Sulis (the modern city of Bath) the locus of its hot springs was transformed into a major Romano-British cult centre.

That the waters of the Red and White Springs also possess transformative, alchemical qualities is not in doubt. The tenth century abbot of Glastonbury, Dunstan, had previously been exiled from the royal court of King Athelstan following accusations of sorcery. At Glastonbury, Dunstan was said to have diverted the waters from both springs to the abbey for use in alchemical experiments. According to some accounts, hundreds of years later John Dee's scryer, Edward Kelley, visited Glastonbury Abbey and found an enigmatic red substance, described as earth or powder, along with a scroll written in an unknown alphabet. In an alternative tale the French writer Nicolas Lenglet du Fresnoy recounts that Kelley purchased the red earth from an innkeeper who had, in turn, procured it from grave robbers; they obtained it from a bishop's tomb.[17] In a further variant of the tale, one Mr John Husey and Kelley approached Dee with a scroll, a book and a quantity of red powder, unearthed near Blockley in the Cotswolds.[18] Kelley firmly believed the red substance was the *ultima materia*, the philosopher's stone, the *lapis exilis*, a claim supported by the seventeenth century alchemist Elias Ashmole. It can be surmised that these powders were the fruits of Dunstan's own alchemy, employing the waters of the Red and White Springs. They represent the alchemical Red King and White Queen, the two vital ingredients for attaining the mysteries of the *lapis exilis* or charged Graal.

The numen of the Red and White Springs are the Well Maidens, tutelary spirits who haunt the springheads. In legend these nymphs were once numerous, serving wayfarers with food and drink from golden cups, until King

17 Wooley, 190–191. See also Hughes, 17–19.

18 Kassell, 132–135. The book was reputedly 'The Book of Dunstan,' an alchemical treatise outlining four variants of the philosopher's stone: vegetable, mineral, angelic and magical. The magical or prospective stone granted the power to see into the past and the future, and to understand the language of animals – abilities very similar to those ascribed to Merlin, thereby implicitly linking the wizard to alchemy and attainment of the *lapis exilis*.

Amangon defiled one of them and stole her treasures. His vassals then did the same. The thirteenth century poem the *Elucidation* describes how, as a result, 'ill luck was to come of it, for no maiden served again, or came forth from that well to help any man who happened by and requested sustenance there... In this way the land went into decline... [It] was so wasted that no tree ever bloomed there again, the grasses and flowers withered, and the streams dried up.' Amangon's rape of the cupbearers can be understood as an inversion of the act of ritual congress between the sacral king and the Magna Mater, symbolised in the proffering of a vessel or Graal from a woman embodying sovereignty. In drinking from the cup, the king was granted authority over the land and the otherworldly accord maintained.

The subtext of the the *Elucidation*'s tale is clear: the king and his men violated their sacral oaths by committing a desecration of Nature, embodied in the Earth Mother, the divine feminine. Their subjugation of both the land and its feminine aspects broke a covenant, a taboo, giving rise to the wasteland. Its restoration was only possible once the Graal was found. The *Elucidation* describes the Graal as bearing food and drink, much like the golden cups of the undines. Thus, the Graal represents the contract between sovereign and goddess; matter and spirit. The wasteland is a state of schism, a rejection of natural synderesis. The Graal may only be properly obtained, and the contract restored, if the apostate becomes the illuminate, if the disunity of the self is transformed and made verdant.

There are parallels with the geography of the Red and White Springs in relation to the Tor, and the three sacred springs or wells of Norse mythology: Urðarbrunnr, Mímisbrunnr and Hvergelmir. Each is located at the foot of the world-tree Yggdrasil, just as the Red and White Springs rise at the 'root' of the world-hill of the Tor. In particular, the three Norns of Urðarbrunnr, the Well of Urðr, are bound to and born of the well's holy waters. As such, they can be understood as undines in addition to their fateful and protective roles. By comparison, the Well Maidens of Arthurian myth are not merely passive guardians of the sacred wells, but weavers-of-fate through their granting or withdrawing of regnal sovereignty, embodied in the cup or Graal.

¶ INTERMISSIO: SACRED DIRECTIONALITY

Directionality, orientation, alignment and the spacial layout of buildings, settlements and landscapes were profound concerns for ancient cultures. They determined oppositions and thresholds, cosmologies and the geographies of myth, the locations and domains of deities, the points of ingress and egress for the souls of the dead, the separation of sacred and profane, and all their concomitant ritual activities.[19] Intentional structuring of architecture based on four (quadripartite) directions is a recurring theme, although those directions may not necessarily be cardinal. However, north-south alignments can be seen at the Forbidden City in Beijing, the Great North Road at Chaco Canyon, Casa Rinconada, and the Giza pyramids.

Roman town planning, based on Greek and Etruscan models, consisted of an axial layout. A north-south road – the *cardine* – was intersected by an east-west road – the *decumanus*. At the centre was the crossroads and *groma*. Four gates marked the entry and exit points of this orthogonal layout, which in some cases were oriented to sunrise or sunset, and to certain landscape features. A variety of functions, statuses, symbols and tutelary spirits known as *lares* were assigned to each quadrant. Similarly, the Viking-era Trelleborg fortress in Sweden was constructed as a circular monument, subdivided into quadrants by the intersecting axes of two roads, suggestive of a sun wheel. The Domsteinene stone circle at Nordsjøvegen, Norway, is arranged as an octagram; a holy tree was thought to have once been located at its centre.

On a smaller scale, the old farm culture of Norway incorporated ritual layouts in its settlements: north represented death and the spirit, where burial mounds were located, along with the farmstead's sacred tree, a proto-Yggdrasil that provided shelter for the farm's *vættir* or land spirits; south was associated with life and humanity; west was male; east female. This concept extended to farm buildings. Days of the week were assigned to the cardinal and intercardinal axes, which determined the ritual spatio-temporal rules for both mundane tasks and seasonal festivities, as well as for managing the interactions between humans and spirits.[20] A similar focus on directionality can be found in the layout and structure of Iron Age roundhouses, where entrances

19 See Ruggles for an introduction to this broad-ranging topic.

20 See Doxtater.

appear to have been oriented towards the midwinter or equinoctial sunrise and the domestic layout was zoned according to specific activities.

This preoccupation with directionality is inextricably linked to the cosmos, the predictable movements of stars, planets and asterisms throughout the year, as viewed from axes mundi – typically high places such as hills, mountains or ziggurats – that also functioned as celestial observatories. It has been argued, for example, that dozens of Maltese megalithic temples are in fact constructed to enable stellar observation, being oriented to the rising of Sirius.[21]

The rising and setting of celestial bodies served a practical purpose as heralds of seasonal events and agrarian activities. The ancient Egyptians divided the sky around the ecliptic into 36 constellations or decans and used their passage as a time-measure. The annual procession began with the heliacal rising of the brightest star in the sky, Sirius / Sothis in the eastern horizon, indicating the imminent inundation of the Nile. The Zuni people of New Mexico used the Pleiades cluster as an agricultural calendar. When the Pleiades disappeared into the western dusk in spring, it was safe to begin seed planting.

At a magicko-mythic level, this sidereal transit narrated the perennial interplay of deities and heroes, who were simultaneously represented by stars and constellations and wholly reified by them. In the context of a specific culture's worldview, the appropriate ritual actions were performed in response to these celestial events, whether planetary conjunctions in their ecliptic journeys through the houses of the zodiac, or the heliacal rising and setting of stars and constellations, or the solstitial rising and setting of the sun.

The orientation and alignment of natural landscape features and human monuments to celestial events, especially the liminal points of rising and setting on the horizon, are acts of sympathetic magick, an expression of the maxim 'as above, so below' where divinity is given a bridge to cross into the mundane realm. It expresses a magickal intent to integrate and synchronise the subastral world with the machinations of the upper and lower world, to bring the three realms into union. By attuning the landscape to the predictable movements of an orderly cosmos, in tandem with proper ritual conduct, harmony and balance is maintained.

It is unsurprising that the Sun occupies a preeminent position in the ritual annual cycle. As part of the process of cosmic congruence, the systematic

21 See Reedijk. This theory is contentious due to the author's early dating of the temples, and therefore largely rejected by mainstream archaeology.

calibration of the terrestrial year is derived from the sun's movements across the horizon. It is the provider of light and life to the middle world, a source of fecundity such that harvests can thrive or fail at its behest. The sun is omnipotent and sees all things beneath it. It traverses the sky by day then descends into the underworld at night, thereby having knowledge of both realms. At the winter solstice, when it is weakest, the sun nevertheless defies the chthonic powers and rises in triumph.

The solstices were significant annual markers, heralding changes in social structure and occasions of seasonal congregation and dispersal, as far back as the last ice age. In magicko-religious terms, they were liminal times of the year, when the sun stood still and the worlds froze in response. Boundaries between the upper, middle and lower realms became permeable and spirits, the living, and the dead could freely pass between them.

The Sun's associations with fertility and prosperity are intimately bound up with ideas of kingship. Celtic cultures in particular inculcated a belief system linking the sun as a source of divine inspiration to the craft of royal rule. The sun was associated with speech and poetry, which in turn was related to truth and authority. The king's right judgement was responsible for the flourishing of Nature and community; his decisions made Nature bloom and transform. Conversely, poorly exercised kingship would see the beneficent action of the elements quickly turn against him.[22]

The Dagda of Irish myth, chief of the Tuatha Dé Danann, trailed behind him a wheeled fork – a phallic solar symbol. It was a means of defining sovereignty and kingdom, and reflected the primordial mating of sun and soil, a theme also echoed in the Old English Æcerbot Ritual. This union of opposites, the mating of the Earth Goddess and Sun God, was enshrined in a sacred union, a hierogamy. The goddess-as-the-land required the sun to quicken it to fertility. Thus, a connubial rite enacted by the king as an hypostasis of the sun god, and a woman representing Terra Mater, reflected the fertilising union of the earth mother and her male consort. It was nothing less than an act of seasonal sex magick.

The magicko-religious significance of the solstices is evident in the numerous monumental ritual structures such as Stonehenge, Brú na Bóinne, Maeshowe and Newgrange, oriented to the midwinter or midsummer sunrise and sunset. Several ancient Egyptian temples are aligned to the solstices. At

22 Enright, 87, 126, 206, 237.

Karnak Temple in Luxor, the rays of the winter solstice sunrise pass through its eastern gate of the Precinct of Amun-Ra and into the inner sanctum, within which a statue of the sun god was illuminated.[23] The ancient Greek historian Ephorus of Cyme divided the entire inhabited world into four zones based on the solstice angles of the Sun, occupied by four races: Celts, Scythians, Indians and Ethiopians. Etruscan culture relied on a set of rites performed by an augur to establish the location of its towns. As a reflection of the heavens, the town and its skyscape were structured according to a quadripartite layout; its axes being oriented to the solstices. In particular, the location of the ritual centre was significant. As an axis mundi, it provided the interface between the celestial and terrestrial. This omphalos was capped with a stone, which was periodically removed to allow spirits of the underworld ingress into the human realm. The north-east, the domain of the summer solstice sunrise was auspicious, occupied by deities most favourable to humankind; gods of Earth and Nature dwelled in the southern quadrants; the north-west, the abode the infernal gods of fate and destiny, was ominous, demarcating the point on the horizon where the sun 'died' and descended into the underworld.[24] Divination occurred as a result of the augur observing the movement of birds, the distribution of the seats of the gods, the weather – especially lightning – and celestial bodies in relation to the quadrants they occupied.[25] In this way, the location and movement of all sky-borne and earth-bound things within and across the four solstitial thresholds informed the process of prognostication. Similarly, the third century BCE Iguvine Tablets describe the acts and rites of early Roman religion, performed by a priesthood known as the Atiedian Brethren. As part of a ceremony of annual lustration, a priest sat upon an augural high seat atop Mount Ingio, facing the intercardinal directions, to perform ornithomancy. The species of bird, its height and position in relation to the augur, and its movements, determined the auspices.[26]

In Britain, excavations of the Roman city of Calleva at Silchester revealed a portion of the urban plan conforming to an earlier Iron Age layout, which was oriented to the solstices.[27] And four of the nine highways decreed by the leg-

23 See Furlong.
24 Pennick & Devereux, 97.
25 Castagnoli, chapter 4.
26 See Poultney, Introduction.
27 Fulford, 70–100.

endary fourth century BCE British King Belinus are reckoned to lie on solstice bearings, intersecting at Oxford; these were designated *chimini regales*, or royal roads, as depicted in Matthew Paris's thirteenth century map *Schema Britanniae.*[28] Further afield, a number of 'medicine wheel' monuments of the Rocky Mountain region in Wyoming track various cosmic cycles, including solstice sunrise and sunset, the precession of the equinoxes, the Moon's phases, lunar and solar eclipse cycles, the heliacal rising of stars and planets' orbital cycles.

The organising principles of the twelve-tribe scheme, of which Atlantis is alleged to have provided the prototype, recurs throughout ancient history. Schematics show twelve tribal regions or kingdoms arranged around a sacred centre. The correspondences of the twelve-fold plan include zodiacal houses, months of the year, deities, constellations and mythic cycles. Strabo and Aristotle describe a symbolic twelve-tribe foundation plan centred on the Acropolis at Athens, surrounded by twelve amphictyonies, which identify the locations of seasonal councils.[29]

These concerns with directionality persist into the modern era. The elaborate ceremonial calendar of the Hopi people is based on a solstitial quadripartite cosmology, where the entire visible landscape is divided into four equal parts, the axes oriented to the rising and setting of the midwinter and midsummer sun. At the centre is the axis mundi, usually a hilltop settlement. These divisions are not geometric abstractions but a means of embedding mythic narratives and magicko-religious significance in the landscape. Theirs is a sacred geography, where directionality defines numerous correspondences and determines the time and place for ceremonial and ritual right action. This quadripartite cosmology is reflected in the medicine wheel symbol and the accompanying exhortations to the four quarters of the world. The Warao indigenous Amerindian peoples recognise a cosmic landscape where the earth is bounded by a chain of mountains, beyond which lies the encompassing world-ocean. The earth's peripheral and axial regions are populated by deities, accessible only by certain shamanic orders (dark shaman, weather shaman, light shaman, priest-shaman.) In Warao cosmology, shamanic domains are distributed across the cardinal, intercardinal and solstitial points of sunrise and sunset. Each shamanic order functions as a gatekeeper and magicko-religious specialist, able to access the divine powers of its domain via ecstatic trance

28 Taylor & Taylor, 39–40.

29 Michell and Rhone, chapter 2.

and other shamanic techniques. The most powerful deities are those who reside on hills at the earth's edge, at the solstitial corners of the universe.[30] Indeed, it might be argued that sacred directionality per se is fundamentally shamanistic.

The concept of guardians or tutelary spirits presiding over the domains of a four or eight-fold cosmology recurs throughout myth, religion and magick. In Chinese astronomy the four directions are governed by four asterisms – auspicious beasts: Qinglong, Zhuque, Baihu and Xuanwu. In Hinduism they are collectively known as Lokapālas and are named Kubera, Yama, Indra and Varuna. In Norse myth they are dwarves: Norðri, Suðri, Austri and Vestri. In Chinese Buddhism they are the Four Heavenly Kings who reside on the lower slopes of Mount Meru, the holy mountain and world hill situated at the centre of the earth; watching over the cardinal directions, their names are Vaiśravana, Virūḍhaka, Dhrtarāṣṭra, and Virūpākṣa. In Chinese folk religion, the sky-god Nuwa and earth-goddess Fuxi, frequently depicted as human-headed snakes, sired four gods – Qing Gan, Zhu Sidan, Bai Daran and Mo Gan – who became associated with the four directions and four seasons. In ancient Egyptian theology, the four gods of the cardinal points are the four spirits of Horus: Hpi, Tuamutef, Amset and Qebhsennuf. In western magickal tradition, the presiding guardians of the four quarters are Watchtowers or Archangels: Michael, Raphael, Gabriel and Uriel. The *Clavis Inferni* of St Cyprian identifies their opposite numbers, the four Demon Kings, as: Paymon, Maimon, Egyn and Oriens. The *Lemegeton* posits alternative Demon Kings, while the *Hygromanteia* assigns many demonic spirits to the directions. Additionally, it is commonplace to correlate a cardinal direction with one of the four Elemental Kings. The Tetramorph of Christian art, with its origins in the Babylonian zodiac, designates four cardinal creatures – the lion, eagle, ox and angel – to the cardinal directions, in addition to numerous other correspondences. Since antiquity, the cardinal and cross-cardinal directions have included a magicko-meteorological aspect in the form of eight divine winds. The second century BCE Tower of the Winds within the Roman Agora in Athens contains a frieze depicting eight wind deities: Boreas, Kaikias, Apeliotes, Eurus, Notus, Livas, Zephytus and Skiron. The virtues of each compass direction are borne on the breath of its respective aeolian god.

30 See Wilbert.

During the ancient Roman festival of Compitalia the *lares compitales*, or guardian spirits of the crossroads, were honoured. Although the *lares* were commonly *genii locorum* associated with a variety of terrestrial thresholds – primarily points of intersection – the *lares compitales* were held in high esteem, being tutelary spirits of Rome's own sacred boundary and quadripartite layout: the *cardine*, the *decumanus* and their crossing-point. During the festival, social conventions were suspended; citizens inhabiting each of the four regions performed lustrations and offered sacrifices of honey cakes at the crossroads. Compitalia took place immediately after Saturnalia, which spanned the winter solstice. It is notable that the mother of the *lares* was Mater Larum, a chthonic aspect of the Magna Mater.[31]

¶ THE GATES OF THE SUN

If the Holy Island is the nexus and crucible for the root-religions of solar and serpent veneration, then consideration must be given to the practice of heliolatry. Widespread cosmological beliefs about the celestial voyage of the sun may be detected at different times and in different parts of Europe over a period of at least two thousand years.[32] Mythic depictions of the sun carried by a boat or chariot are especially prevalent, not least in Celtic material culture. The Petrie crown, the Battersea shield and the Aylesford bucket all show a sun disk ensconced in a boat with a bird-headed prow and stern. Contrapuntal imagery suggests that the sun was understood to sail from left to right on its westward journey from rising to setting, and from right to left in its nocturnal journey through the underworld towards the east. Notably the Trundholm 'chariot of the sun,' a world-renowned Bronze Age solar symbol, features differing designs on the face of the sun disk and its obverse, suggesting a different sun is present in the upper world versus the lower world.[33] This chthonic sun is identified as Sirius, the Sut-Nubti or the black-and-gold one; Sirius and the Sun combined. In certain New Age traditions, the Sun is the heart centre of the cosmos; Sirius is the Ajna centre or third eye. Human and planetary evolution is predicated on raising energy from the heart / Sun to the Ajna / Sir-

31 Woodward (2006), 111–112.
32 Waddell (2015), xiv.
33 Waddell (2015), 36–47.

ius.[34] A further common mythic motif posits that the Sun's quotidian voyage is made possible by two gates, granting access to and from the netherworld. Egyptian and Greek myth suggest that the 'portals of the Sun' are opened daily when the sun meets the horizon.

The Egyptian Book of Gates describes a series of entranceways through which the sun must pass in its journey from setting to rising. The first is guarded by the serpent Sa-set. It is located on the horizon in the western lands, personified by the goddess Amentet, and marks the point of ingress to the underworld from the mortal world. Akhet is the boundary of those two realms, the horizon where the sun rises and sets. The twelfth and final gate is the point of egress, of rising and return from the netherworld. This portal is located in Aaru in the east, guarded by the serpents Sebi and Reri.[35]

The Proto-Indo-European root of this model, of twilight deities – specifically goddesses of dawn and solar gates – is well attested. These portals to and from the underworld, transited by the Sun, are also present in a passage from Homer's *Odyssey*. On the cusp of the great river ocean separating the mortal realm and Hades lay the island of Circe, known as Aeaea, in the west. As an enchantress, Circe is cognate with Morgen or Matrona, the seeress and goddess of Arthurian legend, and has been compared with the female Dactyls of Mount Ida.[36] Her island is referred to in relation to the Gates of the Sun, implying that the points at which the sun rises and sets on the horizon can be understood as portals to and from Hades, and are located on Circe's island. Thus, her island demarcates the boundary between night and day, life and death; Circe herself performs a role as guardian of the threshold.[37]

The Myth of Er, as recounted in Plato's *Republic*, describes a metempsychotic cycle via 'two openings in the earth, and above them two openings in the heavens' by which the cleansed souls of the virtuous descended from the heavens and the weary souls of the immoral ascended from the earth. Their reincarnation took place in the Field of the Middle, situated in the sky between the gates of Heaven and the gates of Earth.[38] In *Timaeus*, Plato also mentions a crossroads in the sky or heavenly intersections, which are determined by

34 See Wilson, 143.

35 McCarthy's interpretation of the Book of Gates is highly recommended.

36 Stratton-Kent, *Geosophia*, vol 1, 141.

37 Marinatos, 193–197.

38 See Stratton-Kent, *Geosophia*, vol 1, 160–179 for a translation of, and commentary on, the Myth of Er.

the meeting of the ecliptic and the Milky Way at the solstices.[39] Similarly, the Greek philosopher Heraclides Ponticus recounts a vision of one Empedotimus of Syracuse, who describes three interconstellational gates by which souls ascend to, and descend from, the celestial Hades.

This model is fundamental to gaining a sorcerous insight to the Holy Island's arcana, which similarly contains many portals to the netherworld of Annwn. Chief of these are the Gates of Descension and Ascension. Their opening occurs at sunset and sunrise and may be gained after imbibing the elixirs held within the Graals of Egression and Admittance. The Adytum at the Tor's summit is an observatory for determining the directions of sunrise and sunset and the timing of the gates' opening. While the quotidian unveiling of these two portals grants passage to the underworld, their twice-yearly solstitial opening briefly yields singular access to the upper world. This is made possible by the eliding of the sun upon the horizon – the threshold of the gates – with the intersection of the ecliptic and the Milky Way, presenting a route for anabasis to the heavens.

In mythological and astrotheological terms, the solstices represent especially significant junctures in the annual solar cycle. Interpretations of Sumerian cuneiform signs refer to two cosmic gates in the east and the west, connecting the earth and the underworld, located upon or between a twin-peaked mountain.[40] A further short passage in Homer's thirteenth book of the *Odyssey* yields more evidence of this persistent cosmological phenomenon. Homer describes a cave on Ithaca, the home island of Odysseus, as sacred to the Naiads, nymphs of the waters. Nymphs are inherently liminal, being neither mortal nor divine; in this example they function as mediators between worlds. The cave is accessed by two gates, one to the north, by which men may descend, and one to the south, a divine path reserved for immortals. In an exegesis of these lines, the third century CE Neoplatonist philosopher Porphyry of Tyre comments that:

> Homer was not satisfied with saying that it had two gates, but adds that one of the gates was turned towards the north, but the other which was more divine, to the south... Theologists therefore assert, that these two gates are Cancer and Capricorn; but Plato calls them entrances.

39 See Latura.

40 See Martirosyan.

> And of these, theologists say, that Cancer is the gate through which souls descend; but Capricorn that through which they ascend. Cancer is indeed northern, and adapted to descent; but Capricorn is southern, and adapted to ascent. The northern parts, likewise, pertain to souls descending into generation. And the gates of the cavern which are turned to the north are rightly said to be pervious to the descent of men; but the southern gates are not the avenues of the Gods, but of souls ascending to the Gods. On this account, the poet does not say that they are the avenues of the Gods, but of immortals; this appellation being also common to our souls, which are per se, or essentially, immortal.[41]

Porphyry is referring to the transit of the sun during the solstices, when it enters the zodiacal house of Cancer at midsummer and Capricorn at midwinter. At midsummer the Sun rises and sets at its extreme northerly azimuths; at midwinter at its extreme southerly azimuths. Porphyry elaborates on the Homeric stanzas by stating that the northern midsummer gate is the route by which souls descend from the heavens into their corporeal bodies. By contrast, the southern midwinter gate is the route by which dead souls ascend to the celestial Hades. The solstitial alignments of Neolithic monuments at Newgrange, Maes Howe, Brú na Bóinne and Woodhenge perhaps display congruence with this view: that solstitial sunrise and sunset are liminal times, functioning as portals between the worlds.

The state of affairs described by Porphyry is substantiated and elaborated by the fifth century CE Roman historian Macrobius:

> At this point we shall discuss the order of the steps by which the soul descends from the sky to the infernal regions of this life. The Milky Way girdles the zodiac, its great circle meeting it obliquely so that it crosses it at the two tropical signs: Capricorn and Cancer. Natural philosophers name these 'the portals of the sun' because the solstices lie athwart the sun's path on either side, checking farther progress and causing it to retrace its course across the belt beyond whose limit it never trespasses. Souls are believed to pass through these portals when going from the sky to the earth and returning from the earth to the sky. For this reason one is called the portal of men, the other the portal of gods: Cancer, the

41 See Taylor (1917).

> portal of men, because through it descent is made to the infernal regions; Capricorn, the portal of gods, because through it souls return to their rightful abode of immortality, to be reckoned among the gods.[42]

Commentators have clarified that the crossing-point of the sun and the Milky Way referred to by Macrobius is the solstitial intersection of the Milky Way and the ecliptic, which function as portals between the realms.[43] These celestial gates are the signs of Capricorn and Cancer which, in this era as a result of precessional drift, correspond to the constellations of Gemini in the north and Sagittarius in the south.[44] In numerous ancient cultures, it is the Milky Way that functions as a path of souls granting mortal access to the celestial realms.

At the winter solstice, Sirius approaches its culmination in the northern hemisphere, when it becomes visible in the night sky for the longest period; while the Sun is at its weakest, the occulted sun-behind-the-sun that is Sirius reaches its ascendency. It is also worth noting that currently the winter solstice Sun rises exactly where the ecliptic crosses the galactic equator, the plane that bisects our galaxy. The point marks the galactic centre, the rotational axis of our galaxy. This conjunction of galactic centre and the Sun began in the 1980s and will last roughly 40 years. Thereafter it will not occur again for another 26,000 years.[45]

A final equivalence between Avalonian and Greek myth can be found in the land of Hesperides, the daughters of evening who dwell in a place of orchards to the far west of the world, close to the gates of sunset. The apples of this 'blessed land,' which grant immortality, are guarded by the serpent Ladon. As nymphs, the Hesperides are presented as shapeshifters who direct the Argonauts to a freshwater spring. They have been equated with the Pleiades,[46] and the serpent Ladon with Draco. The parallels with the Holy Island are evident: its status as an earthly paradise in the west and an island of apples (which in

42 See Stahl, specifically the first note of chapter 12.

43 See Mathisen for a detailed overview of the system of celestial metaphor in relation to the solstices.

44 Macrobius's references to Capricorn and Cancer are not to the constellations themselves but to the homonymous signs of Ptolemy's Tropical Zodiac which, in Macrobius's era, designated the galactic constellations then housing the solstices (but are now Gemini and Sagittarius).

45 Mann & Glasson, 103.

46 See Worthen.

Celtic myth confer access to the otherworld); nymphs and freshwater springs; a sorority of maidens associated with the Pleiades; a guardian serpent associated with Draco.[47] These parallels provide further evidence of the consanguinity of mythemes across disparate cultures.

¶ SKY LORE

The geographies of the Holy Island and its environs suggest intentionality in their correspondences between terrestrial and celestial. In particular, the Tor-as-axis-mundi is a focus for solstitial orientation and alignment, an arrangement consonant with other mythic and magicko-religious landscapes. It has been convincingly argued that certain landscape features of the Holy Island serve as a temple complex, a place where orientation and directionality converge; where significant celestial events purposefully align within a ritual landscape for magicko-religious ends. In this worldview, Edmund Hill, surmounted by a man-made mound, is conceived as a Neolithic viewing platform. At winter solstice dawn the rising Sun appears to roll up the steep northern flank of the Tor; the Sun's ascent, at an angle of 26°, is matched by the angle of the slope of the Tor. The winter solstice Sun reaches its zenith over Chalice Hill and sets behind the outer flank of Wearyall Hill. In the Neolithic, the path of the Sun's rise was lower. One suggestion is that the Tor's terraces were cut in order to observe the upper rim of the sun during its thirty-minute ascent to the Tor's summit.[48] Symbolically, the Sun's ascent at midwinter as observed from Edmund Hill represents its rebirth and emergence from the underworld. Gaining the summit of the Tor, the sun becomes united with the world pillar, the axis of the cosmos. It is the *cakrastambha*; the orb that both sits atop the royal sceptre and crowns the staff of the caduceus. The wheel-pillar embodied in the union of Sun and Tor summit is representative of cosmic balance and right order. Also in the Neolithic, the heliacal rising of Sirius – the Sol Niger and dark twin of the manifested sun; the sun-behind-the-sun and the occulted sun of the underworld – followed the same path of ascent.

47 According to *De astronomica* by the Roman scholar Gaius Julius Hyginus.
48 See Mann & Glasson for a full assessment of Edmund Hill as a celestial observatory.

A similar transit applies to the Moon. At the lowest point of its 18.6 year cycle of lunar standstills, the Moon would have risen along the spine of the Tor and grazed the top of Chalice Hill, before setting over Wearyall Hill. Researchers have additionally suggested that the Glastonbury landscape once functioned as a lunar observatory, whereby the hills around the Tor were sighting points for long range observation of the Moon as it rose and set behind specific peaks upon the horizon.[49]

The magickal significance of the solstices within the sacred geographies of the Holy Island is confirmed by the positioning of Gog and Magog in relation to the Tor. Following a systematic survey of major Celtic sites throughout France and Britain, one notable researcher has proposed a hitherto unacknowledged network of Druidic roads based on lines of longitude, latitude, and most importantly, the solstitial paths of the sun. The author, Graham Robb, identifies a solstice angle of 53.13° east of north as the British Standard, the basis for this sophisticated network, reflecting the two 53.13° angles of the Pythagorean triangle. Glastonbury features prominently in this map of protohistoric Britain, sitting at a point of intersection between a north-south meridian and a southwest-northeast solstice path. In support of Robb's Druidic network, a line drawn from the centre of the Tor to Gog and Magog bisects the ancient oaks at an angle of 53° east of north, which suggests an intentional, ceremonial relationship between the Tor and the rising of the midsummer sun.[50] Dion Fortune noted that, beyond the opposite face of the Tor, the well-shaft of the Red Spring opens into a stone-hewn inner chamber oriented to the summer solstice and into which a shaft of light passes at midsummer.

In 4,000 BCE Orion's Belt ascended the northern flank of the Tor in imitation of the rising winter solstice Sun. In Egyptian star lore, Orion is associated with Sokar-Osiris, lord of the underworld and god of the winter solstice. In the context of Glastonbury's ritual landscape, Orion is equated with Arawn, king of Annwn who, in common with that constellation, rises at Samhain with his otherworldly hounds (Canis Major and the dog star Sirius) and embarks upon the Wild Hunt. As Winter King he presides over the night sky from November to April, until his bright white star Rigel is usurped by Scorpius and its red star Antares; with Ophiuchus they represent Gwythyr ap Greidawl, the mortal enemy of Arawn who, in consideration of his solar attributes, is associ-

49 See Thom in Williams (1990).
50 Robb, chapter 13.

ated with the Summer King. Arawn and Gwythyr represent the same polarities as Osiris and Ra, Set and Horus; the perennial struggle between the opposing forces of day and night, summer and winter.

The nine sorcerer-maidens of Avalon are deified in the nine bright stars of the Pleiades; the star Maia is associated with the Magna Mater, who is cognate with the Goddess of Avalon. Its helical rising marks the point of equinoctial sunrise. As an aside, the Bronze Age Nebra sky disc's depictions of celestial phenomena are broadly equivalent to those forming the Avalonian astromythology: the Pleiades astrum, the Moon, the two solstices, and the solar barge.

In Welsh myth the Milky Way, the path of souls, is named Caer Gwydion after the hero-sorcerer of the Mabinogion, and is peopled by the souls of heroes, kings and princes. An Irish epithet is Sliochd Uis, translating as 'the Path of Whiteness.'[51]

King Arthur is commonly associated with the constellations of Ursa Minor (Little Bear) and Ursa Major (Great Bear) due to a proposed derivation of 'Arthur' from a patronym meaning 'bear-warrior-king.' Cosmogramatically, the zodiacal houses rotate around Ursa Major and Ursa Minor, which includes the North Star Polaris, providing a stellar metaphor for the relationship between the king and his knights, enshrined in the form of the Round Table. A prototype for this model can be found in the first century Hamat Teverya zodiac, depicting Helios at the centre – also apt considering Arthur's status as a solar hero. However, in 3,000 BCE, the star Thuban in the constellation of Draco enjoyed the status of North Star, rather than Polaris. As a result of precession, over the centuries Thuban shifted away such that, in 320 BCE the Greek navigator Pytheas of Massalia described the celestial pole as wholly devoid of stars. But by the fifth century CE the Macedonian historian Joannes Stobaeus described Polaris as always visible at the celestial pole. At around 500 CE Polaris became established as the new North Star, and thereafter it was commonly used as a navigational tool. The astromythological symbolism of this transition is clear. Draco is to Uther Pendragon (Pendragon translates as 'head-dragon') as Ursa Minor is to Arthur. The North Star's shift from Thuban in Draco to Polaris in Ursa Minor represents the transition in kingship from father to son, Uther to Arthur. At a more profound aeonic level, the North Star's passing corresponds to a shift from the matriarchal terra-vulvic Aeon of Isis to the patriarchal solar-phallic Aeon of Osiris. Again, this is reflected in Arthurian

51 Cambell, 12.

tradition where Uther represents pre-Christian kingship (this is made explicit in the Pendragon battle standard's associations with the Sarmatian Mother Goddess); and Arthur represents the incoming veneration of Christ as a solar god of death and resurrection. The North Star's transit appears to have lasted 1,000 years, from 500 BCE to 500 CE. Culturally, this coincided with the emergence of ritual king-slaying in Irish Celtic culture, the rise of Ra and solar worship in Egyptian theology, and the establishment of the second temple in Jerusalem, the seat of biblical patriarchy. In human evolutionary terms, it can be linked to the emergence of the ego and self-consciousness.

As the sleeping 'once and future king' Arthur is also associated with the constellation Boötes, specifically the pellucid red-tinged star Arcturus, the brightest in the northern celestial hemisphere. The fifteenth century poet John Lydgate describes Arthur / Arcturus dwelling in repose in the 'crystal palace' of Boötes, which recalls both the otherworldly glass fortress of Annwn and Ynys Witrin, the Isle of Glass. In certain legends Arthur now dwells in the underworld of Annwn until he is called upon to ride forth again. In others, Arcturus is his dwelling place – an arrangement that echoes the Greek concept of the heavens as the celestial Hades. The rising of Arcturus is associated with the arrival of spring which, again, recalls Arthur's status as a solar hero. Because of its proximity to Ursa Major, otherwise known as Arthur's Wain, Arcturus is known as the Guardian of the Bear: the power of Arthur in Arcturus drives his wain across the sky. This is echoed in the arcane geographies of the local islands of Beckery, Godney, Martinsey, Andersey, Westhay, Meare and Panborough which, along with Glastonbury, approximate the constellation of Ursa Major. John Dee may have been alluding to this phenomenon when he wrote of 'Merlin's Secret,' pointing to astronomical and terrestrial correspondences in the landscape surrounding Glastonbury, potentially including its terrestrial zodiac:

> The starres which agree with their reproductions, on the ground do lye on the celestial path of the Sonne, moon and planets ... thus is astrologie and astronomie carefullie and exactley married and measured in a scientific reconstruction of the heavens which shews that the ancients understode all which today the lerned know to be factes.[52]

52 Deacon, 131–133.

Sirius – which means 'scorching' – is the bright silver star of night and holds an especial otherworldly status, being fundamental to the Draconian astro-theology of the terra-vulvic Aeon of Isis, and therefore to the reign of the Pendragon. It is argued by Crowley and others that the matrifocal Aeon of Isis was characterised by veneration of a great ur-goddess; an embodiment of the prima materia who sired the universe parthenogenetically. She is cognate with Chaos, and with Nuit and Isis (conflated as Nu-Isis.) In Kenneth Grant's Typhonian Order this Draconian female is known as Typhon. Her Aeon coincided with the region of the North Star's eliding with Thuban in Draco, when the upper, lower and middle worlds of the cosmos were conjoined in an axis mundi, through which the primal Draconian or Ophidian current flowed – into the land and into all life. This was the presiding power of the Aeon. In Typhonian tradition her first son was Set, the relationship made explicit in the composite deity of the Greek Magical Papyri known as Set-Typhon. Set means 'black';[53] he is associated with the underworld where his mysteries were originally enacted and, by extension, with the nictating star Sirius, specifically the hidden star Sirius B. Also deified as Sothis, to the Greeks its heliacal rising heralded the burning days of summer; to the Egyptians the commencement of the new year and the inundation of the Nile, a phenomenon interpreted in the context of the feminine mysteries as a deluge of menstrual blood.[54] Set represents a tradition of stellar veneration; his eternal enemy is Horus, emblematic of solar veneration. Therefore, Sirius is recognised as the 'sun behind the sun.' It is the subconscious, concealed child; the unmanifested and occulted sun that is only revealed when the exoteric sun descends into the hidden lands, the chthonic realms, and weakens. Thus, Sirius is the sun of the lower regions, the stellar light in the darkness that illuminates the souls of the dead and the denizens of Annwn, the underworld of Avalon. As such, both Sirius and Set are cognate with the Sol Niger, the alchemical black sun. The process of Nigredo is embodied in Set, whose name also translates as 'soot.' His heat is symbolised by the searing power of the black sun, burning away the mundane in order to reveal that which is purified.

It should be noted that within Katherine Maltwood's great terrestrial zodiac – the Temple of the Stars – the station of Aquarius centred on Glastonbury

53 Set's colour is red, however, drawing an interesting correspondence with the chthonic power from 2 Enoch known as Arkhas.

54 See Grant (1994).

is depicted as a Phoenix, cognate with the Bennu bird, symbolic of rebirth and resurrection from the fires of immolation, and the alchemical process of Rubedo – the culmination of the magnum opus. The ancient Bennu constellation claimed Sirius as its chief star. Thus, in Egyptian tradition, the Phoenix is associated with the commencement of the Sothic year, coinciding with the heliacal rising of Sirius. Notably, the lifespan of the Phoenix was thought to equal the duration of the Egyptian Great Year, thereby connecting the lifecycle of the Phoenix with the great mythic cycles of death and rebirth; the descent of the solar god into the underworld and his subsequent rebirth. The pseudepigraphic Second Book of Enoch describes how, at sunrise, two solar creatures, the Phoenix and the Chalkydri, come forth and burst into song as heralds of the Sun's rising. By virtue of these examples the Phoenix is unequivocally a creature of the sun, unifying both the sustaining solar power of the upper world, and the unmanifest stellar Sol Niger of the lower world; the sun behind the sun that is Sirius.

Sirius, it is claimed, is also the faerie sun lying at the heart of their otherworldly cosmos,[55] the *tylwyth teg* being dwellers in the 'Deep Place' that is Annwn, the chthonic realm illuminated by the black sun. Thus, Sirius is not merely the hound following Arawn into the Wild Hunt. Rather, it is the theriocephalic son of the primal Goddess, the darkly pellucid eye that illuminates the otherworld with its Draconian rays, and to whom Arawn and his kin give tribute.

¶ THE AVALONIAN OTHERWORLD

As an axis mundi or cosmic axis, the Tor is a physical nexus connecting the celestial and chthonic realms. Its axis is the pole star, Polaris in this epoch, around which the cosmos rotates. The circumpolar stars in the northern hemisphere, Auriga, Camelopardalis, Cassiopeia, Cepheus, Draco, Lynx, Perseus, Ursa Major, and Ursa Minor, are those that never set below the horizon; they are undying and eternal. The Milky Way is one mythic gateway to the heavens, the glittering bridge by which the dead ascend to the 'celestial Hades,' the realms of the gods amongst the stars. A second gate is the axis mundi itself, a world-pillar providing transit to the stars from the well of souls in the under-

55 Fortune, Lumley Brown, Knight, 190–191.

world. A third is the Gates of the Sun, the portals of sunrise and sunset and, in particular, of the solstices when the ecliptic crosses the Milky Way.

The underworld exists within or alongside the otherworld, although the two are often conflated. The domain of the Magna Mater, it typically comprises the chthonic realms, the abode of the fey, the dead and manifold deities. To venture into the underworld is to descend into the earth itself, into the body of the Mother, wherein the tombs of the dead become a primordial womb; the putrefaction of the corpse is transformed into a seed of resurrection.

Although broadly understood as being located, or at least accessed via gates, below the earth, this is not always the case. Myths tell of manifold realms of the dead, some in an hypogean context, others located above or beside the mortal world. In broad terms, the conditions of each culture's afterworld were determined by the qualities of its occupants: royalty, aristocracy, heroes and warriors typically enjoyed an afterlife amidst a pastoral idyll free of want, toil and pain. Two obvious examples are Fólkvangr and Valhǫll, the abodes of Freyja and Óðinn located above the middle-world, wherein dwelled those slain on the field of battle. The population-at-large abided in a place deprived of sunlight where dead souls endured an aimless semi-existence, neither thinking nor feeling. Sinners, the wicked and the immoral were consigned to the bowels of the earth to endure an eternity of torment in the smothering darkness.

Greek myth describes the journey to the realm of the dead as a horizontal path rather than a descent, where travellers must cross the great river-ocean demarcating the mortal world and the afterworld. Similarly, the Egyptian underworld was originally located above or beside the mortal world, separated by the sea and a range of mountains enclosing a great valley. These geographies recall the mythic Fortunate Lands and Isle of the Blessed, earthly paradises where souls of the dead dwelled in peace. The Holy Island of Glastonbury can be understood in this regard, as both an axis mundi and a worldly Elysium.

Notably, early Irish literature depicts the otherworld as an enchanted, atemporal mirror-world incorporating realms of the gods, the fey and the dead. While to some extent co-existing with the mundane world, it was wholly different and supra-natural. Certain regions were peaceful and plentiful; others dark and terrifying; yet others were places of refuge and protection.[56] Celtic otherworlds were numerous and heterogeneous, consisting of celestial, terres-

56 Waddell (2015), chapter 4.

trial, chthonic, immaterial, physical and liminal places, divided into manifold realms, kingdoms and principalities and populated by heroes, deities, animals and mythic beasts. In addition to Avalon and Annwn, Irish variants included: Tír na nÓg (the land of the young); Tír fo Thoinn (the land under the waves); Tír Shorcha (the luminous land); Magh Mór (the great plain) and Magh Meall (the pleasant realm.)[57] Of particular interest are the terrestrial otherworlds, which were accessed via the mound and enabled a form of bodily ingress and egress; Welsh and Irish tales describe otherwordly journeys by humans who entered freely or bore a 'key' in the form of an apple or branch, and departed bearing physical gifts and goods. As attested by Welsh and Irish myth, those returning from the otherworld were marked by profound transformation; initiated, transfigured and possessed of gnosis and magickal powers, specifically shape-shifting and seership.

The metempsychotic cycle of Celtic belief is inextricably bound up with the otherworld, which in death provided an opportunity for souls to become refleshed and to wayfare certain other realms in a variety of forms. Although far from unique, Celtic burial customs attest to this state of affairs, with grave goods incorporating weapons, clothes, transport, drinking vessels and food such as joints of meat.[58] Re-embodied souls would reside in the otherworld in pursuit of learning and pleasure, or return to the mundane human realm to continue their worldly lives. Pomponius Mela described how Celts would 'defer the completion of business and the payment of debts until their arrival in another world,' implying that one's previous life was far from evanescent. Anamnesis was a function of the soul's transmigration, yielding a continuity of memory, kinship and bond.

The existence of terrestrial otherworlds in Celtic myth explains the status of Glastonbury as an earthly Elysium. The Holy Island does not simply provide a gateway to the otherworld; it is the otherworld. Similarly, the materiality of liminal otherworlds such as Annwn, the realm of the Faerie, is articulated in Western esoteric tradition, where the fey and certain orders of spirits such as land wights are reputedly embodied in some form (Theosophy describes this embodiment as 'etheric.') Within the initiatory cycle of the Great Quest, the catechumen is required to both perceive the otherworld and engage with it. This is achieved via cultivation of the semi-carnate self – the Umbra Animae

57 Heinz, 47.
58 Ross, 356–7.

– and of magickal behaviours that, by definition, reside outside of mundane norms.

Prior to their unification under an homogenous below-realm known as Tuat, each ancient Egyptian city possessed its own underworld.[59] The same may be said for every early culture, which by its nature was rooted in a specific geography typically featuring a ritual centre. Terrestrial portals to the various underworlds are equally numerous: for Irish Celts it was the chamber of Oweynagat in Rathcroghan; for the Mayans it was the Actun Tunichil Muknal cave; for the ancient Greeks it was the cave on Cape Matapan. Egyptian theology posits a series of netherworld gates which the Sun and its entourage passed through to ultimately access Aaru, the paradisal field of reeds. Each gate was possessed of a female tutelary deity whose secret name must be uttered before safe passage was granted.

Of the underworld's many strata, the realm of Faerie, Elvelond or Elphame is considered to be uppermost, where certain dead also dwell. That the Tor is also an otherworldly gateway is evinced in the *Life of St Collen*, the seventh century monk, who ascended to the Tor's summit and:

> saw the fairest castle he had ever beheld, and around it the best-appointed troops, and numbers of minstrels, and every kind of music of voice and string, and steeds with youths upon them the comeliest in the world, and maidens of elegant aspect, sprightly, light of foot, of graceful apparel, and in the bloom of youth and every magnificence becoming the court of a puissant sovereign. And he beheld a courteous man on the top of the castle, who bade him enter, saying that the king was waiting for him to come to meat. And Collen went into the castle, and when he came there, the king was sitting in a golden chair. And he welcomed Collen honourably and desired him to eat, assuring him that, besides what he saw, he should have the most luxurious of every dainty and delicacy that the mind could desire, and should be supplied with every drink and liquor that his heart could wish; and that there should be in readiness for him every luxury of courtesy and service, of banquet and of honourable entertainment, of rank and of presents: and every respect and welcome due to a man of his wisdom.[60]

59 Budge, 172.

60 From a translation by Mary Jones at https://www.maryjones.us/ctexts/collen.html

The king is Arawn, or Gwyn ap Nudd: leader of the Wild Hunt, lord of the fey and ruler of Annwn, the underworld of the Holy Island. As Gwyn ap Nudd he is a companion of Arthur, a warrior, a psychopomp and bulwark against 'the brood of devils' who dwell in Annwn. Nevertheless, in response, Collen casts holy water at Arawn, 'whereupon [he] vanished from his sight, so that there was neither castle, nor troops, nor men, nor maidens, nor music, nor song, nor steeds, nor youths, nor banquet, nor the appearance of any thing whatever, but the green hillocks.' *Gwyn* means 'fair, bright, white.' His association with the Folk can be found in the etymology of 'elf,' which is derived from the Proto-Indo-European root meaning 'bright, shining, white.' The castle of Arawn referred to in the *Life of St Collen* echoes the castles described in *Preiddeu Annwfn* or *The Spoils of Annwfn*, from the *Book of Taliesin*. Arawn's primary abode is Caer Sidi or the Fortress of the Mound. Seven further castles are described in the poem.

The number seven, sacred in itself, is a recurring motif in descriptions of otherwordly locations, either celestial or chthonic. On one hand, seven is linked to the process of creation: there are seven vertical paths within the Kabbalistic tree of life. Terrestrial temples, whether Glastonbury Tor, the Step Pyramid of Djoser or the Sumerian ziggurat of Etemenanki, consist of seven tiers. *The Chymical Wedding of Christian Rosenkreutz* describes the Elixir of Life residing in a tower with seven levels. In numerous spiritual traditions, a seven-runged ladder, stairway or notched pillar enables the descent of gods and the ascent of dead souls to and from heaven. An equal number of downward steps grants katabasis to the body of the earth.[61] The Buddhist sutra 'Discourse on the Land of Great Happiness' recounts a land in the west called Sukhavati, surrounded by seven tiers, seven veils, and seven rows of trees; its lakes contain the seven precious stones. Its westerly location confirms Sukhavati as an isle of the blessed, an Elysium. The seven castles of Annwn correspond to the seven gates of the underworld in the Sumerian account of Inanna's descent into Hell. In both cases the seven portals provide a prototypical map of the underworld, an inner journey through the realms of darkness in order to achieve gnosis and rebirth.

As lord of the Fair Folk, Arawn is explicitly linked with the spiritous realm of Faerie or Elphame. In this respect he is cognate with Norse Yngvi-freyr, *blótguð svía* or lord of blood sacrifices, the god of kingship and the dead who dwells

61 Eliade, 487–488; 274–279.

in Alfheim, the homeland of the elves. His realm is entered via the mound, a point of ingress echoed by the Tor. Other sites of liminality also provide access: threshold places such as caves, sacred trees, groves, wells, springs and stones. They are the points of coition between inner and outer, palpable and imaginal. To paraphrase Tolkien, the shadowy marches of Faerie begin when the human will makes the power of the imagination immediately effective:

> Faërie ... contains many things besides elves and fays ... it holds the seas, the sun, the moon, the sky; and the earth, and all the things that are in it ... and ourselves, mortal men, when we are enchanted.[62]

The consistency of faerie-lore across cultures attests to their mythic reality. Variously known as the *tylwyth teg* (of which the *ellyllon* are a sylvan typology); *aes sídhe* (the 'people of the mounds') or *ailill*, *sìth*, *ielfe* or *álfar*; the origins of these magickal beings are obscure. They may be deities, lesser spirits, an elder Atlantean race, fallen angels or an otherwise occulted species. Certain commentators have supposed them to be the souls of the dead awaiting a return to mortal life as part of the metempsychotic cycle.[63] Reputedly long-lived, their bodies move freely between the seen and unseen worlds. Given that Sirius-Set is the black star that illuminates the chthonic realm of Annwn, and Sirius is claimed to be the sun of Faerie, the *tylwyth teg* can be described as stellar in origin, but now resident in the otherworld. This is supported by the folklorist William Bottrell, who recorded that the fey are 'not of our religion, but star-worshippers.'[64] Draconian in nature and of a tradition venerating the Divine Feminine, they are characterised as capricious, territorial, socially transgressive and magickally potent, and are liable to inflict enchantment, illness, ruin or death on those who fail to observe proper decorum or deference. Let this be a warning. The Holy Island is a place where The Folk wander freely and manifest as 'punkies' – orbs of light – dancing around the precincts of the Tor. They are especially associated with the green mysteries of the earth, its rhythms and tides.

62 Tolkien, 16, 28. Taken literally, Tolkien's quote can be seen to echo Heraclides's Empedotimus, who claimed that the kingdom of Hades contained all things under the sphere of the sun (and, conversely, the sidereal realm contains the underworld.)
63 Spence, 54.
64 Gary, 44.

John Lydgate's *Fall of Princes* declares that Arthur, brought to Avalon for healing by Morgen of the Sororitas Avalonis, lives on as a crowned king in Annwn. When Merlin's prophesy is fulfilled, Arthur will ride out of Annwn to rule Britain as its lord and sovereign. Arthur's astromorphosis into Arcturus does not contradict his status as a regent in Annwn. In many traditions spirits move freely between the realms and one is a reflection or continuation of the other. The dead are both under the earth and in the stars. His regency in Annwn is testament to the sacral nature of his kingship where, through the rites of that office, his rulership across all worlds is asserted.

Finally, consideration should briefly be given to the remarkable similarities between the geographies of terrestrial otherworlds, earthly paradises, shamanic landscapes, Avalon and Atlantis. Each broadly conforms to the same configuration: an island incorporating a central place or axis mundi in the form of a single, primordial world-tree or grove, a cosmic hill or mountain, or a fortress or temple. A number of life-giving rivers emerge as springs, flowing from the centre towards the compass points. Both the biblical Eden and Islamic Jinnah are examples, along with Flath-innis, the Gaelic Island of the Good; the Taoist Kwen-lun; Homer's description of the western island of Ogygia in the *Odyssey*; the city of Brahma from the Hindu Vishnu Purana; the realm of Glæsisvellir in *Eireks Saga Víðförla*; the Land of Promise in the Irish tale *Echtra Cormaic* or *Echtra Cormaic*; and, not least, a fictitious letter from Prester John to the Emperor Emanuel Comnenus describing the marvels of the Earthly Paradise.[65] In the case of Irish myth, a tree or grove lies at the centre of the paradisal realm of Tír na nÓg. Its regent is Manannán mac Lir, King of the Fey, cognate with Arawn, Gwyn ap Nudd and Yngvi-freyr. Nearby is the well or fountain of wisdom; its waters flow out of Tír na nÓg into the mortal world. Thus, in Irish Celtic myth, all earthly wells and springs have their source in the otherworld.

65 See Warren and Baring-Gould chapter 7 for more on this topic.

¶ THE DRAOIDHEAN

Various commentators have suggested the Draoidhean were inheritors of Atlantean wisdom, imparted by the prophet, sorcerer and ur-Druid Merlin. Allied to this notion, others such as the alchemist Albertus Magnus claimed that alchemy was a continuation of the religion of the Druids. Blavatsky asserted that the Druids were the descendants of the last Atlanteans – a position that likely influenced Dion Fortune – and venerated a deity in the form of a mighty serpent, even referring to themselves as 'Snakes.' She argues that 'the Atlanteans of the middle period were called the Great Dragons, and the first symbol of their tribal deities ... was that of a giant serpent.'[66] Proof of this supposedly lay in the myriad *dracontia* or serpent temples found across all regions of the earth, not least the British landscape. The term 'dracontia' was used by the eighteenth-century antiquarian William Stukeley and the mythographer Jacob Bryant in reference to megalithic sites comprising circular features and avenues, in particular Avebury, which they erroneously attributed to the Druids. Bryant saw these serpentine temples representing the union of sun and earth, solar and ophite religions.[67]

Manifold assertions have been made in relation to Glastonbury and the Druids. Hecataeus of Abdera refers to a legendary northern island inhabited by Hyperboreans, who worship the sun god Apollo upon a wondrous temple, spherical in shape. Some commentators believe this to be Avalon.[68] Further, he alludes to a Druidic college, also located at Glastonbury, along with a perpetual choir to enchant the land and maintain cosmic harmony. And the sorority of witch-maidens who dwelled upon the Tor, led by Morgen, were in all likelihood, in their euhemerised aspect, female Druids.

Prior to Roman invasion under Claudius in 43 CE, British Celtic society was certainly dominated by these priest-rulers.[69] Likely to have been well established in Britain by 600 BCE, Pliny mentions they were still very numerous in Britain in 79 CE, despite their apparent destruction at the Isle of Anglesey – the seat of Druidic power in Britain – some years earlier. The extent to which Druidism persisted after its Roman suppression is impossible to state with

66 Blavatsky (2019), 756.

67 Deane, 364–5.

68 Roberts (1992), 21–22.

69 See Cuncliffe for an excellent, factual introduction to the Druids.

certainty. Excavations at a Romano-British site at Wansborough in Surrey revealed a Roman-era stone temple constructed atop an earlier Celtic *nemeta* surrounding a tree, implying continuity of sanctity. Finds included an elaborate headdress surmounted by a Celtic-style solar wheel. The headdress is not dissimilar to a piece of Romano-Celtic ritual headgear found at Cavenham in Suffolk, incorporating a series of sun discs and chains. A votive group discovered near Bury St Edmunds also contains directly comparable discs and chains. As a whole, these finds suggest that Druidism continued into the Roman era, but likely became assimilated into Romano-Celtic traditions, stepping out of the natural temples of oak, ash and yew and into man-made environments, in imitation of the Roman model.[70] They also support the notion of a persistent Celtic and Romano-Celtic sun cult.

The early Anglo-Saxon cult centre at Goodmanham in East Yorkshire, described by Bede in his *Historia ecclesiastica gentis Anglorum*, draws comparisons with descriptions of Druidic *nemeta*: the Anglo-Saxon shrine consisted of a number of enclosures and altars, surrounded by precincts or hedges. 'Goodmanham' may be derived from the ancient name Godmundingaham, from the Celtic *godo*, an uncovered sanctuary or temple, and *mynyddis* meaning a hilly place.[71] According to Bede, the temple's priest was named Coifi, an anglicised form of the Gaelic *choibhi* or *choibhidh*, meaning 'arch-druid' or high priest.[72] This interpretation is based on Bede's use of a Gaelic word to denote Coifi's station. The seventh century CE political landscape of the region saw the Anglo-Saxon kingdom of Deira abutted by the Brittonic kingdom of Elmet; therefore, Coifi may have represented part of a persistent British pagan tradition with continuity into the Anglo-Saxon era. A few generations earlier, St Brigid, born in 450 CE, was said to have been raised and educated by Druids, after her mother was sold to a chieftain in Connaught.

Druidry was a fundamentally animistic belief system. Additionally, a complex pantheon of deities, many specific to a tribe or locality, were venerated at *temenoi* beside mounds, rivers, streams, lakes, trees, hills and mountains – the same loci of liminality that afford otherworldy access. Chief amongst its deities were the Great Mother goddess Dana, Ana or Anna, and her consort

70 See Watts for the possibilities of continuity of Druidic traditions in Roman-era Britain.

71 See *The East Yorkshire Village Book*, 93–94.

72 Pollington, 125.

Belenos, Beel or Bile, a solar deity and dispenser of light and healing. These two opposing primal deities were likely brought together in seasonal rituals via a form of *hieros gamos*, emphasising the cyclical nature of life and death.

The main spiritual tenet of the Celts, again according to Caesar, was that 'souls do not suffer death, but after death pass from one body to another.' This is the Orphic and Socratic doctrine of metempsychosis, the transmigration of souls. The Mysteries of Eleusis identify the mortal aspect of the self as the *eidolon*; the immortal aspect the *daemon*. Caesar's observation is supported by the Roman geographer Pomponius Mela. In his *Description of the World* written in 43 CE he states:

> And yet they have an eloquence of their own, and their Druids as masters of wisdom. These profess to know the magnitude and form of the earth and the world, the motions of the heaven and the stars, and the will of the gods. They teach the most noble of the nation many things privately, and for a long time, even for twenty years, in a cave, or in inaccessible woods. One of their precepts has become public, namely, that they should act bravely in war, that souls are immortal, and that there is another life after death.[73]

The nineteenth century text *Barddas* by Iolo Morganwg describes four circles of being through which increasingly perfected human souls may ascend: Annwn, the underworld and source of corporeal reincarnation; Abred, the corporeal world; Gwynfyd, the celestial otherworld; and Ceugant, the realm of the godhead cognate with the Kabbalistic crown of Kether.[74] Although of dubious provenance, the model is useful in justifying the existence of a Celtic above-realm of pure spirit, made explicit in the stars and asterisms of the night sky.

Caesar noted that the Druids claimed to be sons of Dīs Pater, the Roman god of the underworld, who is cognate with Welsh Arawn and Irish Midir, ruler of the hollow elf-mounds of Brí Léith. This is notable inasmuch as it establishes an explicit link between Druidic teachings, otherworldly gnosis and the metempsychotic cycle. In claiming descent from a chthonic deity, the implication is that Druids possessed direct experience and detailed knowledge of otherworlds. By extension, we can postulate that the Druids played a

73 Mela, 107.

74 Evans-Wentz, 342–344.

pivotal role in maintaining good relations with otherworldly beings, presiding over rites of death and rebirth, ingress and egress, and generally assisting in the maintenance of a healthy homeostasis between the mundane realm and the otherworlds.

Druids were priest-rulers, aristocrats attached to a royal household as a magickal practitioner; a shaman and shapeshifter; an enactor of rituals and giver of sacrifices; an advisor, arbitrator, lawgiver, teacher and prophet. However, there appears to be some overlap with the Celtic priestly castes of Ovate and Bard, according to Roman commentators. Strabo notes that:

> The belief in the justice [of the Druids] is so great that the decision both of public and private disputes is referred to them; and they have before now, by their decision, prevented armies from engaging when drawn up in battle-array against each other.[75]

The Roman statesman Cicero provides the only eye-witness account of a druid: he describes Divitiacus (meaning 'Avenger') of the Aedui tribe as a diplomat, magistrate and political leader, possessing knowledge of divination, astronomy and natural philosophy. A description of British Druids is provided by Tacitus in his account of the first Roman attack on Anglesey by Suetonius Paulanus:

> On the beach stood the adverse array, a serried mass of arms and men, with women flitting between the ranks. In the style of Furies, in robes of deathly black and with dishevelled hair, they brandished their torches; while a circle of Druids, lifting their hands to heaven and showering imprecations, struck the troops with such an awe at the extraordinary spectacle that, as though their limbs were paralysed, they exposed their bodies to wounds without an attempt at movement. Then, reassured by their general, and inciting each other never to flinch before a band of females and fanatics, they charged behind the standards, cut down all who met them, and enveloped the enemy in his own flames.[76]

75 Strabo, 294.
76 Tacitus, Book XIV, ch.XXX.

In the early Irish text known as *Sanas Cormaic*, Mug Ruith, the chief Druid of the king of Ireland is described as wearing a bull's hide, a feathered bird mask, a coloured cloak and earrings of gold. His powers include the ability to generate water, breathe black mist, summon a firestorm and fly by virtue of a garment known as a *tuigen* (also as an *énchennach*), a covering or cloak made from white and multicoloured feathers. The wearing of feathers is a sign of avian kinship, magickal ability and poetic inspiration. Archaeology in Britain has revealed ritual objects such as sheet metal 'feathers' that recall the *tuigen*. In Celtic tradition birds are otherworldly creatures; in some cases psychopomps and spirit guides; in others messengers of the gods, or even souls of the dead. The ancient Greek historian Diodorus Siculus noted that '[the Druids] predict the future by observing the flight and calls of birds.' The shape-shifting transformation from human to bird – a common motif in Celtic myth – represents the liminal state of the soul; it is located neither within a human body or the unseen realms.[77]

The *nemeta* or sacred spaces of the Celts were not solely groves. The Roman poet Lucan describes a Gaulish Druidic temple thus:

> There was a grove, untouched through long centuries ... It was sacred to no rural Pan ... but gods were worshipped there with savage rites, the altars piled high with foul offerings, and every tree drenched in human blood. On those boughs ... the birds feared to perch; in those coverts no wild beast would lie; on that grove no wind ever blew, no lightning bolt from the storm clouds fell; and the trees, spreading their leaves to an absent breeze, rustled of themselves. Water flowed there in copious dark streams, while the images of the gods, rough-hewn and grim, were merely crude blocks cut from felled trunks of trees ... They also say the subterranean caves often shook and roared, that yew-trees fell and then rose again, that flame glowed from trees free of fire, while serpents slithered and twined about their trunks. The people never gathered there to worship; they had abandoned the place to the gods, and when the sun was at the zenith, or night's blackness seized the sky, the priest himself dreaded those moments, afraid of surprising the lord of the wood.[78]

77 See Slavin for more on this topic.

78 Lucan, Book III, 399–452.

Excavations of sites in Northern France and Southern England reveal Iron Age sanctuaries consisting of rectilinear, fenced or bank-and-ditch enclosures, central pits and east-facing entrances. Some are divided into mortuary and ritual spaces. Commentators have suggested the central pits of the nemeta contained sacrifices, functioning as portals for spirits to descend to Dumnos, the deep darkness of the underworld.[79]

Archaeology reveals that the majority of Druidic sanctuaries are located on high ground overlooking the surrounding landscape and close to coastal areas or rivers. The shrine or cult centre at Hayling Island in Sussex is an exemplar.[80] Glastonbury Tor conforms to this topography, even though explicit associations with Druidry and the Holy Island are difficult to confirm. However, if Glastonbury functioned as an Iron Age cult centre, as both the archaeology and legends suggest, then it is not unreasonable to assume a priesthood was present upon the island.

Most commentators of the ancient world have asserted the practice of sacrifice amongst the Druids. Strabo states that:

> They would strike a man devoted as an offering in his back with a sword, and divine from his convulsive throes. Without the Druids they never sacrifice. It is said they have other modes of sacrificing their human victims; that they pierce some of them with arrows, and crucify others in their temples; and that they prepare a colossus of hay and wood, into which they put cattle, beasts of all kinds, and men, and then set fire to it.[81]

And he goes on to recount the Greek geographer Artemidorus when he states 'that there is an island near Britain in which they [the Druids] perform sacrifices to these goddesses [Ceres and Proserpine] after the same fashion that they do in Samothrace.'[82] While the location of the island is unknown, the quote is notable for its reference to the Druids' supposed veneration of chthonic and fertility goddesses, thereby aligning their religious practices with the death-and-resurrection rituals of the Romano-Greek mystery cults.

79 Robb, 126.
80 See Garland.
81 Strabo, 295.
82 Ibid.

¶ DE SORORITAS AVALONIS

Arthurian lore refers to nine maidens who dwell upon the Holy Isle of Avalon. In his *Vita Merlini*, Geoffrey of Monmouth mentions nine women of the Isle of Apples, seeresses and healers, led by Morgen, Modron or Matrona, the Lady of Avalon. The other eight are named Moronoe, Mazoe, Gliten, Glitonea, Gliton, Tyronoe, Thiten and Thiton, who receive the mortally wounded King Arthur from Taliesin in an attempt to heal him. In her guise as the Queen of Danemarche, Morgan's abode is described as surrounded by an impenetrable 'hedge of air,' which articulates the nature of high places typical of druidic sanctuaries.[83]

The nine maidens of Avalon are cognate with the sisterhood of nine virgin priestesses of the Île de Sein, an island off the coast of modern-day Brittany. First mentioned by the Greek geographer Artemidorus of Ephesus, they were later described as *gallisenae*, female druids, endowed with powers of sorcery, shape-shifting, healing and divination. Celtic coin finds depict what may be a druidess or *bandruí*, adorned with a crown of moons and a snake, suggestive of a priestess's ritual garb. Strabo also tells of an island, which may be the Île de Sein:

> There is a small island lying opposite to the outlet of the river Loire, inhabited by Samnite women who are Bacchantes, and conciliate and appease that god by mysteries and sacrifices. No man is permitted to land on the island; and when the women desire to have intercourse with the other sex, they cross the sea, and afterwards return again.[84]

Preiddeu Annwfn recounts the tale of nine maidens of Annwn who attend the magickal cauldron of Arawn. Recited by the bard Taliesin, he identifies the cauldron as the source of his inspiration; in turn, the cauldron receives its powers from the nine maidens' breath. This draws parallels with the nine Muses, the Greek goddesses of inspiration.

83 The initiatory nature of the Avalonian ennead may possess a galactic equivalent in the Council of Nine, the evolved beings maintaining universal balance, according to channelled communications received by Phyllis Schlemmer and collated by Palden Jenkins – see Schlemmer & Jenkins.

84 Ibid., 295.

This ennead is both benign and malevolent. *Peredur son of Efrawg* from the *Mabinogion* recounts the story of the *Naw Widdon* or *Nine Witches of Caer Lloyw*. Their dwelling-place, the 'shining fortress,' recalls the seven Caers of Annwn. They are fearsome black-clad maiden-hags, mistresses of warfare and magick. In this guise they evoke the Morrígna, the sinister raven-queens of Irish myth and the Scottish divine hag or Cailleach, who leads nine witches. The Cailleach is connected with high places, as evinced by the presence of menhirs known as Cnoc a Cailleach located at the summit of hills and mountains. Other Scottish folklore links the ennead of maidens with winter solstice and dragons, the latter in terms of the waning of pagan belief in the wake of Christianity; the nine are also invoked in various Scottish folk magickal spells.

The cult of nine maidens persists across European mythology, not least Norse myth. The *jötunn* Ægir, a sea deity, sires nine daughters. Their names are Blóðughadda, Bylgja, Dröfn, Dúfa, Hefring, Himinglæva, Hrönn, Kolga and Uðr. The Icelandic tale *Þiðranda þáttr ok Þórhalls* features nine *valkyrja*, while the Old Norse *Helgakvida Hundingsbana* also tells of nine *valkyrja* who prophesy the hero's future and grant him a name, which functions as a gift of eloquence. This echoes the gift of inspiration received by Taliesin from the nine maidens' cauldron. *Eiríks saga rauða* includes a coven of nine *völur* with divinatory powers, linking the cult of nine maidens to Freyja, the prototypical *valkyrja*, goddess of battle, witch-mother and giver of *seiðr*, the magick of the *völur*. *Fjölsvinnsmál* tells of nine maidens who attend to the woman known as Menglöð; guarded by the watchman Fjölsviðr, they dwell in a castle upon the hill of Lyfjaberg, which translates as 'hill of healing.'

In Norse star lore, Freyja is linked to the Pleiades cluster, consisting of nine bright stars. To the Celts the Pleiades was known as *tŵr tewdws*, the 'close pack.' Since antiquity the nine bright stars of the Pleiades have been associated with seven sisters and their parents, Atlas and Pleione. In ancient Greece its heliacal rising and setting marked the beginning of spring and autumn and the sailing season, which also defined the period in which initiation into the Mysteries of Samothrace occurred.[85]

The cult of nine maidens can also be extended to St Brigid, whose sacred fire at Kildare was attended by nine virgins. Nine female companions were said to have accompanied Brigid in her journey to Abernethy in Scotland. The Sororitas Avalonis may also be considered as female variants of the nine

85 Adams, 27.

Idaean Dactyls or *daimones* who dwelled upon Mount Ida in the service of the Magna Mater.

These exemplars of nine maidens or sorceresses are consanguineous with their earliest ur-myths: the Magdalenian cave painting at El Cogul, near Lleida in Catalonia, is approximately fifteen thousand years old. It depicts nine women and an ithyphallic male figure – thought to represent the Sun – in a ritualistic arrangement.[86] Earlier still, the Kikuyu people claim descent from a group of nine sisters who dwelled at a place called Mũkũrwe wa Gathanga close to the sacred Mount Kenya. The nine *mousai* or Muses of ancient Greek religion echo these primordial myths: the nine sisters, givers of inspiration, were daughters of Gaia the Earth Mother and Ouranos the Sky Father; they resided upon Mount Helikon in Boiotia, the location of their cult centre, and were led by the sun god Apollo.

Gender aside, the *paut* of ancient Egyptian Heliopolis, the great company of the gods, was nine in number. Further, nine chief forms of Horus are given in the Pyramid Texts, of which four are the 'spirits of Horus,' the four gods of the cardinal directions.

The veracity of the nine maidens cult is confirmed and elevated by its antediluvian origins: the sorceresses are deities, associated with creation, healing, prophesy and fertility. They dwell upon an island, hill or mountain. As such, they sit at the crossroads of the cenobitic priory, the oracular priestess's temple and the forest-dwelling coven, all located at places of isolation and liminality in dedication to their Arte.

86 See McHardy for more on the Nine Maidens cult.

¶ THE GRAAL

Glastonbury lore tells of Joseph of Arimathea arriving at the Holy Island with two cruets: one containing the blood of Christ, the other his sweat. Hidden beneath the Tor (or Chalice Hill), they manifest in the phenomena of the Red and White Springs. Yet the Graal possesses no ontic reality. Any attempt to comprehend it in purely noetic terms will result in falsehood. Over time the Graal has been variously identified as: a crucible, a stone, the bloodline of Christ, a cauldron, an oracular severed head, a Marian cypher, the crescent moon, the tarot, the Orphic bowl, a tray, a jewel, the two cruets, a chalice, a book, a krater, a foundation stone, a dodecahedron, the Sophia or wisdom of god, the cup of the last supper, the Omega Point, a symbol of the Pelagian succession, and a gnostic expression of initiatory vegetation rituals.[87] It is all and none of these things.

In Arthurian tradition, the Holy Graal is sought as a means of healing the wasteland, of restoring fertility to the earth and reestablishing harmony between the otherworld and the physical world. The wasteland was brought about as a direct result of men wilfully desecrating Nature and its in-dwelling spirits. The Graal therefore represents Magistery: transformation, healing and balance. The Graal Quest is a perennial inner journey for renewal of the self, an eternal act of becoming. It is a resolution of humankind's emasculation, which itself is a consequence of its separation from divinity in all its forms. The trials and privations of the quest lie upon the path of initiation, which leads to revelation and gnosis. The quest must be undertaken in order to transfigure the postulant into the illuminant, to bring the disunity of the self and the universe, mortality and divinity, into one body. Only then, when the covenant between spirit and flesh is restored, can the Graal itself be approached. The microcosm of the sanctified, verdant self will then witness the wasteland's transformation into a virid realm, a fecund conjunction of natural and supernatural grace; the subtle alchemy of the Graal Quest works through the body of the catechumen to glorify the world-at-large.

One Graal myth in particular merits further attention. It concerns an emerald struck from the brow of Lucifer by the Archangel Michael, which fell to the earth and was discovered by Hiram, King of Tyre (it should be noted that an

87 See Weston (2011) for an exploration of possible links between the medieval Holy Graal romances and ancient fertility rituals.

earlier king of Tyre – Ithobaal III – is associated with Lucifer in Ezekiel:28.)[88] The emerald was fashioned into a bowl and given to King Solomon. Hiram assisted Solomon in construction of the Holy Temple in Jerusalem by commissioning the master mason Hiram Abiff, a widow's son and the central figure in Freemasonry's allegorical tale of fidelity and secrecy; he was murdered for refusing to divulge his masonic secrets and mysteries. The emerald bowl, the *schethiya*, is cognate with the foundation stone, the 'stone of perfection' or the *lapis fundamentalis*, which was situated above the Well of Souls in the Holy of Holies, the temple's inner sanctum, axis mundi, and location of the Ark of the Covenant wherein the name of God dwelled. The *schethiya* was employed in ceremonies practiced by the temple's priests; in certain traditions it imparts an understanding of angelic speech, which recalls the Enochian language received by John Dee and Edward Kelley.

A Talmudic legend posits that, upon their exile, Adam and Eve were given a gift from the angel Raziel: a stone glowing with divine illumination, the light of the first day, known as the *tzohar* or stone of Abraham, which granted nourishment and healing to those who approached it. The stone was passed to Jacob, who placed it in a cup, and thereafter to Moses, who was instructed in a dream to take the glowing stone from Jacob's coffin and place it in the Tabernacle, where it became the *ner tamid*, the eternal light that burns above the Ark of the Torah in every synagogue. The legend continues that the *tzohar* or *schethiya* was later acquired by Joseph of Arimathea, was used at the Last Supper and thereafter to capture blood from the wounds of the crucified Christ, whereupon it became the Graal. It is consonant with the *lapis exilis* or philosopher's stone, the ultimate goal of traditional alchemy, which grants rejuvenation and immortality. One final example resides in Iranian symbology, which refers to Mount Qaf – the Rosicrucian cosmic mountain or Hill of Vision; the locus of mystical initiation and meeting point between the spiritual and material worlds. Upon its summit lies an emerald stone, cognate with the Emerald Tablet of Hermes Trismegistus, upon which are inscribed the secrets of alchemy.[89]

The verisimilitude of these myths should be considered in relation to this discourse on the Holy Island and the Graal. In conformity with the sacred configuration of the Holy of Holies within the Jerusalem Temple, the Tor is

88 For the genesis of this legend see Von Eschenbach, 240. See also Hall, 258, for a useful summary.

89 Rebisse, 151–153.

also a templum and an axis mundi located above a Well of Souls, and is the symbolic resting-place of the Graal. The qualities of the *schethiya*, *tzohar* and *lapis exilis* include: nourishment, rejuvenation, pleromic utterance and illumination. These are comparable to the attributes of the four graals of the Holy Island, the four cauldrons of Welsh myth that grant: transcendent inspiration, resurrection of the dead, sustenance to the brave, and the rhapsodic gift of poetic speech. The assertion that the Graal originates with Lucifer should not be overlooked; in certain traditions, Lucifer's emerald Graal-stone fell from the star Thuban in the constellation of Draco when it held the status of the North Star. Its descent denoted the fall of draconian light into the body of man.[90] Consideration should also be given to the significant liminal times of twilight when the planet Venus, the light-bringer or Lucifer of the dawn, and the night-bringer or Noctifer of dusk, is most visible.

The vessel, the chalice, is a central motif in western esoteric tradition. One of the four suits of the tarot, it is a feminine symbol, associated with the direction of the west, the Moon, the Earth and the element of water. It stands in opposition to the masculine sword in the east. Both the vessel and the sword are represented in Avalonian lore: the vessel is the Arthurian Graal; the sword is Excalibur, which was cast into the lake beneath Pomparles Bridge. A cornerstone of magickal doctrine is concerned with the manipulation of these two atavistic, polarised energies, the divine masculine and feminine. The cup is the womb, the menses, the mystery of the word made flesh, of spirit and blood. In receiving the logos or seminal fluid of the sword or phallus, the vessel or vulva contains and transforms. This is the arcanum of the Graal: it embodies not only the vessel itself, but the synthesis of both the vessel and its contents; the Graal is made whole only when it is full. This secret lies behind the tradition that the Graal contains the *soma* or *amrita*, the draught of the immortal gods. Thus the Graal represents one-pointedness; the bringing together of two polarising, but ultimately harmonious, aspects of divinity. In Fortunean tradition, the polarity-working is achieved by the manipulation of power by both physical and etheric aspects of the self. This congressum – the charged Graal – is an act of reunification and fertilisation. It incubates and gives birth to the magickal.

A second arcanum concerns service. The answer to the question 'whom does the Graal serve?' is this: it serves everyone. The answer to the question

90 Chumbley, 374–5.

'who serves the Graal?' is: the illuminated few, the synomosy of those who seek it and, in turn, have drunk its transforming elixir. Dion Fortune observed that the spiritual graal quest is resolved when the cup is restored to its true female custodians. Yet in the crucible of the Graal, the forces of opposition are unified and brought into the service of one another. Theirs is an inexhaustible fountain of giving and receiving, an eternal cosmic rite forever coming-into-being.

Wolfram von Eschenbach's *Parzival* equates the Graal with the *lapis exilis* or philosopher's stone, the alchemical marriage of the Red King and White Queen. As a mystical process of personal transmutation, of refining and unifying the base metals of the self into a rejuvenating elixir, the alchemical Great Work and the Graal Quest are synonymous. Both are concerned with spiritual gnosis and prolongation of life; with the *henosis* of opposing forces, embodied in the primal materials of red sulphur and white mercury. Their concomitant powers are the Red Serpent and White Serpent, symbolised in the caduceus of Hermes, alchemy's patron and teacher. The legend of the warring red and white dragons, understood on one level as a spagyric drama, were interpreted by Merlin in his prophesies as the struggle between the Britons and Saxons. The Arthurian Graal quest was a means of restoring the wasteland of post-Roman Britain through the union of these two opposing, warring factions. Taken as a synoptic whole, the Graal is inextricably linked with the polarised red and white powers recurring through Avalonian lore. It is the means by which the red and white are united and transmuted, becoming the charged Graal of illumination.

The transformative power of the Graal in its atavistic cauldron alias is described in the Welsh tale *Hanes Taliesin*, which recounts how Gwion, helper to the witch-goddess Ceridwen, inadvertently consumes three drops of *awen* from Ceridwen's cauldron. In anger, Ceridwen pursues Gwion, who shape-shifts into various forms to escape her clutches. As a grain of wheat, he is eaten by Ceridwen and gestates inside her until she gives birth nine months later. She sets the baby Gwion adrift, who is found by Elphin mab Gwyddno. Upon seeing the child's forehead, Elphin declares 'behold a radiant brow,' and so names him Taliesin. The child subsequently grows to become a Bardic seer-shaman figure. That Gwion is consumed by a dark goddess and then reborn in an illuminated state is noteworthy, as is the allusion to the seasonal agrarian cycle of death and rebirth. The cauldron's elixir – the *awen* – is the *amrita*, the ensorcelled liquor giving rise to Gwion's transfiguration into the 'radiant-browed' Taliesin.

¶ THE VESICA PISCIS

The *vesica piscis* describes two circles, side by side yet overlapping; their overlap allows each circle to share the centre of the other. This intersection is the mandorla. To Pythagorean philosophers, the vesica piscis represented the separation of the Monad, the first and singular deity, the Essence or the Foundation. The unity of the Monad gave way to the Dyad, yielding two opposing powers: masculine and feminine, heaven and earth, spirit and matter. In this conception, the vulvic mandorla represents unity, fertility and creation; the conjoining of male and female; the divine Androgyne. In other traditions it symbolises the unity of heaven and earth; or humankind – itself a coming-together of spirit and matter; or the eye of the adept, capable of seeing through the veil of the worlds. Thus the vesica piscis is synonymous with the Graal as a symbol of the *coincidentia oppositorum*, the unity of opposites.

One of the chief arcana of Glastonbury is that its landscape is a tangible expression of these dualistic, but ultimately harmonious, magickal currents. It is no coincidence that the vesica piscis is worked into the gates of the Chalice Well entranceway and the stonework of its path. Most significantly, it is present upon the circular lid of the well head. These symbols depict the vesica piscis bisected by a sword, spear or wand and are emblematic of the esoteric vessel or vulva receiving the sword or phallus, the very act of magickal creation.

A further relevant example can be found in the pink granite basin of Bibracte, part of an excavated Celtic *oppidum* at Autun in Burgundy. Bibracte was the capital of the Aedui tribe, one of the most significant hillforts in Gaul and a place of initiation into the Celtic Mysteries. Blavatsky quotes the French author Jean-Marie Ragon:

> [Bibracte was] a town equally famous for its sacred college of Druids, its civilisation, its schools, in which 40,000 students were taught philosophy, literature, grammar, jurisprudence, medicine, astrology, occult sciences, architecture, etc.

And she adds, 'Such was the last city in Gaul wherein died for Europe the secrets of the Initiations of the Great Mysteries, the Mysteries of Nature, and of her forgotten Occult truths.'[91]

91 Blavatsky (2003 ed.), 295–296.

The pink granite basin, originally filled with spring water, is located at the main entranceway to the *oppidum* and carved in a mandorla form, its dimensions conforming to Pythagorean geometry. Its two sharp corners are oriented to the winter solstice sunrise and the summer solstice sunset.[92] Thus, the basin as a whole imparts a mystery of Druidic cosmology: that solstitial sunrise and sunset were intimately linked with the symbology of the mandorla, the unity of opposites, and with the energetic properties of water.

¶ SOVEREIGNTY AND THE SACRAL CYCLE

Both Caesar and Mela confirmed the Druid's belief in the Orphic and Socratic doctrine of metempsychosis and the primacy of the soul, which is eternal, and after death passes from one body to another. This perpetual cycle of renewal is known as *neheh* in Egyptian theology and is intimately linked to both the solar cycle and the practice of 'sacral kingship,' from a tradition with its roots in Proto-Indo-European prehistory spanning millennia. The origins of sacral kingship may lie as far back as the Paleolithic, where evidence of seasonal variations of social structure suggests that authority figures gained prominence at certain times of year, only for their rule to be dismantled later[93] (there is a loose esoteric parallel here with the Equinox Ritual of the Golden Dawn, where the vernal and autumn equinoxes herald a change of Hiereus.) It has been argued that the origins of sacral kingship and its associated rites of death-and-rebirth lie in shamanism; over time, the shaman as ur-magician developed into a priest, and thence a sacral chieftain or king.[94] This may be attested in certain persistent traditions involving the magickal flight of sovereigns, such as those performed during the Egyptian rituals of Heb Sed, when the monarch ascended to the stars via the axis of a stellar temple.

In relation to Celtic and specifically Irish kingship, regents were unique figures in the social order, marked off from others as a result of their divine descent, their priestly functions, magickal and numinous knowledge, and their ability to bestow prosperity through a ritual seasonal marriage to the

92 Robb, 123–124.

93 See https://www.theguardian.com/news/2021/oct/19/unfreezing-the-ice-age-the-truth-about-humanitys-deep-past

94 Devereux, 77.

land. The Irish tradition's essential practice involved the ritual slaughter of the priest-king – an hypostasis of the sun god – at a propitious time in relation to the solar cycle, typically Samhain at the commencement of the month of Giamonios – the start of the winter half of the year. Because his life force was so sympathetically bound up with the prosperity of the land, as his powers failed the king was sacrificed and another chosen. His death was not equated with annihilation, but rather participation in the cosmic cycle of death and rebirth. The blood and flesh of the sacrifice lived on, distributed amongst the community; parts of the body were buried in the fields to ensure the harvest. Heaven and earth were united as his vital energy renewed the kingdom; in life and death he was a bridge between the worlds. Sacrifice freed his soul, to return to the underworld where, in some cases, the king also enjoyed regnal authority. He resided there throughout the winter period and ultimately became united with a new body. The regent's cycle of kingship was a seasonal drama; a microcosm of the same mythic cycle of the solar year, reflected in dying-and-rising corn gods: the mysteries of Adonis, Osiris and Isis, Demeter and Persephone, Dionysus, Attis and Mithras. The Arthurian Green Knight myth may also be interpreted in terms of the death and resurrection of a seasonal deity.[95]

Irish sacral kings were wedded to the land, embodied in the Earth Mother or Terra Mater, by a ritualised act of congress or *banais rígi*. The priestess, as representative of the deity, selected her new monarch by offering a cup of mead. Sovereignty was granted in a symbolic act of hierogamy and the king became her consort. One exemplar from Irish literature describes king Cormac Mac Art receiving a cup from a mysterious woman. The cup burst apart when a lie was told and was restored when a truth was spoken. Another example tells of King Conn of the Hundred Battles, who received an otherworldly cup from a woman embodying sovereignty. In drinking from the cup, the king was granted custodianship of the land. Both examples reveal the role of the cup or Graal in bestowing sovereignty and upholding sacral oaths.[96] As cupbearers,

95 Frazer's notorious nineteenth century opus *The Golden Bough* has been disparaged by scholars for its assertion that all religions have their origins in seasonal fertility cults organised around the ritual slaughter of a sacral king. However, there is now considerable evidence to support the existence of a form of sacral kingship, tied to the fertility of the land, in Celtic, Scandinavian and Germanic cultures. See Klæðskeri for an overview.

96 See Waddell (2015) and (2018) for a detailed discussion of specifically Irish sacral kingship and ideas of sovereignty.

the Well Maidens of Arthurian myth can be understood as brokers of the covenant between the king and the land, the human world and the otherworld and, ultimately, the king's fate. A further parallel can be found in the relationship between the sorceress-deity Circe and the Homeric hero Jason. Circe's cup, which intoxicates and transforms, is employed to provoke Jason into a magicko-religious union; he becomes a mortal consort of the goddess. Additionally, the correspondences between the traditions of sacral kingship and the rural, archaic rites of ancient Greece should not be ignored: these included mythic dramas oriented around a fertile goddess, a consort representing the Sun, a semi-deified royal or priestly figure, and roles incorporating chthonic aspects, all of which may have been early precursors to the Mysteries.[97]

A king's successful rule was determined by his ability to fulfil his oaths, conduct the communal seasonal rites, and observe the *gessi* or taboos given to him by the gods. The seasonal ceremonies included a blessing-circuit by the king, who circumambulated his kingdom throughout the year, conducting sacrifices and mating with women-as-hypostases of Terra Mater.[98] Alternatively, a wagon-drawn effigy of the deity was accompanied by its male or female consort, as evinced by the Icelandic text *Ögmundar þáttr dytts*, and Tacitus' account of the wagon-circuit of the Germanic goddess Nerthus. An equivalent means of fertilising the land can be seen in the phallic cult centre at Høgberget at Skatval, Norway, where stone phalluses were carried through the agricultural landscape to ensure a good year and peace. The seasonal cycle of the king's death-and-rebirth likely evolved over time. Mela and Tacitus suggest that the reign of a regent was extended to a period of years and incorporated a symbolic death, or a scapegoat sacrifice in lieu of the monarch. However, this did not prevent the populace from rising up and enforcing a royal blood offering if the king's conduct was deemed unsatisfactory. In the case of the Ynglinga line of Swedish kings, both King Dómaldi and King Óláfr Trételgja were poor regents, slaughtered by their kinsmen as sacrifices for good crops.

Irish kings were expected to deliver true and moral judgments. Correct behaviour, reflected in proper and truthful speech, was a sign of royal legitimacy and upheld the very nature of kingship. Speech was associated with ideas of projection, casting and throwing. Poetry was the truest form of speech, related to truth, authority and kingly judgement, and the source of poetic inspiration

97 Stratton-Kent (2010), vol. 1, 141, 236.

98 See North.

was the Sun. It provided a legitimate and truth-speaking king with his power and wisdom. In turn, through an understanding and veneration of the Sun's progress marked by seasonal customs, the king became aligned with the cosmos; his behaviour was synchronised to the predictable movements of the solar body.[99]

If the king ruled unjustly, signs would appear that his land would fall to ruin through the sovereign's falsehood. Fruit would rot, grain would be scarce, milk cows would go dry and famine would occur. King Amangon's raping of the well maidens is a profound expression of this. His defilement represented 'the single sin of the sovereign' – an irreparable act that destroyed the bonds of sovereignty. By failing to observe the covenant between the human realm and the otherworld, 'the grasses and flowers withered, and the streams dried up.' Only the Graal, as a symbol of unity and balance through the proper observance of sacral oaths, could undo the dis-ease of the wasteland. The maimed Fisher King of Arthurian myth is a further expression of the symbiosis between the health of the regent and the health of the land, enshrined in the maxim 'the king and the land are one.' As a Graal-keeper, the Fisher King suffers from a wound that does not heal and exists in a condition of dead-aliveness in the Graal castle. As a result of his weakness, his kingdom has become a wasteland. Thus, 'sovereignty' in the context of sacral rule describes not just governance of a specific territory, but careful custodianship of the land and the things that dwell upon it, both seen and unseen. The regent is a protector and steward of Nature, and the prohibitions conferred upon him are tests of his ability to fulfil this role. For how can a monarch execute the office of sovereign of the land when he is unable to maintain sovereignty over the self?

The sacred union between regent and deity conferred fecundity upon the land until the goddess grew old and withered, whereupon she would select a new consort, with whom she would symbolically mate, to return her to youth, vigour and beauty. This ritualised *conjunctio* of Sun and Earth, male and female is as old as human civilisation. A Sumerian rite involving the sexual union of priest and priestess, within a temple atop a ziggurat, was enacted to heal the division of earth and sky. The ziggurat-as-world-mountain possessed the power to reconnect the separated elements and restore the universe's right order through an act of magicko-sexual congress.[100]

99 See Enright for occasional references to solar cults and Celtic kingship.

100 Robert M. Scoch, in White (2016), 217.

The fundamental message of the station of sacral kingship is this: the land is gifted by deity to human based on the recipient's rectitude; the transaction is spiritual, enshrined in a symbiotic covenant between the otherworld and the human world. It is also temporal – the pact can be broken if its injunctions are not fulfilled, or if the term of stewardship is completed. Contravention of the agreement results in a collapse of that essential symbiosis and balance, giving rise to a literal and metaphorical wasteland. This is in stark contrast to the modern mindset where land is seized and exploited through the dominion of unjust actors. For untold centuries our so-called leaders have abandoned any pretense of rectitude. Their sovereignty is a sham, unjust and autocratic. Service and self-sacrifice are unknown to them. They care naught for the well-being of the land, of the things that dwell above, below and upon it. And because of this they are the very source of our present dis-ease. It falls instead to us to pick up and dust off the mantle of custodianship; to reenact the mythic cycles of sacral regency and, in so doing, forge a new covenant.

The four stations of that office conform to the quadripartite cycle of the Great Quest:

- *The first station* is the division and burial of the old king's corpse, distributed to the four corners of the kingdom. His eternal daemon or spirit learns the fleshless mysteries in Annwn and is reborn as an eidolon or mortal, or ascends to the celestial Hades to reside amongst the stars.

- *The second station* is the dawn of the new king, his somatic, enfleshed manifestation, coronation and rites of admission to the office of regent.

- *The third station* is the granting of sovereignty of the land to the king by the Terra Mater. The priestess as hypostasis of the Goddess proffers the Graal to the king; their union is confirmed in a *hieros gamos*, which confers prosperity upon the land and represents a cosmic *congressum* or unity of opposites. The king rules at the height of his powers as consort of the Goddess.

- *The fourth station* marks the dusk of the king, his ritual slaughter as his powers, and therefore the vigour of the Goddess, begin to wane. The unity of the king is sundered, separating into dead flesh and eternal spirit, which descends to the chthonic realms.

This metempsychotic cycle is a greater key of the Quest and its four stations. The sacral king undertakes a form of graal quest in his pursuit of sovereignty and true kingship; the catechumen undertakes a sacral cycle in pursuit of personal sovereignty and transfiguration of the self unto wholeness.

The metaphysical death-and-rebirth of the catechumen, derived from the stations of Celtic sacral kingship, has a noteworthy alchemical parallel. The sixteenth century treatise *Pretiosa margarita novella de thesauro, ac pretiosissimo philosophorum lapide* ('The new pearl of great price, a treatise concerning the treasure and most precious stone of the philosophers') by the Italian physician Petrus Bonus includes fourteen illustrations or emblems depicting the life, death and rebirth of the king. Enthroned, his servants before him, the old king is pierced with a sword and his corpse interred in a sepulchre. His bones are then removed, spread upon the ground, and blessed by divine providence in the form of an angel wielding a bone. The new, resurrected, transfigured king is enthroned once more, but now able to impart his gnosis to the assembled servants. The old king represents the matter to be worked upon, the consciousness requiring cleansing and illumination. The blackened, exhumed bones correspond to the alchemical state of Nigredo. The angel represents a succession of processes, from Albedo and Citrinas to the final state of Rubedo, which is illustrated in the king's resurrection. Thus, through magickal transmutation, a *solve et coagula*, the initiatory Great Quest ultimately transfigures and revitalises. The base metals of the self are refined and unified into the *lapis exilis*, the Graal itself.

¶ THE ARTHURIAN ARCHETYPES

The wise acknowledge the tremendous potency of archetypes, which are in essence the totality of the cosmos (the human-apprehended universe) – its *materia* and *asomata*; its corporeal and spiritual multiplicities – codified according to human experience and recorded in myth as exempla. It is therefore commonly asserted that deities are archetypes inasmuch as they too are codified aspects of the cosmos, and therefore of human origin. This does not discount their veracity as emanations of divinity. Magick is the prism through which the macrocosmic *prima materia* meets the microcosmic *terra Adamica*. The ancestral experience of the cosmos, resident within the genetics of the theurgist, rises to meet the individuated divine being, who corresponds to the same ancestral experience. Thus, specific deities are evoked and invoked according to cosmic laws governing the sympathetic relationships between divinity and humanity.

The Avalonian mythos is replete with archetypes, being in large part derived from Arthurian tradition. Dion Fortune and her cohorts in the Society of the Inner Light have provided an interpretation of these atavisms in *The Arthurian Formula*. Although space prohibits a detailed exploration of this expansive topic, two archetypal figures merit specific attention: Merlin and Arthur.

The two polarised expressions of divinity united and resolved in the alchemical marriage of the charged Graal, the *lapis exilis*, are forever ebbing and flowing according to time and tide, shaped by great and aeonian imperatives beyond mortal ken. The only certainty is the protean, evolving nature of their eternal dance. Upon the Holy Island the feminine principle has waxed large. Over time the arcana of the Goddess and her aspects have become unveiled and the land, mantled with her breath, is nothing less than a verendum; her ontophany is found in the very earth of Avalon. The wise recognise this and honour the Matrona, the Magna Mater, accordingly.

In contrast, the masculine aspect, although manifested in the island's terraqueous features in the form of the White Serpent and the White Spring, is in abeyance. The reasons for this exiguity are manifold. In terms of the Avalonian mythos it can be seen in the failure of the Arthurian project: of its two key actors, one maintains a life-in-death existence as a king beneath the hill, waiting to fulfil his destiny as the once and future king; the other is imprisoned, alive but impotent, in either a hawthorn tower, a tree, a cave, or a pit. Both are tragic figures. Another explanation lies in the text of the *Elucidation*. King Amangon's rape of the Well Maidens provides an allegory for the persecution of the divine feminine, for misogynistic aggression and environmental exploitation. Through this act the symbolic contract between the Terra Mater and the regent-as-solar-hypostasis remains broken. Until such time as it is restored, masculine estrangement from the redemptive powers of the divine feminine will persist. Related to this state of affairs, modern Goddess spirituality has focussed on a cosmogenetic narrative where a primordial ur-goddess exists as a self-fertilising creatrix resistant to male insemination. Through her alone the cosmos came into being; thus, the divine masculine is rendered obsolete.

Yet the terra-vulvic and solar-phallic must both participate in the ophidian dance. As complementary forces they transform each other and transmute into one another in an eternal interchange. Together they generate and manifest life. Notably, in recent years intimations of a rejuvenated, evolved masculine power stirring upon the Holy Island have begun to circulate.[101] Some identify this with Arawn or Gwyn ap Nudd (even though he also represents a separate but no less significant elvish current), and with a resurgent Arthur and Merlin.

the artifex

Far from embodying the wise wizard of popular imagination, Merlin is without doubt the most complex, inscrutable figure in the Arthurian repertoire. In his earliest incarnation, Myrddin was chief bard to the Cumbrian king Gwenddoleu; a related legendary figure is the Scottish truth-teller Lailoken. Later, Gerald of Wales distinguished between two Merlins, both prophets: Merlin Ambrosius and Merlin Silvester. In Geoffrey of Monmouth's *Vita Merlini* Merlin appears in a different guise, as 'Merlin Caledonius.' The predominant characteristic of these early incarnations is their status as *wodewose*, a wild man of the forest. In this mode, Myrddin fled in madness to the woods after witnessing his king's defeat in battle, where he became Myrddin Wyllt (wild Merlin). Initially regarded as bestial, subhuman, aggressive and hypersexual – the cultural antithesis of civilisation – the wodewose later became sympathetic figures; noble savages living in a state of nature.[102] Merlin sits between the two positions: on one hand, he is a deranged figure, self-exiled from society, lamenting the follies of mankind. On the other, he is a pseudo-shaman figure; a silvan cunning-man and beast-master, with power over wild animals, and a wolf as a companion.

In Robert de Boron's *Estoire de Merlin*, part of the sprawling Vulgate Cycle, Merlin is a wild man from birth, as a result of his status as a cambion, a child formed from the union of spirit-being and mortal human. The legend states that his father was an incubus (or in some tales Satan or Lucifer) and his mother a daughter of the king of Dyfed. *Estoire de Merlin* describes how a band of demons intended to perpetrate great evils upon the world by means of a human agent. To achieve this, one of them seduced a virgin. Immediately after giving birth the young mother baptised the infant, who was none other than Merlin, thus thwarting the demons' plans to bring an antichrist into the

101 See Pearson Appendix 1 and Mann & Glasson (2010), 37.

102 Stock, 24.

world. Some commentators have questioned the true nature of Merlin's father, suggesting an otherworldly or faerie origin. Others have drawn comparisons between Merlin and the biblical Nephilim, offspring of the Watchers, the fallen angels who imparted forbidden knowledge to humankind. Yet others have offered an allegorical interpretation, one that alludes to Merlin as a 'Son of the Serpent' – an initiate of the Mysteries. This corresponds to Dion Fortune's belief that Merlin was a Manu or Cosmic Initiator of an Atlantean root generation, one of the Masters of the Ancient Wisdom and a being at the highest level of Initiation, along with Sanat Kumara, Gautama Buddha, Maitreya, the Maha Chohan, Djwal Khul, Narad Muni and Melchizedek. All these interpretations result in a similar portrait: Merlin is a spiritual being in human form, symbolic of transformed consciousness. He is a teacher, a bearer of ancient wisdom. His preternatural powers are both innate and learned, diabolic and supernal, and include: knowledge of the past; prophesy; a perception of otherworldly realities; and an ability to both understand wind and see into stone. Nevertheless, it should be borne in mind that his mere existence as a union of spirit-being and mortal was unnatural; he was perceived as a breach in the cosmic order.

Merlin supposedly lived in the sixth century, emerging from post-Roman Britain, yet his chronology is muddled. As a Manu and escapee from the dying Atlantean civilisation he is immortal, arriving in Britain and teaching the Druids the Mysteries. Geoffrey's young Merlin supervenes much of the Arthurian corpus; he receives tuition from the bard and seer Taliesin, one in a line of master teachers. Taliesin was taught by the monk Gildas, who in turn was tutored by Saint Illtud, reputedly a cousin of King Arthur and custodian of the Graal. Geoffrey's *Vita Merlini* recounts a story of Merlin's formative years, drawing on an earlier legend from the eighth century *Historia Brittonum* by Nennius. The boy Merlin, referred to by his earlier name of Ambrosius, is selected as a sacrifice to ensure the stability of King Vortigern's castle. Vortigern fears the boy's supernatural powers, which Ambrosius uses to discern the presence of warring red and white serpents beneath the castle. He divines a subtext to their presence, namely that the red serpent represents the Britons, the white serpent the invading Saxons. This tale is pivotal in establishing Merlin's connection to Avalon, and its larger role in the Matter of Britain.[103]

103 The corpus of medieval literature and legend concerning Great Britain and Brittany and their associated Kings and heroes.

In the sixteenth century a mythology of alchemy developed proposing that the Royal Arte evolved in England, and the philosopher's stone sprung from the earth of Glastonbury. The person behind this was Merlin, who was acknowledged as the founder of British hermeticism. The legend of Vortigern's warring red and white dragons was partly understood in esoteric terms as an alchemical drama, describing the conflict between red sulphur and white mercury. But its exoteric meaning, interpreted by Merlin in his prophesies as the struggle between the Britons and Saxons, was also lauded as a form of alchemy, one where Merlin restored the wasteland of post-Roman Britain through the union of these two opposing, warring factions.[104] He also foresaw the coming of Arthur – the Boar of Cornwall – as a saviour of the Britons. Thus, Merlin was hailed as the alchemist and prophet who orchestrated and supervised the birth of Britain under Arthur. The means of attaining this unity - the *conjunctio* of red and white polarities - was given shape in the form of the red and white cruets brought to Britain by Joseph of Arimathea; these constitute the Graal, which is cognate with the *lapis exilis*, the goal of alchemy. The Graal in turn is reified and localised in the red and white springs of Avalon. Merlin is linked to the Graal through his prophetic abilities to articulate its history and power. And the alchemical secret of the nation's birth became linked to Glastonbury through its unique congressum of natural phenomena. This explains John Dee's preoccupation with the Holy Island.

Historically, this facility to shape a nation's destiny through occult means was a hugely influential aspect of the Merlin tradition; one that entangled occult traditions with politics.[105] John Dee, as a magus and a royal advisor, can be viewed as an Elizabethan 'Merlin.' Yet despite its seductive possibilities, the truth of Merlin's influence as a power-behind-the-throne is tragedy and failure. Through his ability to see into the past and divine the future, Merlin was ideally placed to manage the vicissitudes of power. According to Dion Fortune and others, as chief engineer of Arthurian genealogies, Merlin's original plan involved the breeding of a race of sacral priest-kings by merging the native aristocratic Pendragon line with an Atlantean priestly aristocracy in the form of Ygraine. But Arthur's disastrous marriage to Guinevere, orchestrated by Merlin, failed to produce an heir, largely due to her tragic affair with Lancelot – a human raised in the realm of Faerie by the *Dame du Lac*, the Lady of the

104 Hughes, chapter 2.
105 See Young for more on this topic.

Lake. In certain traditions Guinevere is of faerie rather than human descent and this common ground is the source of their attraction. The failure of the Pendragon bloodline is symbolic of the persistent schism between man and nature, human and faerie, flesh and spirit. This disharmony creates conditions in which Mordred – a figure equated with Set, in opposition to Arthur's solar hero – can flourish and, ultimately, dismantle Merlin's plans. Under Merlin's auspices the Graal is sought but not returned to Camelot; the Round Table is broken and the knightly order disbanded.

The failure of Merlin's great project can be attributed to a weakness of nature and character. Through his unnatural conception and occult knowledge he is imbued with power. On one hand he represents the union of opposites, the alchemical homunculus. He is a graal in which the polarities of beast and human, demonic and heavenly, secular and sacred, magic and science, madness and sanity, pagan and Christian commingle. On the other he occupies an equivocal position halfway between one state and another:

> [He is] the half-formed trickster who miscreates the world, not because of any malefic intent but rather because of the incompleteness of his creative power... [Which] is replete with the ambiguities of the demiurge, an ironically creative force that somehow goes awry.[106]

In this respect he resembles the Scottish Old Grey Magician or the Irish Fear Doirich, the powerful and capricious dark Druid of folklore.[107]

Merlin's weakness lies in his overweening personal ambition; a desire for god-like control; to see his will done on earth. This is a fundamental occult lesson that the adept and the magus will acknowledge: a magickal act may reverberate through the vast and subtle web of *wyrd* with a life of its own, in ways unplanned by its creator. Yet Merlin's ultimate downfall occurs as the consequence of a more mundane weakness. His grand plans are undermined by a humiliating and destructive passion for the Lady of the Lake, otherwise known as Nimue or Viviane. Throughout the literature their relationship is complex and fraught. Traditionally, Merlin teaches Nimue his occult secrets (but not his innate skills of seership) while simultaneously pursuing an unrequited sexual relationship. Out of frustration and cruelty, Nimue uses

106 See Kimball.

107 See MacPherson for more on this enigmatic figure.

Merlin's own Arte to imprison him. One scholar has proposed that Merlin wielded the Pendragon dragonhead standard, a version of the Roman military's Dacian Draco and a totem of the Sarmatian great Mother Goddess Satanaya, a prototype for the Arthurian *Dame du Lac*.[108] Under this state of affairs he is the herald of the Lady of the Lake on the battlefield, proclaiming her dominion and influence; a disciple and adorant. This is appropriate given that she can be understood as a goddess of sovereignty and an incarnation of the Magna Mater. She is also synonymous with the undines and Well Maidens of the *Elucidation*; a white-clad queen of the *tylwyth teg*. In this respect, Nimue's imprisonment of Merlin can be interpreted less as an act of wanton cruelty and more as an imprecation against his taboo behaviour. His sexual advances transgressed a prohibition against the Matrona and were punished. Merlin's incarceration can be seen as a concision, halting the metastasis of sexual impropriety against otherworldly women, begun with King Amangon.

The great mystery of Merlin's narrative is this: why should he devote himself to the Arthurian project in the full knowledge of its failure, and his eventual defeat? The answer lies with the Jungian Mercurius, the 'world creating spirit' with whom Merlin is associated.[109] Mercurius is an integration of light and dark, material and spiritual, the beginning and the end of the alchemist's quest. Mercury represents its commencement; Mercurius the conclusion. Mercurius is the older, sagely version of Mercury; the self transformed by the trials of earthly existence into a fulcrum, where the primordial forces of Nature achieve balance (however, it is apt that Merlin is allied with Mercury; trickster, god of magick and cognate with Óðinn and Woden, deities with whom Merlin has much in common.) Yet the dual nature of Mercurius also acknowledges the quest as cyclical and without end. The self must eternally descend into the earth and return in order to become wiser and yet more refined. Merlin, an evolved but incomplete artifex, understood this and, through his prophetic ability, foresaw that his power was not eternally broken. In Fortunean tradition the implication is that, although Merlin was physically imprisoned, he was able to traverse the otherworld and pass on his knowledge to the Elementals. He will be freed from darkness when the cosmic wheel turns and the gods of the New Age begin to manifest in the souls of the folk.[110] This is one

108 See Malcor.

109 See Jung and von Franz in Goodrich, 278–285.

110 Fortune; Lumley Brown; Knight, 51.

aspect of the masculine current that now rouses upon the Holy Island. While not in any sense qliphothic or diabolic, it is potent, ambiguous, unpredictable, amoral and protean, but also sagacious and beneficent.

the servitor

If Merlin is the artifex behind the birth of Albion, Arthur is its servitor. A moonchild, a baby conceived under magickal auspices, his purpose was to bring harmony to Britain and, as progenitor, establish a bloodline of sacral kings. That Arthur is granted sovereignty of the land is not in doubt: the drawing of the sword from the stone, the symbolic drawing of the masculine from the feminine; and the gift of Excalibur from the Dame du Lac attest to this. Further evidence is found in the Irish tale *Eachtra an Mhadra Mhaoil* where, in common with Irish tribal leaders, who are typically also sacral rulers, Arthur is bound by sacred prohibitions or *gessi*: 'there are many *gessi* upon me … [but] I shall not break my *gessi* … for [one who does] is a person without prosperity.'[111]

The early, pre-medieval depictions of Arthur portray him as a warrior and chieftain; a violent hero of prodigious fighting prowess. In the account of Arthur's twelve battles by the ninth century British chronicler Nennius, Arthur and his warband fight and prevail 'with all the kings and military force of Britain' against the invading Saxons. In the final battle of Badon, he single-handedly kills nine hundred and forty foe. In this early incarnation he draws parallels with the Irish hero Fionn mac Cumhaill. As a warrior and commander, a cauldron-hunter and guardian of Britain he is comparable to Brân the Blessed.

Arthur's relationship with the otherworld and its denizens is ambiguous. On one hand, he is identified as the cousin of the Welsh god-hero Culwhch, whose retinue includes various otherworldly figures: Mabon the Hunter and Gwyn ap Nudd. On the other, he conducts forays into the otherworld to rescue individuals imprisoned there and to steal fabulous treasures, not least the cauldron of the Chief of Annwn, belonging to Pwyll, Prince of Dyfed, albeit at great cost in warriors' lives. Otherworldly conflict is not uncommon in Welsh literature. *Cad Goddeu* and *Culhwch and Olwen* both describe internecine battles. In the latter, Arthur occupies a position of authority and judgement, ruling on the conditions by which Gwyn ap Nudd and his sworn enemy, Gwythyr

111 Macalister, 5.

ap Greidawl, must abide in their dispute over the maiden Creiddylad. In the medieval chivalric romances Arthur is elevated to a courtly king of Britain. Yet, either because of or in spite of this, he becomes a less compelling character, seemingly constrained by the office of kingship. He is the *roi fainéant*, the 'do-nothing king' whose even-handedness results in stasis and, ultimately, decline. Chief amongst these sins of quiescence is the dysfunctional relationship with his wife. Arthur is unequivocally a solar hero, the hypostasis of the sun god. Yet his marriage to the Magna Mater, embodied in his faerie-wife Guinevere, is barren. As she is drawn into an affair with Lancelot, Arthur becomes emasculated, a cuckold. In turn, Guinevere is denied the full cycle of womanhood and Merlin's grand plan collapses. This is Arthur's tragic flaw: although he is wedded to the land, as all sacral kings must be, his marriage is never literally or symbolically consummated, and the otherworldly contract, the faerie accord, remains unrestored. Arthur is an incomplete king.

Amangon's rape of the cup-bearing Well Maidens was an inversion of the *hieros gamos* between regent and Terra Mater. The *Elucidation* describes the consequences of that act when, under Arthur's watch, a retinue of anti-knights known as the Rich Company emerges and predates the land. They are half-human, half-faerie beings, the bitter fruits of Amangon's crime. They set themselves up in opposition to the Round Table knights and bring greed, war and oppression to the kingdom, creating a wasteland. Only a prolonged and concerted effort by Arthur's knights can defeat them.[112]

If the Graal represents the means to transform the wasteland into a fecund and harmonious realm, Arthur has little involvement in its quest. He is perhaps even equivocal about its purpose, knowing it will cost the lives of many of his knights. This proves to be the case and the quest reveals their unworthiness, save for Galahad. Towards its conclusion, Bors, Percival and Galahad travel through the wasteland to the Graal Castle at Corbenic, thought to be Castell Dinas Bran in North Wales. There, Galahad assists in the healing of the maimed Fisher King. The Graal is then transported by boat to Sarras, an island lying on the route taken by Joseph of Arimathea, who first bore the vessel to Britain. The Ascension of the Graal completes the journey and only Bors returns to Camelot to tell the tale. Whether Arthur should have undertaken the quest is a question he asks of himself, but he was unable to do so, being bound by oaths of sovereignty to protect his own kingdom.

112 Matthews (2019), 329–336.

Although divinely ordained, the Graal Quest exacts a heavy burden on Arthur. His spirit is further attenuated by his wife's love affair and the rise of Mordred, which culminates in the final Battle of Camlann, where Mordred is killed and Arthur mortally wounded. The king is transported by barge to Avalon and tended by the Sororitas Avalonis, the nine sorcerer-maidens led by Morgen. Chroniclers disagree on Arthur's fate. Geoffrey of Monmouth makes no comment. Layamon's *Brut* tells how Arthur, anticipating his own demise, foresees his journey to Avalon to be healed. Layamon adds that Merlin had prophesied the king's return at a future time. The Vulgate Cycle implies Arthur does not survive and the Alliterative *Morte Arthure* is explicit. However, Malory asserts that Arthur will rise again from a tomb bearing the legend *Hic jacet Arthurus, rex quondam, rexque futurus* (Here lies Arthur, the once and future king.) And John Lydgate's *Fall of Princes* declares that Arthur lives on as a crowned king in Faerie (Annwn.) When Merlin's prophesy is fulfilled, Arthur will ride out from Annwn to rule Britain as its lord and sovereign. This is interesting inasmuch as, like Merlin, Arthur is able to continue his affairs in the otherworld, even though physically incapacitated. The claim that he enjoys a regnal status in the otherworld may be attributed to his companionship with Gwyn ap Nudd, or that the otherworldy denizens acknowledge Arthur as regent across all the realms of Albion, mundane or otherwise.

Perhaps because of his parallels with Fionn mac Cumhail, who lies sleeping in a cave surrounded by his Fianna, his retinue of hunter-warriors, and with other legendary monarchs, Arthur's status as an archetypal king-beneath-the-hill has become canonical. Into the nineteenth century Arthurian revival and beyond, the notion of Arthur as a messianic national hero grew more persistent. The writer Howard Pyle suggests that the sleeping Arthur suffers from a pseudo-Dolorous Stroke and, when the timing is propitious, 'his dreadful wound be healed and then will he return.'

The Avalonian current encompasses the arcanum of Arthur's reawakening and return, and is manifested in the initiatory cycle of the Great Quest, which is concerned with the renewal of the self through a descent to, and return from, the otherworld as part of a symbolic Graal rite. If the Graal reveals the hysterema of the world and the self, the Quest is the means by which the latter is transfigured; in turn, the former is made whole. This is a greater key of the Holy Island: the catechumen who, by participating in the initiatory cycle of the Quest, will restore the accord between matter and spirit; through the catechumen, Arthur will rise to become a complete king.

¶ INTERMISSIO: MAGICKO-RELIGIOUS CONTINUITY

Ancient Egyptian material culture provides profound insights into the workings of a society where magickal practice was central to its organisation and function. Its traditions were expansive and sophisticated, yet unequivocally inheriting topoi from the earliest myths. As such, an examination of Egyptian magicko-religious practice helps to elucidate the sacral aspects of the Holy Island of Glastonbury, its uses and ritual arcana, which are in propinquity with the earliest sorcerous landscapes. Such a comparison deciphers Avalon's topography, revealing consanguinity of purpose through threads of commonality. In short, it justifies the Holy Island's preeminent status as a locus of power and sanctity.

Egyptian theologies were numerous and fluid, evolving over centuries and with untold deities falling in or out of favour according to the vicissitudes of the times. A chief innovation were the spiritual technologies engineered to guide the souls of the deceased, not least those of royal descent, through the realms of the afterlife. At the point of death, the *ka*, the etheric body of the deceased, remained with the corpse and was nourished by offerings from the living. The *ba* was free to travel to the heavens and commune with the gods by day, but was required to return to the corpse at night. For royalty, this cycle could be broken by transforming the *ba* and *ka* into an eternally combined spirit, the *akh*, which dwelled amongst the Undying Stars forever, free to return to the earth as desired via the Gates of the Sun.

In Egyptian cosmology, the sky is the abode of the supernal gods and the regal dead. Tuat is the unseen sky below the horizon, the underworld and the dwelling-place of chthonic gods and beings. Akhet is the boundary of those two realms, the horizon where the Sun rises and sets. The liminal threshold of Akhet provides transit to and from Rostau, the abode of Sokar-Osiris, Lord of the Underworld and god of the winter solstice, which is located at the boundary of the sky. Rostau functions as a cosmic gateway. Its portals are the two Sun Gates, becoming the celestial gates of the solstices when the ecliptic crosses the Milky Way. Sunrise and sunset at midwinter enable the righteous dead to ascend to the Imperishable Stars – the circumpolar stars that never set – along the Winding Waterway, the River of Heaven. At midsummer sunrise and sunset, souls descend to earth. In other words, spirits come from, return to, and are the stars; a state of affairs that lends a novel interpretation to Crowley's assertion 'every man and woman is a star.'

The god Sokar-Osiris is usually depicted standing upon a primeval mound, or Island of the Egg. The island is described as surrounded by water with a field of reeds upon its shore. Within it lies the underworld of the soul, a further route into Tuat for the deceased regardless of status. It is entered via the Place of the Well. Commentators suggest that, within the Giza complex, this primeval 'well of souls' may be physically located at Gebel Ghibli, a hillock 300 metres dues south of the Great Sphinx. At certain times of the year, inundation of the Nile would once have surrounded the hill with water.[113]

Sokar is additionally associated with the Djoser funerary complex at Sakkara (which derives its name from that deity), comprising the oldest known pyramid structure, plus temples, courts, tombs and altars. A boundary wall surrounded the complex, which was itself enclosed by a moat. Originally the site was approached by boat via an artificial lake. The rites of the winter solstice during the Festival of Sokar were likely enacted there. The Djoser complex is notable for its step pyramid, potentially comprising seven levels in its original form. This stepped construction was a deliberate conceit, reflecting the regent's authority to climb to the upper world of the supernal gods. The nearby pyramids of Teti and Unas contain the earliest examples of so-called Pyramid Texts, describing ritual procedures enabling the monarch's ascent to the heavens in both life and death.

Of the various courts within the Djoser complex, one was reserved for use during Heb Sed, a festival where the sacral king, wearing the red and white double crown, asserted his sovereignty over all the realms and confirmed his own immortality. Its rites, reflecting the content of the Pyramid Texts, included the king's magickal exhortations to the cardinal directions – possibly in honour of the four spirits of Horus – from a stepped dais, representing Sokar's primordial mound. After the symbolic destruction of his physical body at the hands of the god Set, the king was resurrected, enabling his spiritual ascent to, and descent from, the stars through the axis of the stellar temple. The purpose of these rituals was to bring his physical kingdom into conscious alignment with the unseen world, which upheld and fecundated the middle world, to ensure an harmonious connection between the two and the wellbeing of both. As earthly ruler, the sacral king functioned as a subastral incarnation of the Sun, a governor of the cosmos. Through the rites of stellar and solar congress, the regent not only asserted his dominion over the stars,

113 Collins, 176–178.

confirming his place amongst the gods, but also acknowledged his responsibilities in maintaining cosmic wellbeing.[114]

The relationship between the Sun and kingship was enshrined in a reciprocal exchange of Ma'at, simultaneously both the goddess of balance and daughter of the Sun (Ra, Aten, Horus, Temu, Atum or Khepera), and an embodiment of right conduct that, properly enacted, upheld the cosmic order. The Sun sustained both nature and society, while its quotidian rebirth was sustained by sacrifice, magick and ritual, all expressions of an ordered kingdom. The temple was the earthly locus of this careful balance, a liminal place where the functioning of the cosmos was observed and its stability maintained through a structured daily cycle of prayers and hymnals.[115]

Taken as a whole, the parallels between Avalon and the Egyptian myths, geographies and magickal practices elucidated above are evident: a seven-tiered structure within a funerary landscape, surmounted by a temple and surrounded by water; a primordial mound presided over by a god of the underworld and the winter solstice, beneath which a portal to the chthonic realm is located; a ritual landscape oriented to the solstices; a central place occupied by a presiding priest-magician; a symbolic and magickal nexus of sovereignty, equilibrium and beneficence. In light of this, the specific configuration of the Holy Island's landscape becomes a recension of ritual geographies evolved from the earliest myths; herein lie the roots of its status as a place of unique sanctity and power. The clear comparisons between Egyptian and Celtic notions of sacral kingship, with particular reference to the regent as hypostasis of the Sun god, should also be borne in mind.

114 White (2016), 193–199.
115 Oesterdiekhoff, 54–58.

the quaternities of the holy island

THE SORCEROUS GEOGRAPHIES

Our earlier exposition of magickal directionality identified a method for dividing the land into a quadripartite cosmology, its axes defined by the solstice angles of the Sun with an axis mundi at the centre. Upon the Holy Island the axis mundi is the Adytum of the Tor; the sacred crossroads; the *crux decussata*, the diagonal cross of sacrifice and point of ingress to and egress from the celestial and chthonic realms.

The summit of the hill, being an incarnation of the world mountain, grants an uninterrupted vision of the land in every direction to the horizon, the rim of the Graal. The hill's zenith is the sacred centre of the Holy Island, its Temenos and Adytum. The stepped slopes of the Tor, the world-mountain-as-ziggurat, encompass the Templum. Beyond the immediate threshold of the Tor lies the Inner Precincts; thereafter lies the Outer Precincts, extending to the shores of the Holy Island. The direction of north represents the depths of the sunless realms, wherein the catechumen is emancipated from the body and the phenomenal world. The south represents the heights of the solar realms, wherein the catechumen is a fulgid unity of soul and body. East and west denote the Sun's equinoctial rising and setting.

¶ THE FOUR INITIATORY QUEENS

The Avalonian powers are localised reflexes of the cosmic; polarised but complementary, they are revealed in two ways. Firstly, as the telluric, serpentine forces that simultaneously fructify the island and are transformed in the crucible of the Tor, becoming progressively reified initially within the Holy Hill's dual acquifers, and then as the Red and White Springs, their loci of rising being the points of final emanation and manifestation. Secondly, as deities who dwell upon the island. Firstly, the feminine principle, identified as the Goddess of Avalon, becoming divided into the nine-who-are-one, the ennead; they are the very fabric of the Holy Island. The male principle simultaneously exists beneath the Holy Island in Annwn and in the celestial Hades above. This masculine current manifests in various ways: as Arawn or Gwyn ap Nudd, monarch of the stellar-Draconian race of fey; as Arthur, the eternal, archetypal solar regent and king-beneath-the-hill, and as Merlin, the mercurial, inscrutable and ungovernable trickster-magus.

Further beings of the insular otherworld include the denizens of Annwn – the Fair Folk; the ancestors and the wandering dead; the guardians, nature-spirits and *genii locorum*; the Watchers of Avalon – the monkish fraternity contacted by Frederick Bligh Bond and Dion Fortune;[1] the mythic zootype of the Phoenix, and the elemental forces associated with the Tor invoked by her 'Chant of the Elements.'

The presiding deity is the Goddess of Avalon, a terrestrial and insular incarnation of the primordial chaos-goddess, the unmated mother of all things. As the Island's Terra Mater, her further archetypal aspects are unveiled through an octernity of deities or Matronae. Of this sorority, the Terra Mater is the ninth Matrona and the *prima inter pares*, the symbolic centre of the circle.

Four Matronae correspond to the cardinal directions. The guardians of those airts are widely understood in terms of their traditional associations with the four elements. However, the four goddesses of the intercardinal directions are less understood, but perform a significant role within the context of the Great Quest, being threshold deities of change; as teachers and attendants they guide the initiand through the metempsychotic transmutation of the self. The cross-cardinal axes define the Roads of these four Queens, extending to the horizon, and passing through the Holy Island's

1 Selby, 146.

figure 3 The Domains and Roads of the Four Queens

landmass, dividing it into quadrants. Through the sympathetic correspondences between land and presiding deity, certain landscape features acquire an eldritch significance, and these are elaborated below. Thus, for the purposes of the Great Quest, the four initiatory Queens can be said to govern one of four realms and one of four Graals. The catechumen undertakes the Great Quest by passing through each Domain in turn. Traversal of the northern half of the otherworldy landscape requires a descent to, and ascent from, the chthonic realms, accessed by two gates located on the Templum of the Tor. Their positions are varied but predictable, being spatiotemporally bound to the transit of the Sun. Thus, the Gates of Descension and Ascension are revealed in homothesis with the points of sunrise and sunset upon the distal threshold of the horizon.

The polarised ophidian deities known as the White Serpent and Red Serpent converge in a *coincidentia oppositorum* upon the Adytum, the summit of the Tor temple, giving rise to life and fecundity. Through their entwining, serpentine dance the Holy Island is kept verdant. Their fertilising union represents the true Graal which, if unattended, would give rise to the wasteland. These ophidian powers are also emanations of the primal Magna Mater; they are in the service of the terrestrial Goddess of Avalon, presiding as she does over the Island entire, which is her demesne above all others.

¶ THE LINEAMENTS OF THE ENNEAD

Through an understanding of the Holy Island's geosophy, the delineations of its spirit-guardians may be known. The Avalonian legendarium describes it as an Elysium; a realm of healing and rest; a gateway to the underworld and an abode of the fey; a locus of power and sanctity; a place of initiation and emergence, one central to the destiny of the island of Albion. Therefore, some aspects of its powers can be understood as goddesses; as guardians, psychopomps, healers, hierophants, seers, rulers, mystagogues, necromancers and mediators. The insular feminine powers of Avalon – the ennead, the nine-who-are-one – do not merely preside over the Island; they are the Island. One is an expression of the other and their relationship is more than symbiosis. This systasis between Goddess and land, as old as myth itself, lies behind the sensation vividly experienced by many: that Glastonbury as an entity is autonomian and bound to a divine telesis. Via communion with the Island, as simple to initiate as placing feet and hands upon its earth and breathing its air, the sensation is confirmed and grows only stronger over time. The feeling that the land remembers; that, if earned, there is kinship and trust, is impossible to ignore. The land is not a backdrop; rather, it asserts itself everywhere and is foremost in the minds of all. This protensive sentience is most embodied in the Tor, which, in overseeing its domain, irresistibly draws the eye and raises the heckles. The divine panopticon is inspiring and unsettling in equal measure.

By examining the traditions of the nine maidens cult, further delineations of the Sororitas Avalonis can be gleaned: they dwell upon a high place (the Tor temple); they are *bandruí*, sorcerers and shapeshifters; they are explicitly related to Brigid and the Morrígna and, by extension, are givers of poetry and sovereignty, and bringers of death. Through their association with the Sun they participate in the cosmic cycle of life, death and rebirth.

The Regina Insulae, the Terra Mater, is not transcendent but immanent. She is present in the land; as old as its geology yet forever evolving. Her will is spoken of in the industry of the birds and the buffeting winds; her entelechy can be discerned in the waxing and waning of shadow. All the qualities of the Island are hers. Thus, she delights in those who participate in her perpetual cosmic dance, where Nature, the stars, the Sun, the otherworld and the underworld, all turn towards and around her centre, which is the axis of the Island. Such directed engagement enchants the land, and this is the primary concern of the Goddess in all her aspects. By harmonising its natural order with the predictable movements of the cosmos, the homeostasis of the island is sustained and preserved. In fulfilment of this the catechumen undertakes the microcosmic Great Quest to become part of the Island's natural polity and, by extension, the macrocosmic congress.

In the same way that the study of specific organisms reveals a wider ecology, so too does the study of deity unveil a culture's relationship with spiritual ecosystems. Yet that culture's depictions of its gods and goddesses are essentially metaphorical – or sometimes literal – masks. Perhaps they are an expression of alterity, or the deities' powers, loyalties, places and traits, or they are anthropomorphised for the benefit of the human psyche, or they reveal its archetypal root. But their surfaces do not necessarily provide any deeper insight than a pupa tells of the life contained within, or a fetish object tells of its indwelling spirit. Rather, apprehension of the otherworld requires a dismantling of the hegemony of sight. It is sensed rather than seen and it transcends that which the eye perceives. Emotion, intuition, feeling and touch are preeminent. The otherworld is felt and Glastonbury is charged with feeling. The mysteries of the Avalonian landscape are held in the mind. Its powers are intuited in the rites of sunrise and sunset, in the day's inhale and exhale.

The ennead can therefore be understood in a variety of ways, as:

- Presiding *genii locorum* of the Holy Island.

- Deities euhemerised in the Arthurian legendarium as nine sisters ruling over an earthly Elysium.

- Governors and protectors of the Holy Island's health and sanctity, maintained by influencing and directing the activities of things dwelling within or passing through its precincts, both explicitly and implicitly, whether energetic, animal, human, meteorological et al.

- Sentinels of the cardinal and cross-cardinal directions and their associated correspondences (winds, Graals, initiatory bodies, alchemical processes) within the Avalonian cosmology and its related ritual landscapes.

- Guardians of the gates to the Avalonian otherworlds, including the gates of the Sun and the celestial gates of the solstices.

When perceived by visionary means their alterity is manifested in several guises: whirling, dancing entities; many-limbed beings; therianthropes; fulgid or tenebrous forms; or simply as women cowled and robed, barefoot and draped in simple habiliments. They resist decoration, being unadorned and requiring no elaborate ceremonials or extravagant offerings. This latter expression provides the catechumen with an accessible means of visualising the four initiatory queens, and gives an indication of how they desire to be understood: as liberated, unsubordinated, autonomous, independent feminine powers; not defined in opposition to the masculine, nor lacunae waiting to be filled; they are in and of themselves. They are not cyphers, even though they may conform to certain archetypes for the benefit of their adorants.

They are not of the Welsh or the Irish pantheons, being insular deities of the Holy Island, although they may contain aspects of those goddesses. They are not misandric, although their attitudes to, and relationships with, masculine powers are complex (witness their textured and wildly differing interactions with Arthur and Merlin.) They are unity-in-division and therefore can be said to contain some characteristics of the perennial fourfold Goddess and her quaternity of archetypes. Yet the virgin, the lover, the mother and the crone do not encapsulate the rich and variegated natures of the Four Matronae, who cannot be defined in terms of their childbearing status or servitude to the needs of men. Indeed, pursuit of the Great Quest reveals only certain aspects of the Four – those which assist the initiatory process. The devoted disciple may come to know them *in toto* after much resolute practice.

As keepers of their four stations and domains, the quaternity can be said to embody the waxing and waning of the year, for within them resides the cosmic cycles of life and death; the metempsychotic wheel fundamental to the quest's arcana. These four fundamental stations are staves of reckoning in time's eternal orrery. They mark the drawing in of night, the seeping into the joints of another winter, the reality of death. But they also identify the Matronae as the Isis who breathes life back into the dead; who heals and restores. The great mystery of the four initiatory Queens is this: as takers and givers of life, as bestowers of sovereignty, they are empowered to grant fecundity to the Holy Island, or to withdraw it and render its swards and orchards a wasteland. Yet they require a recipient of their gifts and prohibitions; without a Graal-seeker, there is no change or progress; without a novitiate, there is no-one to process through their domains. Thus, the relationship between the catechumen and the divine ennead is symbiotic: without the former, the goddesses-who-are-the-land will wither; without the latter, the catechumen will never acquire gnosis. The consummation of this mystery – the interdependence of physical and spiritual, outer and inner – is made possible by the sorcerous geographies of the Holy Island itself.

As land deities, the four initiatory Queens are subject to, and yet expressions of, the same stations of life and death we as mortals must undergo. Throughout the cycle of the Great Quest, we follow their skein of crimson; the circle of their blood, mingled with amniotia, milk, urine and chymus. But their presence at each station marks them as welcome companions. They are with us, to guide and to comfort. And, at death, unlike the beast that goes into hiding in anticipation of extinction, we need not be alone.

☙ *the dark queen*

The Dark Queen, the Mortifer, is also known by these names: the Goddess of Shadows, the Destroyer, the Initiatrix, the Mistress of Darkness, Queen of the Wasteland, and the Gajamo-rriẏėn. Hers is the domain where the earth receives the spent waters. She represents the waxing of the esoteric, unconscious self.

From the Temenos, in a northwesterly direction, the road of the Dark Queen extends to the horizon, being the solstice station of midsummer sunset, the gateway from otherness when souls descend from the stars into the underworld. The domain of the Dark Queen approximates to the portion of the Holy Island betwixt the directions of west and north, through which the Templum receives the in-flowing powers of the Red Serpent. It is the place of solar darkness and winter. The abbey and Edmund Hill are part of her dominion.

As psychopomp and death deity she receives the sundered pilgrims upon the Great Quest from the Roseate Queen and initiates them into the fleshless mysteries. Hers is the Realm of Spirit, the well of souls that is Annwn where, in the stillness and abeyance of her chthonic halls, the process of Nigredo, the excarnation and blackening of the self, begins and is accomplished. The Goddess of Shadows is a tutor, being the gatekeeper to many realms and pathways. For those in pursuit of the Graal, her esoteric teachings are concerned with ritual purification, the confrontation and cleansing of the manifested self and existence. She is a sorceress and seer, a witch and a healer; through her the tongues of the dead are stirred into speech. For those upon the quest, she imparts the most profound of secrets: that in the midst of crisis and division, the Corpus Noctis will ascend again as a 'radiant-browed' luminary, enlightened by self-knowledge and otherworldy wisdom. Death is but a stage in the process of life. Yet the catechumen must first partake of the Graal of Spirit, charged with the gift of Quiescence, the *awen* or elixir ensorcelled with witchbreath. This is the nature of *awen*: inspiration may only be truly attained once certain abyssal trials have been overcome. The drops that fell upon Taliesin's brow are chthonic in origin. Thus, the Corpus Noctis must taste the gnosis that comes from a return to primal chaos in order to be reborn in wisdom.

The Black Mistress is cognate with aspects of Hecate, Ceridwen, Calleach, Adsagsona, Nicnevin, Hel, Black Isis and Ereškigal. Her totem birds are the Corvidae; the crow, the raven and the magpie, birds of death and bodement. In conformity with the Celtic wheel of the year, she is associated with winter, the feast of Samhain and the Gaulish month of Giamonios.

the pale queen

The Pale Queen, the Lucifer, is also known by these names: the Goddess of Ascent, the Teacher, the Revelatrix, the Mistress of Trembling, and the Brewant-rriẏen. She is the Virgin aspect of the Feminine. Hers is the domain where the air meets the earth in a mandorla of twilight. She represents the waning of the esoteric, unconscious self.

From the Temenos, in a northeasterly direction, the road of the Pale Queen extends to the horizon, being the solstice station of midsummer sunrise. The Domain of the Pale Queen approximates to the portion of the Holy Island betwixt the directions of north and east, through which the Templum gives the out-flowing powers of the White Serpent. It is the place of solar dawn and spring. The ancient oaks known as Gog and Magog, demarcating the oaken path, the chief ceremonial route to the Tor, are part of her dominion.

As high priestess and tutor in the mysteries of resurrection, the Pale Mistress receives the purified souls upon the Great Quest from the Dark Queen and reveals unto them the arcana of rousing and return. As Midwife of Souls she shares some attributes of the Calleach, who is also linked to Brigid. Hers is the Realm of Ascent, a spiritous domain of Annwn, where the initiand drinks from the Graal of Admittance, charged with the gift of Anamnesis. The Corpus Aurora is stirred from repose to awakening and proceeds towards reunification of soul and body. The Pale Mistress is a prophet and chaste protector of neophytes embarking upon the mysteries of ascent, those who stand upon the cusp of rebirth. The eternal, unattainable virgin-priestess, she belongs to no-one but herself and has no need or desire for union in order to be whole, but presides over the process of Albedo, the awakening of enfleshed souls, nonetheless. She is the embodiment of primal innocence, of divine purity untainted by experience. Through the Gates of Ascension, she leads the catechumen from the darkness of Annwn to the moon-lit greenswards of the physical world, the esoteric rebirth of the initiated self.

The White Queen is cognate with aspects of Brigid, Tlachtga, Artemis, Athene, Veiled Isis, Cybele, Hausōs, Mater Matuta and Volla. Her totem birds are the Anatidae: the goose and the swan, birds of otherworldly transformation; and the Columbidae: the dove and the pigeon, birds of peace and sacrifice. In conformity with the Celtic wheel of the year, she is associated with spring, the feast of Imbolc and the Gaulish month of Elembivios, which etymologically is related to the stag.

the aureate queen

The Aureate Queen, the Ardorifer, is also known by these names: the Goddess of Glory, the Inciter, the Idolatrix, the Mistress of the Sky, and the Samo-rriyėn. Hers is the domain where the air is ignited with argent fire. She represents the waxing of the exoteric, conscious self.

From the Temenos, in a southeasterly direction, the road of the Aureate Queen extends to the horizon, being the solstice station of midwinter sunrise. The domain of the Aureate Queen approximates to the portion of the Holy Island betwixt the directions of east and south, through which the Templum gives the out-flowing powers of the Red Serpent. It is the place of solar zenith. Her realm includes the neck of land connecting the world-at-large to the Holy Island, its threshold bisected by the earthwork known as Ponter's Ball.

The Golden Mistress embodies the cultivation of an exalted lust for life; strength, joy, liberation, ecstasy and courage. She is the glory of life and the world, presiding over the Dionysian mysteries where holiness is found in the physical. As a deity of worldly desire, she stands in opposition to the raven-winged Dark Queen, even though her adorants acknowledge the complementary energies of sex and death.

Under her terrible gaze the process of Citrinas is realised: the timid and innocent self is transfigured into the Corpus Lux; the innocence of the Corpus Aurora is sacrificed upon her altar. By imbibing the gift of volition from her Graal of Flesh, the catechumen is granted the courage to embrace worldly experience and accept change without fear. Beneath the sustaining full power of the Sun, the Goddess of Glory grants sovereignty to those who please her. Yet even as the Sun begins to weaken unto death as it passes its zenith, so too will her consorts – those who receive her connubial and concupiscent rites – taste the elixir of mortality.

The Aureate Queen is cognate with aspects of Medb, Rhiannon, Babalon, Inanna, Ištar, Freyja, Bright Isis, Rosmerta and Nynyve / Niniane. Her totem birds are the Accipitridae: the eagle and the hawk, birds of the Sun, and the Turdidae: the thrush and the blackbird, birds of song and worldly delight. In conformity with the Celtic wheel of the year, she is associated with summer, the feast of Beltane, which traditionally lasted for three nights, and the Gaulish month of Samonios, the first month of the Celtic year.

the roseate queen

The Roseate Queen, the Noctifer, is also known by these names: the Goddess of Descent, the Mother, the Imperatrix, the Mistress of the Altar, and the Sido-bremo-rriẏėn. Hers is the domain where fire is extinguished in the waters of the Island. She represents the waning of the exoteric, conscious self.

From the Temenos, in a southwesterly direction, the road of the Roseate Queen extends to the horizon, being the solstice station of midwinter sunset, the gateway to otherness when souls ascend to the stars from the underworld. The Domain of the Roseate Queen approximates to the portion of the Holy Island betwixt the directions of south and west, through which the Templum receives the in-flowing powers of the White Serpent. It is the place of solar dusk and autumn. The Red and White Springs and Wearyall Hill are part of her dominion.

The Red Mistress is the goddess of completion, resolution and balance, standing in opposition to the Pale Queen, who represents birth, initiation and commencement. As an incarnation of the Terra Mater the Mother receives the harvest of souls, those who are approaching a resolution of the Graal's quest-cycle. Theirs is the Corpus Tenebris, representing mastery of the self, cosmic balance and right order. In her realm, the process of Rubedo is undertaken, the *coincidentia oppositorum*, yielding the philosopher's stone and attainment of the Great Work. Her Graal of Egression, bearing the gift of Utterance, grants the transcendent arte of poetic speech – an expression of unity, gnosis and authority.

Yet even while her realm is peaceful, fecund and prosperous, the Sun declines towards the horizon and the regal Roseate Queen must lead the catechumen towards the Gates of Descension. At dusk, the Dark Queen stands upon the threshold of death to receive those pilgrims who, even though they bear the arcanum of vivification, through sacrifice will become sundered once more. Such is the cyclical doctrine of metempsychosis and the perennial quest for the Graal, where continual initiation yields access to greater and more potent mysteries.

The Roseate Queen is cognate with aspects of Arianrhod, Rosmerta, Ceres, Demeter, Nerthus, Isis Unveiled, and Gerðr. Her totem birds are the Ardeidae: the heron, cognate with the Bennu bird and the Phoenix, the mythical bird of regeneration; and the Strigiformes: the owl, bird of wisdom and dusk. In conformity with the Celtic wheel of the year, she is associated with autumn, the feast of Lughnasadh and the Gaulish month of Anagantio, the time of ritual ablutions.

¶ THE FOUR GRAALS OF THE HOLY ISLAND

That the Graal is cognate with the cup of the tarot is evinced by the four treasures of the Tuatha Dé Danann: the Lia Fáil stone, the Spear of Lugh, the Sword of Light or *claidheamh soluis*, and the Cauldron of the Dagda or *coire anseasc*. These treasures correspond to the shield or pentacle, the wand, the sword and the cup and are the chief artefacts of Arthurian tradition. In Dion Fortune's milieu, these same symbols – the stone, the lance, the sword and the Graal – are known as the Grail Hallows and form the basis of a Holy Grail Rite.

The link between Celtic myth and the Graal Quest, the Celtic cauldron as the ur-Graal, is made explicit in the Irish tale *The Prophetic Ecstasy of the Phantom*. It is the primogenitor of the Graal legend's major tropes, specifically in relation to sovereignty.

In Celtic myth, the Graal-cauldron is a vessel of the Goddess, originating in the otherworld, and possessed of various powers: illumination, renewal, courage and utterance. Welsh myth tells of four cauldrons, each representing a station in the perennial quest-cycle of the Graal. The first is the Cauldron of Ceridwen, goddess of transformation and inspiration. It the vessel of the underworld from which Taliesin received three drops and was reborn as the 'radiant-browed.' This the Graal of Spirit, charged with the gift of Quiescence, the *hun-međ*. Its elixir is the *don lionn iomhas*, the *awen* that imparts the arcana of death, tribulation and resurrection, giving rise to illumination. Its inspiration is received when the self has been sundered, passing from unity to separation; the bifurcation of flesh and spirit. The Graal of Spirit is cognate with the extasis or theomania of initiation, the emancipation of the soul from the body and its purification from the phenomenal and the sensuous. The guardians of the Graal are the Sororitas Avalonis, the nine sorceresses whose witch-breath ensorcels the Graal's elixir. In the stillness and repose of the chthonic realm the Graal of Spirit reveals the fleshless mysteries of the 'deep place' that is Annwn.

The second is the *pair dadeni* or Cauldron of Rebirth, empowered to resurrect the dead. It is the Graal of Admittance, bearing the gift of Anamnesis, the *biw-međ*. Once the soul is illuminated by the fleshless mysteries, and receives the concomitant purifying rites, the flensed self proceeds towards reunification: somatic and worldly ingress. The elixir of revivification kindles the light of new life, beginning the process of embodiment, of awakening and re-emergence into the material world. It marks the esoteric rebirth of the re-initiated self. The Graal of Admittance is cognate with the extasis or theomania of prophesy, the province of the seer-priestess whose foresight reveals the life-yet-to-be-lived.

The third is the Cauldron of Diwrnach, the vessel that grants sustenance to the brave and would not cook food for cowards. It is the Graal of Flesh, charged with the gift of Volition, the *exoβn-með*, cognate with the extasis or theomania of erotic love, the bewitching power that reveals the divinity within the physical. The Graal's elixir instills the innocent and untainted self with full bodily consciousness and an awareness of worldly experience. Like the Sun, it sustains the courageous life-affirmers and yea-sayers, life's adorants who glorify the world and the body, who embrace change without fear, and live in terms of their own volition. It bears the promise of revelation, ultimately leading to an intimation of one's True Will.

The fourth is the Cauldron of the Head of Annwn, the pearl-rimmed vessel that grants poetic speech. It is the Graal of Egression, bearing the gift of Utterance, the *barðọl-með*. Attainable only at the culmination of the quest-cycle, the accumulated knowledge and wisdom of the catechumen is transfigured by the elixir of fruition into poetic utterance, which signals divine truth, authority and right judgement. Poetic speech is the expression of cosmic balance and order, the unity of opposites. It represents the final stage of initiation before the soul's irresistible descension into the underworld. The Graal of Egression is cognate with the extasis or theomania of poetry, the rhapsodic, inspired and transcendent arte of magickal word-weaving.

¶ THE FOUR BODIES OF THE QUEST

The catechumen possesses four bodies, transfiguring into each to resolve the perennial quest-cycle and acquire gnosis.

The first body is the Corpus Noctis or *kreθ-tiβ̃uil*, the sundered self that descends into the chthonic realm of Annwn. It is cognate with the alchemical state of Nigredo. Upon drinking from the Graal of Spirit, the catechumen is blackened with the death and decomposition of the old self, ego, and of worldly identity. A cleansing of impurities is followed by an illumination of the fleshless mysteries. The sepulchral arcanum of Nigredo is made explicit in the alchemical acronym VITRIOL (*visita interiora terrae rectificando invenies occultum lapidem*, which translates as 'visit the innermost of the earth and by rectifying you will find the hidden stone.') Further, the Sol Niger or Black Sun of Nigredo is synonymous with the sun of the underworld, identified as Sirius. When the midwinter sun weakens and descends to the chthonic realms, it is extinguished and reignited in the black flame of the unmanifest nocturnal sun. Through katabasis, the catechumen must similarly pass through the underworld and become purified in the *niger ignis*, in pursuit of the 'hidden stone' – the *lapis exilis* or philosopher's stone, which is cognate with the Graal.

The second body is the Corpus Aurora or *kreθ-bọrẹy*, the purified self that prepares for ascension to worldly life in a unity of spirit and flesh. Upon drinking from the Graal of Admittance, the catechumen is initiated into the arcana of renewal and return, the giving of form to life. The Corpus Aurora is cognate with the alchemical state of Albedo, which brings light and clarity to the *prima materia* through its unity of two opposing principles: soul and body. The initiand becomes the light of the awakened soul in the darkness; primal innocence, the moon bathed in the first blush of dawn.

The third body is the Corpus Lux or *kreθ-dið*, the fully incarnated and conscious self firmly rooted in the corporeal world. The Corpus Lux is the vehicle by which the self, embracing the glory of the phenomenal, learns volition and True Will. The adorant's voluptuary journey is marked by the passage of the Sun from dawn to maximal solar light. Innocence is replaced with experience: attraction, *agape*, ecstasy, concupiscence, manifold life and fecundity, giving rise to courage and liberty. The Corpus Lux is cognate with the alchemical state of Citrinas, the dawning of solar light and the transformation of the timid and innocent self.

The fourth body is the Corpus Tenebris or *kreθ-diweð*, the inspired, fully manifested self. It is the harvest of a life lived according to its True Will. The Corpus Tenebris is the charged Graal, representing mastery of the self, cosmic balance and right order, the unification of opposites. It is cognate with the alchemical state of Rubedo, the culmination of the magnum opus and the Great Work. It is the union of the hermetic king and queen, the attainment of the *lapis exilis*, even as both the Sun and the self weaken unto dusk.

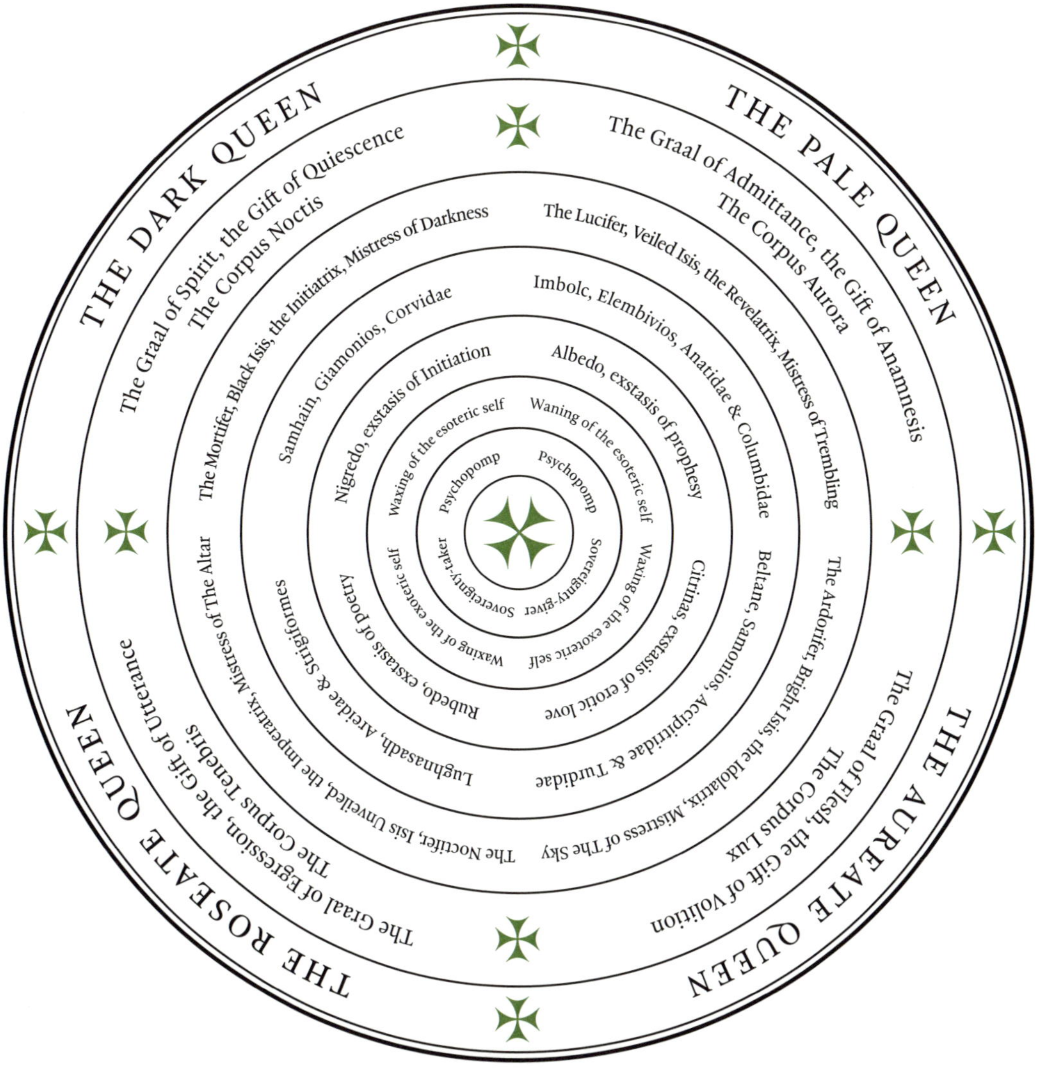

figure 4 The quadripartite correspondences of the Four Queens

LIBER MYSTERIA

When the purple of night presses down onto the thin copper of day
And planets rise like the souls of the dead;
When the chthonic sun has leeched all noise from the land
And a dark peace settles into the folds;
When, in deep sleep, the hour teeters on the brink of new
And churchyard-dwellers wander the lanes of their youth;
When hedgerows glisten with silver leaf
And things formless ride on a single, saved breath;
When the tree-cusp tells of nothing except blank expectation
And every branch is straining to hear;
When the reasoning mind, standing dumbly by,
Waits upon those who soar in unfettered joy;
When the borders of glorious derangement are yet to harden;
Then, oh then, is the time
To do the wondrous deeds of which I speak.

the outer precincts

¶ SUMMARIUM

Glastonbury, the Isle of Avalon, the Hieronesos, possesses an unparalleled magicko-mythic status. As an elevated landmass, rising from 175 to 450 feet, it embodies the hill-as-island mytheme, an expression of divine unity bifurcated into primordial opposites: water and land. In the earliest ur-myths the waters separated and gave birth to the earth in the form of a primeval mound, surrounded by a field of reeds. This in turn recalls the Egyptian paradisal realm of Aaru and echoes Avalon's status as an earthly Elysium closed to the profane world. In numerous mythologies, Islands of the Dead such as the Irish Tech Duinn are located in the west, surrounded by a great river-ocean or inland sea. Separated from the world-at-large, they are inherently withdrawn and isolated. The Druidic island of Anglesey; the Iron Age cult centre at Hayling Island in Sussex; Circe's island; the Île de Sein, whereon dwelled nine virgin priestesses, are all exemplars of islands as private loci of heterodox, occult practice.

The Tor itself embodies myriad cosmological and magicko-religious functions. As a world hill it is located at the centre of the cosmos within the Avalonian ritual landscape. Cultures variously venerate this central place as a hill or mountain, a ziggurat or pyramid, a pole or pillar, a rope, a ladder, or a tree. In Taoism the world hill is the mythological Mount Kunlun, the 'mountain at the middle of the world.' In Irish myth it is the Hill of Uisneach, burial-place of the gods. In Mesopotamian myth it is Mount Mashu, beneath which flow the Waters of Death.

As an axis mundi the Tor is the point of coition between a chthonic well of souls – the underworld of Annwn – and the celestial realm. As a place of otherworldly ingress, it conforms to a model of descent to the lower world based on a septenary structure, reflected in the Tor's terracing and echoed in mythological accounts of the netherworld.

In western esoteric tradition the Tor is Mount Abiegnus, the Rosicrucian Mountain of Initiation or Hill of Vision. Beneath the hill is the Cavern, the secret place of meeting and initiation. Above the Cavern is the Hall of Learning, the Chapel of the Graal and the Watchtower.[1] In Fortunean terms it is also the Atlantean Sun temple atop the sacred mountain, whereon a fire burns in perpetuity.

Both archaeology and myth agree on its status as a temple or *nemeton*. The Tor is the abode of nine ruling sorcerer-priestesses, the Graal guardians, a state of affairs consanguineous with the earliest myths of nine female deities and, later, with nine witch-maidens who reside on a holy island or high place. As such, the Tor conforms to the strict definition of a templum: an open space to conduct augury; a ritual space dedicated to deity; and a place of celestial observation. In this respect it is a reflex of the seven-tiered temple, exemplified in the Sumerian Etemenanki ziggurat, the Prang Pyramid at Koh Ker in northern Cambodia, and the Egyptian Djoser Step Pyramid.

As an elevated Templum with uninterrupted views to the horizon in every direction, the Tor becomes a place where solar and celestial observation determine the propitious times for rituals of directionality, specifically sunrise and sunset. Its numerous solstitial orientations and alignments imply a status as ceremonial centre where the intercardinal axes of a quadripartite cosmology converge. Its summit is an Adytum where deities and threshold-guardians of the sorcerous landscape below may be systematically evoked and entreated; these are chiefly the Four Queens, aspects of the presiding Matrona, the Magna Mater.

That the opposing telluric currents of the Red Serpent and White Serpent converge upon the Tor marks it as a nexus of power. They are earthly embodiments of the twin primal aspects of divinity: masculine and feminine; kteis and phallus; menstrual blood and semen. Their union upon the Holy Hill represents the ophidian marriage of sun and earth; the alchemical distillations of white mercury and red sulphur. The relationship between the Tor and the Red

1 Fortune (2012), 51.

and White Serpents is made explicit in the transformative waters of the Red and White Springs which rise at the base of the Holy Hill. The waters gestate in the liminal womb of the Tor, at the confluence of the above-world and the netherworld, nurtured by their respective currents. The waters are terraqueous reifications of this spiritous eliding and, in common with the Graal, are given freely to all-comers. Indeed, the relationship between the Graal and the waters is conveyed in the red and white cruets of Avalonian tradition, which, as we have mentioned, contained holy blood and sweat and are symbols of divinity.

As a mythic resting-place of the Graal the Tor is a realm of *henosis*; of initiation and revelation. The Red and White Springs are the primary *materia magica* of the Great Quest, their waters employed to lustrate, consecrate and ensorcel. All those who taste of them are brought into the precincts of Magistery, unwittingly or otherwise. The Great Quest therefore is a conscious engagement with the arcana of the Holy Island. The catechumen becomes a sacral hypostasis, a cosmic pilgrim circumambulating four realms and four initiatory stations in pursuit of personal transmutation.

The Call to Avalon, otherwise known as the Glastonbury Experience, is a phenomenon experienced by many pilgrims. It has been described as an accelerated process of personal spiritual growth; an emotionally painful confrontation with hidden and repressed aspects of the self, leading to personal trauma but ultimately healing. It has been recognised as equivalent to the fiery purification process meted out by Shiva upon Mount Arunachala, where anything not aligned to one's true self is brought to the surface, magnified, rooted out and incinerated in Shiva's fire of transformation.

Through an undertaking of the Great Quest, the catechumen deliberately participates in this process, inviting transfiguration by the Magna Mater of the Holy Island. By partaking of four Graals, and through a ritual cycle of metempsychosis, of descent and ascent, death and rebirth, the microcosmic wasteland of the self is transformed. In standing upon the crossroads, the *crux decussata* of the Adytum at the summit of the Tor, the catechumen becomes the mandorla, an embodiment of cosmic unity. Through gnosis, the covenant between spirit and flesh is restored and the *lapis exilis* or charged Graal of personal sovereignty is gained. This is the essence of the Graal tradition. At the Quest's completion, of those to who the mysteries of the Holy Island are unveiled, but a few become members of a rare synomosy; dedicants protecting and upholding the Avalonian *prohairesis*. For those who would not proceed along the path of initiation, turn back now.

¶ INTERMISSIO: THE UMBRA ANIMAE

One of the greatest deprivations of western materialism is its rejection of concepts of the soul, a position largely predicated on the waning of religious belief upon which, it is argued, the existence of the soul is necessitated. Across cultures and histories, the soul has been conceived of differently and this, in turn, defines an understanding of the self, the world and existence. An ontology in which ideas of the soul are absent is inherently prejudiced against, and denuded of, spiritual meaning.

In the *Phaedo*, Plato, the father of substance dualism, presents a series of proofs for the immortality of the soul. Yet, ironically, in *Timaeus* he argues for the existence of a world-soul, a creation of the demiurge occurring before the introduction of matter, of which the human soul is also fashioned. Thus, the human soul becomes a microcosm of the ensouled world and the ensouled universe, a relationship which ultimately defines the teleology of western occultism.

In tandem with an increasingly atheological western philosophy, substance dualism found its apogee in the Cartesian notion of the soul as nothing more than an individualistic mind. In Decartes's view, the mind / soul is wholly disconnected from the body. Further, Nature at large possesses no 'thinking soul' at all and is entirely mechanistic. The physical and biological world becomes inanimate and desacralised, with no intrinsic beauty or purposiveness. If Nature consists solely of matter, all things may legitimately become controlled and exploited for human gain.[2] This position is the absolute antithesis of animism. In truth, the hylic philosophies of western culture are not absolute; they are rather illative chains encumbered by scientific bias, in the service of economic imperatives. Be aware that manifold cultures have, still do, and will continue to regard the world as an ensouled realm, and the enfleshed human as a retinue of co-located ecosystems, intelligences and organisms; a vessel for its divine hypostases.

The catechumen must reject or, at least, suspend adoption of the dominant western materialistic worldview, for the Great Quest requires careful cultivation of the Umbra Animae or *skọd-kuilð*, which is the catechumen's liminal body, dwelling at the intersection of matter and spirit. The Umbra Animae is not transcendent but dwells within the flesh, yet functions as an intermediary

2 See Hickman for more on this topic.

for higher spiritual congress. Broadly cognate with the etheric double which, along with diverse other forms, spirits and intelligences, comprises the Bodily Retinue, its chief organ is the Oculi Magicka (the *hud-llugad*), which enables the otherworldly realms and their denizens to be discerned and contacted. Three energetic foci are also part of its fabric: the Rubeus Lapis, the red seed; the Albus Lapis, the white seed, and the Lapis Viridis, the green seed. The red and white seeds are microcosms of the Red Serpent and White Serpent; the polarised powers that ensorcel and vitalise the Holy Island. The green seed is their fecund union; the emerald henosis of those procreative powers. It is the Graal-stone of one-pointedness; the Lumen Naturae, cognate with the light of the divine monad already resident within the subtle body's heart-centre. Through these three foci, the body of the catechumen communes with the Body of the Island. The subtle self may also be sent forth as a famulus to cross the Gates of the Holy Island and apprehend the chthonic realm of Annwn beyond.

In very general terms, the cross-cultural non-physical aspects of the self can be said to typically incorporate a spirit – the sustaining breath of life or *pneuma*; and the soul – the immortal, divine and individuated self. Alchemically, the body, spirit and soul correspond to salt, mercury, and sulphur. The mind – the thinking, judging, rational intellect – may be considered an additional aspect. Brythonic and proto-Celtic words for breath, mind, spirit and soul reflect this asomatous composition. The vital, etheric or subtle body is yet a further aspect. Interpretation of the nature and extent of a human's Bodily Retinue varies widely, yet the etheric body, the *soma pneumatikon*, features in numerous traditions, not least eastern religious practice and western esotericism.

The material of the etheric body is roughly analogous to the Platonic fifth element or aether, and the medieval alchemical quintessence. It is also cognate with *prana* and *qi*, the vitalising energy of which the Red Serpent and White Serpent are composed, along with the fey, spirits and guardians of the land. It is the least dense of the four physical states – including gas, liquid and solid – and is similarly present throughout Nature. It interpenetrates the material body, being a counterpart in terms of form and structure. Some traditions posit that the etheric body is eternally present; others that it must be consciously created by the magician. Whichever is the case, it typically includes a subtle physiology, which may be expressed as focal points (e.g. chakras in eastern traditions), channels, energies and fluids. Through this rarefied system, it becomes the medium by which the higher, transcendent, immaterial selves conjoin with the lower, dense body and through which the higher exerts an influence on the lower. This is the doctrine of emanation in microcosm. In chaos magick, ether is cognate with *potentia*, a half-formed probabilistic substance containing all possibilities, certain of which the consciousness and the will of the magician can bring into manifestation.[3]

A primary function of the etheric body is to receive the abundant life-sustaining currents poured out from the Sun, which incorporate the planetary powers, and to distribute them over their physical counterpart. In this way, the heavenly bodies exert themselves upon the body of matter. Heraclides Ponticus proposed that human souls, in the form of a fiery light, are comprised of 'luminous aether,' as is the cosmos at large and the infinity that lies beyond. Sunlight is the medium of thought, which is most powerful at midday.[4] Thus, by force of attraction of like to like, both the fiery light from within us and the infinite living mind are drawn together by the power of the noonday Sun. Sunlight is the medium by which human and cosmic effluences flow and meet. And aether, the underlying element common to all things, is the binding link between inner vision, psychic awareness, the celestial bodies and divinity.

Through its sympathetic attachment to the dense body, one regulating and affecting the health of the other, the etheric body recalls the Anglo-Saxon *hama*, a protective membrane that remains with the body in life. In folklore, witnessing the etheric body detached from its corporeal counterpart presages death. And at the point of physical extinction the etheric double may be seen close by its physical counterpart as a wraith, a state of affairs reminiscent of the Egyptian *ka*. Although the dense and etheric bodies are not normally separated during earthly life, the latter may be deliberately disengaged from the former and sent forth, for example as the so-called 'free soul' of certain shamanic traditions. The etheric double may even possess a degree of autonomy or identity distinct from its host. In certain traditions it is known as the Carrier of the Will. This blurring of the border between self and famulus is illustrated in old Norse mythology, where the *hugr* is the mind-spirit or personal soul, able to shape-shift and become detached from its material counterpart. Related to the *hugr* is the *hamr*, the visible part of the soul or physical presence. The *fylgia* or *vǫrðr* is the shadow-body and guardian, the warden-spirit

3 See Carroll, 18–19.

4 See Reiche.

of the incarnated soul from birth to death (the word 'wraith' is derived from *vǫrðr*.) The relationship with its owner is symbiotic, akin to the bond between the dense and etheric bodies. One function of the *fylgia* is to enable the *hugr* to roam unencumbered by the physical self as a free soul. The *hamingja* is a second warden-spirit, associated with the fetch of traditional witchcraft and potentially even cognate with the Holy Guardian Angel. The *hamingja* determines its owner's luck and general happiness, much like the *eudaimon* of ancient Greek tradition. It is capable of travelling independently while assuming its owner's *hamr* or appearance; the wandering *hugr* may also adopt the *hamr* of its corporeal body and thus be apprehended as a second self or doppelgänger.[5] In certain traditions, the act of etheric intercourse may give rise to offspring with no corporeal existence, an outcome with parallels to the willed creation of an egregore.

The Bodily Retinue of the catechumen is the *terra Adamica*, the 'Earth of the Anthropos,' the first man who is symbolic of the alchemical *prima materia*. The actions of the Great Quest are performed on the operators themselves: the Frater Mysterium and Soror Mystica. The invisible denizens of the Holy Island's terrestrial otherworlds are united in their etheric composition, which is the medium shared by the catechumen's subtle body, Thus, by developing a knowledge of, and propinquity with, the Umbra Animae, the catechumen becomes attuned to the great etheric currents that sweep from the astral realm across the earth, flowing through the Red and White Serpents into the fabric of the Holy Island. It is the tool for discernment of, and communication with, the Avalonian otherworlds.

5 See Frisvold and Pollington for a thorough overview of Norse and Anglo-Saxon conceptions of the soul.

¶ THEORIA

Certain preparations must be made prior to commencement of the Great Quest, including an apprehension of the Bodily Retinue's mysteries. This is achieved via the following exercises, which are the Quotidian Meditations, and, as the name suggests, should be performed daily.

☙ Lie in stillness with eyes closed. Breathe deeply and attend to the corporeal self until it is in abeyance and wholly succumbed to heaviness. See a many-faceted, almond-shaped white jewel residing within the skull; above the top of the spinal cord and behind the pineal gland, to the rear of the head. Emitting a mild, milky radiance, this is the Albus Lapis, the masculine white seed. Below it and behind the umbilicus, see a second red jewel of identical shape and size. As dark as swirling menstrual blood, this is the Rubeus Lapis, the feminine red seed. Betwixt the red and white, within the torso, see a third emerald jewel, its marquise-cut form perpetually aflame with tongues of iridescent green. At its very centre sits a single mote of pellucid, golden light. This is the Lapis Viridis. Apprehend all three as a trinity dwelling within the subtle body; three treasures housed in the etheric temple of the Umbra Animae.

Direct your attention back to the corporeal self. Become attuned to the body of matter and acknowledge it as a living entity; an intricate anatomical composition quivering with life. Attend to the interior of your biological reality, in particular the autonomic functions performed without your conscious participation: the perpetual exchange of impulses across your nervous systems; the unceasing flow of blood, lymph and hormones through their respective networks; their cleansing and purification; the processing and absorption of nutrients; the autonomous interpretation of sense data. Focus on the bodily signals indicating your corporeal existence: pulse, heartbeat, breath, sensation, emotion, thought, movement. Direct your attention further inwards, drawing awareness into the bones that comprise your skeleton: from the extremities of the feet and hands to the pelvis, the vertebrae, ribs and skull; attend also to the organ of the brain and its neural mass, giving rise to bodily consciousness. And in so doing, also apprehend the white Albus Lapis and know that it generates and governs these anatomical parts through a body-wide network of subtle capillaries.

Now focus on the muscles of the body, the connective tissues that enfold the skeleton, on the heart and the other viscera. Attend to the circulatory system through which the body's lifeblood courses, and its relationship to the lungs: breathe and know that each in-breath bestows oxygen to the body through the blood; the blood returns waste carbon dioxide to the lungs, where it is expelled in the out-breath. See the Rubeus Lapis and know that it generates and governs these anatomical parts.

In esoteric teachings, the physical body is frequently demeaned as a mere shell or a gaol for the eternal soul. In truth, it is a wondrous creation through which phenomena are experienced; a creation that defines our reality, for better or worse. The body is the corporeal manifestation of the Bodily Retinue, our living self; a home rather than a prison. Yet, for all our intimacy with it, it remains veiled; the body of flesh is acknowledged but unknown. The purpose of this meditation is therefore to retrieve the exoteric body through a directed exploration of its interior; that which is anatomically hidden. This is necessary in order to cultivate interoception, to understand its relationship to the subtle body, which is wholly dissimilar and yet interconnected, and to the Bodily Retinue at large.

Discerning, stirring and projecting the Umbra Animae requires practice. Its mysteries lie in its relationship to the self, inasmuch as it is part of the Bodily Retinue yet divorced from normal sense-perception. It is simultaneously self and non-self or, more specifically, it is part of the esoteric, occulted self and is therefore usually unattainable. Yet it can be apprehended. In time, the catechumen will become versed in calling it forth and alternating attention between the hylic and psychic selves at will. Interoception of the Umbra Animae is also frequently accompanied by a unique paresthesia; a sensation with which the catechumen will become familiar. This can be employed to swiftly attune oneself to the umbral body. An incipient relationship with the etheric self begins with the following exercises.

Sit in stillness, with eyes closed. Be free of all disturbances, using earplugs and an eye mask if required. Breathe deeply and focus on the mechanical functions of the exoteric body of flesh: heartbeat, pulse, sensation, and so on. Conduct a body scan in order for the corporeal self to become serene and dormant, such that a heaviness of limb resists all movement. Transfer attention to your breathing, which grows slower and deeper. With each out-breath, the corporeal body relaxes into a state of even more profound calm, its mass becoming as heavy and immobile as bronze. Attend now to the three lapides and see them brighten gently with each in-breath. Maintain this until the *lapides* are purified and lustrous with vitality. Simultaneously, the physical body fades into insensibility and its boundaries become permeable. Now, know and trust that the Umbra Animae exists within you. Seek it calmly and become attuned to its ontophany, know that it has an objective reality. Focus wholly on the incorporeal dark self within; the etheric interior of that which you identify as 'I.' Feel it extend beyond your mundane thresholds. Delight in the sensations afforded by this acquaintance for, in this moment, the subtle body possesses greater truth than your physical counterpart. Maintain this conjoinment for as long as possible, ensuring the umbral body remains an absolute cynosure. Then, alternate attention between the exoteric body (the fleshy anatomy described above) and the subtle body, attending to the qualities and the sensations accompanying each.

Once a heightened limpidity and conscious awareness of the etheric body are attained, dissociation may commence. Attain a state of deep physical stillness so that the mundane body becomes passive and devoid of sensation. As its fleshly confines fade to naught, turn your attention to the Umbra Animae and feel it grow in substantiality. Even as an awareness of the mundane body wanes, your incorporeal self strengthens, becoming ungoverned by its mortal counterpart. Focus on the white Albus Lapis, the subtle jewel located above the top of the spinal cord and behind the pineal gland, to the rear of the head. Feel it slowly rise upwards and transit from the boundaries of the skull. The Albus Lapis becomes an anchor for one's locus of consciousness such that, as the etheric self ascends beyond the borders of the flesh, so too does the seat of awareness, being thus tethered. Through the process of ascension, which may be accompanied by sensations of bodily lightness, vertigo, disorientation, or energetic prickling, the umbral self becomes dissociated and wholly freed from its resting fleshy carriage. Feel your consciousness continue to rise upwards into the firmament. It may then go forth to explore the Inner Island and perform remote acts of autoscopy via the Oculi Magicka – the eye of the etheric self. This is the first step towards a refined percipience, and mystical comprehension of Avalon's haecceity. The catechumen may choose to experiment with alternative or preferred techniques for achieving dissociation of the subtle body and / or remote viewing.

The Umbra Animae may also be put to use whilst still resident within the corporeal form. Given that the etheric body is sensible to the etheric world at large (namely the terrestrial otherworlds), it can be employed as an agent of guile to discern that which is hidden to the mundane senses. While wayfaring in Nature, rouse the etheric double and relax into a mild trance, where the gaze rests on all things and no thing. Bid the Umbra Animae to lead you to a place of telluric power, or where a particular spirit resides, or where the land is afflicted. Surrender yourself to its impulses and insights. Allow yourself to be guided (It is notable that dowsing is positively affected by this technique.) By this means may secrets be revealed, as visionary telaesthesis is fundamental to the Great Quest's praxis.

As a final exercise, stand before the sun when it has attained its zenith. Feel its emanations upon the surface of the corporeal body. Now, focus your sensorium wholly on the etheric double's receipt of the sun's blessings, such that its virtues are intuited as golden motes, untold in number, settling onto the subtle body's contours, which extend a short distance beyond the physical. See those manifold but meandering motes of golden sunlight become absorbed into the central Lapis Viridis, which reflects and refracts its brilliance in an endless cycle. Being the bridge between the astral and the corporeal, the Lapis Viridis distributes the sun's virtues to the red and white lapides, thence to the physical body. Now, in contrast to this unceasing autonomic process, consciously draw the inflowing motes of sunlight to the central jewel. Upon each in-breath, see them swiftly gather towards the emerald stone as a shoal of light and become consumed; in turn, as the Lapis Viridis receives the sun's auratic emissions, see its golden centre blaze akin to breathing on an ember. Feel its emerald flames flare and grow in vigour with each breath. Repeat this process until the jewel is fiercely incandescent, its flames tall and mighty. Attend to the accompanying sensations, then stop and allow the Lapis Viridis to becalm and return to its normal state. See the excess of vitality drain out of the body through the feet as ribbons of emerald light. This is one of a number of techniques to raise power, energy or *mana* in conformity with the pedagogy of the Great Quest.

¶ PAROUSIA

Whether a resident in the modern town of Glastonbury or a visitor to the Holy Island, the aspirant should undertake the initiatory trials as a pilgrim, *sub rosa* and in solitude, and in a meditative state of devotion and humility. Throughout, profane and worldly distractions should be shunned. The external borders of the true inner Holy Island should rarely be crossed. The timing of the undertaking is at the discretion of the individual, although the solstices and equinoxes are especially propitious, as are the days preceding the moon's swelling unto fullness.

The initiand will require the following tools: a small wooden or earthenware bowl, carefully selected; two sealed vessels for carrying water; nine candles and holders; honey and fruit; red wine and mead, preferably cyser or apple metheglin; an incense burner; fumigant herbs and fragrant incense; a needle; four small jars; a compass; a notebook; a small bell or chime; and sacred entheogens if desired.

The Great Quest commences with a formal declaration to the tutelary powers of the Holy Island. By day, wayfare to an isolated place in the Outer Precincts, amongst trees and meadows. Do not dwell in the Inner Precincts or ascend the Hill – the Templum – at this stage. Be still and know that you stand upon earth that is preeminent amongst Albion's virid tapestry, and has been marked as sacred for untold years. Listen. Feel the sun and wind upon the contours of your flesh. Breathe the air of this place. Know that its spirits will attend to you when called upon. Ring your bell or chime such that a single clear peal is sent forth. Face in the direction of the Templum, wherever you stand, and utter this objuration:

> *Mad llano spïrïd-tʉd, naw gwrageð, pedwar rriyaneð, ʉn duɨwissa.*

The phonetic spelling is:

> *Mad laano spirid-tood, naw gwrageth, pedwar reeganeth, oon deuwyissa.*

> *Hearken to me ye guardians and spirits of this Holy Island. I come in pilgrimage, in all humility and of my own free will, to undertake the Great Quest. I call upon the Nine, the priest-maidens who dwell upon the summit of the Templum. I call upon the Four, the Keepers of the Graal who preside over the Domains of this country.*

I call upon the One, the Matrona, the Goddess herself. Judge me according to my deeds, that I may be deemed worthy of your Gifts.

Sit and place your hands upon the earth. Listen. Observe the flight of birds, the direction of the winds, the scudding of clouds. Close your eyes and, with your sensorium alive to your surroundings, become attuned to the quiddity of the Holy Island. After a time, rouse, stand, bow towards the Templum and depart in silence.

¶ CULTIVATING THE OCULI MAGICKA

The act of wayfaring the Precincts of the Holy Island serves many purposes: it familiarises the pilgrim with its topography, its flora and fauna and its energies; it facilitates spirit congress with the myriad entities that reside in its meadows, hedgerows, hills and clefts; and it prepares the initiate for the revelations to come. Wayfaring, by its nature, should be conducted on foot, and in solitude. Cultivation of the Oculi Magicka, the *hud-llugad*, is essential in order to fully comprehend the true *ousia* of the Holy Island, which to profane minds remains veiled and unattainable. Thus, when wayfaring, the pilgrim should remain focused upon the act of walking, where each step establishes contact with the living earth of the sacred land and where each breath is an act of giving and receiving. The mind should be unburdened of habitus, of petty and worldly trifles, and instead focused wholly on the minutiae of the here-and-now; the turn of a tree root, the flight of a bird, the whisper of the wind through leaves. Such attentiveness will attune the pilgrim to the numen of the Island and quicken the flow of gnosis. Furthermore, the Holy Island is atemporal and eternal, ungoverned by clock or calendar. Therefore, all time-reckoning should be conducted by observation of the Sun and Moon's transit, the waxing and waning of shadow. When the etheric self is sent forth into the otherworlds of the Inner Island and Annwn, a distinct attribute of its phenomenology is the dissolution of time-consciousness, a condition not dissimilar to entheogenic alterity.

Whilst wayfaring, a state of mild transcendence may be achieved by attending to the Umbra Animae. To the profane, the enfleshed frame that conveys its non-corporeal bodies is a barrier to an apprehension of the numinous yet, as already described, the material and spiritous selves can become unshackled. By these and other techniques may the Oculi Magicka be cultivated and primal aesthesis achieved.

The Inner Island – that is, its otherworldly, untainted and archetypal aspect – can be discerned through the Oculi Magicka by means of directed vision. Through the mind's eye, as the pilgrim roams the Island, perceive an expanse of water girding the land (refer to the map and commit to memory the land that sits proud of the tidal estuary.) When perceiving the Templum, do so such that the tower upon its summit is absent (when looking towards the Templum, repeatedly obscuring the tower from vision will effect this change); in place of roads and buildings see only trees, launds and greenswards. From time to time, relax your gaze and absorb the vista before you *in toto*, settling into a mild trance while retaining a sensation of the land as water-girdled. In so doing the pilgrim will become unburdened from the tyranny of the moment in favour of an inner mythic dreamtime, a primordial vision that grants access to the true and eldritch geographies of the Inner Island.

Further revelations may be obtained by sending forth the Umbra Animae when the physical body is quiescent, as outlined elsewhere. When cognisance resides wholly within the Umbra Animae, the catechumen may go forth into the Inner Island, apprehending the land through the Oculi Magicka in all its glory.

¶ THE NUMEN OF THE OUTER PRECINCTS

First and foremost, the pilgrim should wayfare in physical form far and wide across the Hieronesos, the Holy Island, always cultivating the Oculi Magicka, always avoiding the profane, always attentive to the ever-unfolding qualia. The pilgrim should become intimate with the salient aspects of the Outer Precincts, its geography and topography, venturing even to the shores of the Inner Island. The countryside to the north and east is especially mild and peaceful. Consult the map herein and walk to a place where the waters of the Levels would lap against the meads of the Inner Island. Via application of the Oculi Magicka, look out across the watery vista; see the sun glistening upon the great inland sea and distant islands rising from it. Know that the many crowns and clefts of Avalon are all girdled with water; feel a modulation of perception as you intuitively acknowledge the visionary reality of this place as a sacred island-country.

An excursion to Pontis Vallum at Havyatt is worthwhile, demarcating as it does the threshold between the Holy Island and the world-at-large. Difficult to access, it is best reached via the route running to the south of Edgarley. The linear earthwork should be understood as a cordon sanitaire, an apotropaic incision, warding the only land-based entry route to the peninsula. Its presence identifies Glastonbury as a place of otherness. Do not stray to the eastern bank, but remain in the west. Again, look and discern the waters enclosing the Holy Island to the north and south, which would infill the extent of the ditch. Observe the lands beyond this liminal delving, the world-at-large, and know that the island where you stand was once a holy precinct, and through its mysteria it remains an Elysium, withdrawn from the world beyond. Look back towards the island's interior and the great Hill rising from its rolling launds; meditate on its status as a temple, an observatory and a panopticon: those who dwell upon it see and know all. Nothing escapes their gaze.

Walk in pilgrimage along the neck of land extending to the west of the Holy Island, leading to Wearyall Hill. Alas, the blight of industry and commerce scars the area to the north, yet these modern disfigurements may be passed over by the Oculi Magicka, whereby they are not present, their foundations being submerged beneath the waters of the great inland sea. Discernment of Avalon's veridical island status can be quickened here, where water inundates the surrounding land on three sides. Wearyall Hill's western extremity undoubtedly formed a point of ingress and egress to the Holy Island, its spine a processional route to the interior. John of Glastonbury states that a monastery of holy virgins, St Peter's convent, was located upon the hill – a Christian mirror to the heterodox community of sorceresses who once dwelled upon the Temple of the Tor.

According to legend, when Joseph of Arimathea arrived on Wearyall Hill, he planted his staff in the ground, which burst into flower, giving rise to the Holy Thorn. The Glastonbury Thorn has been subject to numerous attacks, most recently in 2012. Some years thereafter, the landowner wholly removed the tree from its dwelling-place on Wearyall Hill. However the thorn has been widely propagated and another grows in the grounds of Glastonbury Abbey.

The southern tip of Wearyall Hill was once connected to the mainland by an early medieval bridge, first erected in 650–780. Known as Pomparles Bridge, its name derives from the Latin *pons perilis*, the Bridge Perilous, where Excalibur was returned to the Lady of the Lake after King Arthur's final, fatal battle. To the northwest the tidal estuary extends to the horizon. To the southwest a long spur of land bearing the Polden Hills rises from swamp and marsh. From the hill's summit a majestic view towards the Templum will rouse and stir the pilgrim.

To the northwest, beyond the shores of Wearyall Hill, rises the island of Beckery. Pilgrims would visit here prior to their arrival at Glastonbury proper, and it is where, in legend, the mortally wounded Arthur was transported by barge and attended by the four goddesses. The dutiful pilgrim will wayfare to this place through an unlovely industrial estate where those leading an itinerant life are required to do so at the town's margins.[6] At the site of Bride's Mound the remains of the Norman chapel dedicated first to Mary Magdalene, then to St Brigid, were excavated in 2016 (note that these are no longer visible.) The mound and surrounding meadows are a tranquil retreat amidst the canker of modernity. Offerings of honey and fruit should be made to the tutelary Maidens of Bride's Well which, although now lost, is marked by a stone to the west, close to the River Brue. In so doing, the pilgrim presents a small reparation for their historical violation and, by association, the desecration of the Goddess-as-Terra-Mater. Meditate also upon the visitation to Beckery by St Brigid who, it is said, remained upon the island for some years. A syncretised form of the goddess Brid, she is a virgin aspect of the sacred feminine and cognate with the Pale Queen. The chaste protector of neophytes entering the Avalonian Mysteries, she stands as sentinel to the two chief ceremonial routes into the Holy Island: the Oaken Path to the east and Wearyall Hill to the west.

In 1885 Dr John Arthur Goodchild purchased an apparently ancient blue glass bowl. In 1887 he underwent a visionary experience and was commanded to take the bowl to Bride's Hill in Glastonbury in order for it to be passed into the possession of a woman who would unveil new spiritual truths. A year later his book *The Light of the West* was published, outlining a thesis where Celtic theology was matrifocal, Ireland being a centre of Goddess-veneration, of whom Brid was an aspect. He asserted that the redemptive power of the sacred feminine was essential for earthly peace and harmony. In 1889 Goodchild took the bowl to Glastonbury and buried it in the waters of Bride's Well. Seven years later he experienced two further visions: one of a sword

6 It might be argued that the persecution of New Age travellers, begun at least forty years ago following their designation by Thatcher's government as the new 'enemy within,' continues today as their lifestyle grows ever-more incompatible with mainstream society.

in the east, another of a cup in the west. Goodchild recounted his visions to his friend Wellesley Tudor Pole, who in turn received a message in vision, explaining that three maidens should go to a well at Glastonbury and search the waters for a sacred object. Three women, including Wellesley's sister Kitty, did exactly that and discovered the blue bowl at Bride's Well, believing it to be the Graal. The blue glass bowl is now held by the Trustees of Chalice Well at Glastonbury.

The ruins of Glastonbury Abbey are an impressive relic of Church authority and dissolution. Hallowed as the earliest seat of Christianity in Albion, its establishment upon the Holy Island attests to the sanctity of the Summer Country. Yet the venality of its cenobites resulted in a profanation of the Arthurian tradition, through their falsification of Arthur's tomb. The ruins shrink from the all-seeing glare of the dwellers upon the Templum, hidden as they are by the intervening mass of Chalice Hill. Nevertheless, the Abbey remains part of the sacred tapestry of Avalon. Its grounds are peaceful and expansive, attended and guarded by their own spirits of place, and therefore worthy of respectful attention.

The final destination within the bounds of the Outer Precincts is Edmund Hill, or Windmill Hill. Now surrounded by modern dwellings, the presence of this artificial mound is underwhelming. Yet for those fortunate enough to stand and witness the winter solstice dawn, when the rising Sun appears to roll up the steep northern flank of the Templum, there can be no doubting the deliberate positioning of this mound in service of the Holy Island's arcana, fulfilling its function as a solar and stellar observatory.

A mystery of the Great Quest is service. Not obedience or servitude, but simple assistance, given freely and without expectation of reciprocity. It is service that sustains and nurtures the Holy Island. Its denizens, spirits and deities, the Graal and the Land itself are all, by degrees, in service to one another. Therefore it befits the pilgrim to exercise service, even as a novitiate, through small acts. 'Crow work' – litter picking – is a simple expression of service that both encourages ascesis in the pilgrim and maintains the homeostasis of the Holy Island. Defilement of its sacred earth is unrelenting; in response many attendants do, of their own volition, collect litter from the lanes and meadows. Such ostensibly humble acts will not go unnoticed. By these deeds and others will the catechumen be judged, for any agency that glorifies the realm of Avalon draws the Outer Island into conformity with the Inner, and brings the actions of the intercessor into harmony with the will of the presiding powers.

Furthermore, the pilgrim should remain the exemplar of courtesy when encounters with the spiritual and corporeal denizens of the Holy Island take place. Its subtle arcana are frequently manifested in the bonds that bind one entity to another, which are veiled and enigmatic; a seemingly trivial meeting may later be revealed as one of great import, according to the weave of the destinies involved. Such is the revelatory nature of the Quest, which itself is an expression of the Goddess's inscrutable will and the Holy Island's entelechy.

¶ ACQUIRING SPIRIT ALLIES

The Holy Island teems with spirits, collectively referred to as the *spïrïd-tʉd*. They are its mighty dead and autochthons and, as such, are wellsprings of wisdom. Therefore, establishing contact, rapport and kinship is an essential condition of the Quest. While wayfaring far and wide, initially through the Outer Precincts and later the Inner Precincts, encounters will be had. Through the faculty of the Oculi Magicka, the pilgrim may be drawn to certain rocks, landscape features, animals and plants, wherein or close by their tutelary spirits reside. In particular, many venerable trees dwell upon the Holy Island: great arbors of oak, ash, beech, sycamore and maple; crooked and tortile hawthorn; ancient apple laden with mistletoe. Some stand alone, others as members of the synomosy of the hedge or the copse. Certain of these trees are named and venerated: the Avalon Oaks of Gog and Magog; the Glastonbury Thorn; the Apple King and Queen; Grandmother Lime upon Bushy Coombe. Further, many of Avalon's mighty dead are buried, unmarked, in fields and meadows.

Time, solitude and stillness amongst the secret green places of the Holy Island are the foundations of spirit-congress; a studied relationship with Nature is in itself a form of initiation. By wayfaring here and there, and by employing the Oculi Magicka, the pilgrim will learn to intuit the numen of diverse places through a heightened receptivity to subtle intimations. Dowsing may be employed to locate especially receptive or cooperative *genii locorum*. Once discerned, they should be approached slowly, with obeisance shown when drawing near. Use this salutation:

Mad llano spïrïd a'n gwɨrð ɨnɨs.

The phonetic spelling is:

Mad laano spirid an gwirth euneus.

In stillness, extend the Umbra Animae into that virid temple such that its spiritous essence is discerned; pay heed to the play of light, the wind's breath, the fragrant terpenes and odiferous emissions. The adorant may discern a rippling or haze within that grove, or an irresistible presence from a particular direction. Creatures may reveal themselves, in triplicate if the attendant is especially fortunate; these are the *famuli* of the *genius loci*, its guardians and servants, or the enfleshed form of the spirit itself, or its totem-animals. When the adorant is certain of even a subtle congress, ask for permission to attend to the corporeal sanctuary. Make libations of honey, fruit, milk or weak alcohol. Place these on the ground, rather than upon the dwelling-place of the numen. On no account dress a tree or shrub with clooties. No fires should be lit nor any thing proffered which cannot naturally rot, or would harm the homeostasis of that sanctum.

Reach out and discern its aura and, if permitted, touch its corporeal form. The received sensation may be subtle or quite potent. Step back, close your eyes and see its inner aspect. Ask the genius to come forth. The tutelary spirit may then unveil itself in therianthropic, humanoid or zoomorphic form. Explain aloud who you are and your purpose is; that you are a pilgrim and catechumen upon the Great Quest. The spirit may ask you questions, or tell you its name, or offer you something. If you are asked to leave, do so immediately.

All being well, abide there in peace and stillness for a time, always attentive to the numinous qualities of the sanctum wherein you presently dwell. Then, offer thanks, genuflect and depart.

Repeated ventures to encounter the spirits of place are advised, to establish trust, rapport and concord. The catechumen should establish new conclaves often, as the unseen denizens of the Holy Island are myriad and diverse. Ongoing congress will hasten gnosis and open doorways upon the Great Quest that are otherwise locked.

The Inner Island may be roamed and these spiritous habitations visited, in repose, by sending forth the Umbra Animae. Indeed, employment of both the Oculi Magicka and the Umbra Animae is the sole means of achieving *synkatathesis*; that is, the discernment of the aeonian otherworld of the Island. In wayfaring its true and eldritch domains, the pilgrim will encounter numerous entities: eidola of the ancestral dead, fey, nymphs, spirit-animals, servants, guardians and deities. The retinue of Arawn may sometimes be glimpsed processing through meadow or grove; or the four Queens of Avalon, attending to their respective domains in purposeful solitude; or wondrous sprites akin to dragonflies dancing above rippling pasture. Meanwhile, baneful and benighted creatures lurk in hidden clefts. Figures may be spied upon the distant Temple of the Tor, from where a pillar of smoke rises into the otherworldly skies. Many temples and shrines are located around the Holy Island's precincts, and should be approached with care. These and other cynosures may be apprehended through visionary aesthesis.

The postulant may experience an occasional phenomenon of both the Inner and Outer Island, best expressed as an inescapable drawing of the self, a magnetism exerted by the powers of the Island, which seizes and directs the pilgrim towards, or away from, certain regions. The Tor Temple and those who dwell upon it wield especial powers in this regard. In vision, the wayfarer may experience sensations of being pulled ineluctably towards the Holy Hill, but this should be resisted with firm resolve. Alternatively, the spiritous self may be hoisted high above the Island upon the tides of a confounding vortex and deposited elsewhere, even within a dim and rayless hypogeum. On other occasions, when interacting directly with certain guardians, ingress to routes and domains may be prohibited. Thereafter, when the Umbra Animae is returned and the Oculi Magicka closed, the catechumen may become attenuated for a time. This is a consequence of a profound arcanum: since your initial declaration at the commencement of the Quest, you have been observed, that act alone rousing the attention of the Island's presiding powers. Your genuine intentions are unknown to them, and they are wary. In truth, the Holy Island is governed according to a spiritous hierarchy of authorities, dignities and sovereignties; all things acknowledge this *prohairesis*. Because of this, the details of your exchanges with the *genii locorum* have been widely propagated. Thus, any phenomena of restriction, attraction and repulsion can be understood as a precaution and bulwark employed by the Island against extraneous, unfamiliar forces. This is why the Great Quest reveals the moieties of Avalon through structured initiation. If any such prohibition is encountered in vision, it is an indication of the Island's vigilance. In remediation, you should reaffirm your positive intentions to the *genii locorum* with who you are now acquainted, proclaiming your enduring trustworthiness, and ensuring your deeds remain respectful and unimpeachable – by these will you be judged.

Do not doubt that sanguinity and concord can be properly established. In time, through diverse bodements, the deeper eldritch aspects of the Holy

Island will become unveiled: meaning and correspondence will be discerned; simulacra will be beheld; synchronicities will proliferate; things will be spied at the edge of vision; entities will form and emerge from the dawn mists; susurrus voices and singing will be descried; time will compress and confound. Certain spirits will become *spïrïd-karant*, true allies, and show their amity through assistance. In short, the Holy Island will be transfigured. Yet the postulant will always sense a watchful presence, and know that they are ceaselessly observed.

the inner precincts

¶ ACQUIRING THE SACRAMENTALIA

The Templum of the Holy Hill is girdled with a ring of sacred ground known as the Inner Precincts, its foison expressed in rolling orchards and meadows. Stepping into this realm, the wayfarer will sense a quickening of the pulse as the Adytum of the Tor Temple, the axis mundi, grows ever closer. To the north, three narrow and sunken lanes – Stonedown, Paradise and Maidencroft – are flanked by ancient hedgerows and canopied by noble arbors. During the hours of dusk, night-time and dawn, spirits freely walk these paths. To the west, Wellhouse Lane leads to the rising Red Spring and White Spring and beyond, lanes weave a route behind Chalice Hill towards the modern town. Chalice Hill is privately owned and cannot be accessed, although Bushy Coombe passes close by its northern edge. According to Dion Fortune, it is the gathering-point of the Wild Hunt and the place where King Arthur sleeps until his return.[1] To the south lies Gipsy Lane, extending as a footpath around the eastern lower slopes of the Tor. The postulant should continue to wayfare widely, nurturing rapprochement with diverse spirits and employing the Oculi Magicka to discern the eldritch geographies of the Inner Island. A number of orchards are located here and there, the ancient apple trees blessed with mistletoe. Its abundance is an indication of Avalon's status as an earthly Elysium and terrestrial otherworld, for the plant, renowned as a celestial gift, is not

1 Richardson, 61.

rooted in the soil, relying on its host-tree for vitality. Thus, being aloof from and untainted by the profane earth, its sanctity remains intact.

Chalice Well and its surrounding gardens should be visited, being a *hortus conclusus* to the Red Serpent and a place of peaceful numinosity. Similarly, the temple of the White Spring within the Victorian Well House invites pilgrimage. The dank, candle-lit interior housing pools and shrines is a true sanctum; a hypogeum with its own quadripartite layout in which the Avalonian mysteries may be deeply discerned.

While roaming the domains of the four Matronae, the pilgrim should be attentive to any natural objects presented upon the path by happenstance, or that lie nearby but demand attention. These may include: rocks, pleasingly shaped stones and hagstones, windfallen wood, feathers, bones and skulls, seeds and nuts. Do not attend to human-made, manufactured *objet trouvé*. The initiand should seek to acquire at least one such item from each of the four realms, preferably associated with the qualities of each respective goddess. To assist in this endeavour, at the outset extemporise an orison to the presiding deity of the domain. Spirit allies may be called upon as guides and pathfinders; the Oculi Magicka will also serve as a tool of revelation. Alternatively, dowsing may be employed. Patience, attentiveness and a calm, detached disposition are fundamental. The process cannot be undertaken in haste and the opportunity for serendipitous discovery must be accommodated. Sublimation of individual will in favour of absolute trust in the telesis of the spirits will yield success.

When the catechumen enters into the ordained object's purview, a noticeable impulsion will be sensed. Kneel before it and lift it from its resting place with great care, providing a libation of honey or fruit in return. Commit to memory the location of this epiphany. Offer thanks to the spirits and the presiding deity. Carry the item about your person; it will become a potent *sacramentalis*, charm-fetish and *telesma*.

¶ THE SACRAMENT OF THE WATERS

The sacred waters of the Red Spring and White Spring are cardinal *noema* of the Great Quest's praxis. Their telesmatic properties are endowed by a rare conjunction of virtues. The waters, which saturate the aquifers beneath the Templum, are in turn saturated with magickal potency from its living bedrock, which forms a tenebrous gateway to the underworld. The in-flowing currents of the Red and White Serpents further fructify the waters of their respective aquifers with potent telluric currents. The waters of the two springs, being thus ensorcelled, are vigorous reifications of the two primal, polarised aspects of divinity. As such, they are actively employed in the rites of the Great Quest. But first, the waters must be gathered in the appropriate manner.

Wayfare to the foot of Wellhouse Lane when the place is empty of humanity and in quietude. Face towards the hill, before the modern well house and the publicly accessible outlets of both springs. Through the Oculi Magicka, see the walls and structures fall away, revealing two verdant groves, one to the left and one to the right, wherein the waters emerge from their stygian source. The modern road is no longer present; instead, a swarth rises towards a copse, obscuring the hill beyond.

The *nemeton* of the White Spring is dank and rupestrian; lime-encrusted dropping-wells are edged with moss, lichen and frounds of emerald fern. The *nemeton* of the Red Spring is a mass of grassy hillocks through which a channel weaves, lined with carmine-stained rocks. Crooked ancient yews stoop over it, abumbrating the ground. Beneath, the waters of both springs collect in two large, deep, rock-rimmed pools, formed into a vesica piscis. The sinistral pool is stained a rusted crimson; the dextral pool is limed and pearlescent. At the intersection of these circular basins is the mandorla, which also bears water, even though its boundary is untainted by the accretions of either spring. Rocks lie across its length, from point to point.

Each *nemeton* is attended by a Well Maiden, who may be envisioned as pale-skinned, barefoot, with long tresses curling over simple vestments; each carries an earthenware amphora and cup. Bow to both, in approbation of these groves as places of especial sanctity. Meditate briefly on their profaning over the centuries; the myriad peoples who have arrogated the waters without acknowledging or thanking the tutelary nymphs. Turn to the Maiden of the Red Spring and speak the following:

Mad llano spïrïd a'n gluiw funtọn.

The phonetic spelling is:

Mad laano spirid an gloow funton.

Maiden of this Hallowed Spring, I ask that I may gather a portion of these waters, to be used with care, as wisely as I am able, in the service of the Great Quest and in exaltation of the Holy Island.

Wait for a response. Turn towards the White Spring and repeat the process. If the Well Maidens assent, step onto the stones of the mandorla and walk across into the *nemeta*, which are their domains. Approach the modern fountain of the Red Spring and fill a vessel. Do the same at the fountain of the White Spring. Step back, bow and offer thanks to both undines. Depart in silence. Clearly mark each vessel to ensure they are not confused.

The postulant may experience the curious magnetism alluded to earlier, but on this occasion emanating from the two water-laden vessels themselves. The still-energetic waters – only just taken from their source and dancing with sinuous, life-enhancing energy – may manifest to the postulant as a pulling or drawing towards a particular direction, typically the Tor Temple, which is their source. After a time, the waters will calm, although their vigour remains intact.

The collected waters from the Red Spring and White Spring should be used solely for ritual purposes, as described herein. If further water is needed, repeat the process outlined above. The waters' first application is as follows: at night-time, immediately prior to slumber, take a sip from the Red Spring. Feel its scarlet vigour flow through and vitalise your corporeal and spiritous bodies, which osmose the liquid's many virtues. See the red seed of the subtle body, the Rubeus Lapis located behind your umbilicus, glow and become radiant. Then, upon rising after slumber, immediately partake of the water from the White Spring; feel its argent energies flow through and seep into your self as a whole. See the white seed located behind your brow, the Albus Lapis, gleam with luminance. Perform these observances daily for the duration of the Great Quest.

In due course the waters will be employed to anoint and purify the body's superficies, prior to ascending the Templum of the Tor and treading the holy ground of its temenos.

¶ THE SACRA VIA OF THE OAKEN PATH

At the crossroads of Maidencroft Lane, Stonedown Lane, Paradise Lane and Wick Hollow, follow the route of Maidencroft Lane north and continue as it wends east beneath a leafy mantle, tree roots cleaving to the bank of the drove. The Tor Temple is obscured from view by the northern edge of Stone Down Hill as the lane descends towards the hamlet of Wick, becoming visible only briefly. Wayfare through Paddington Farm, bear right over the stile and cross the footbridge over the stream where a copse runs its length. Climbing up and into the meadow, the pilgrim will behold a wondrous sight: a sweeping arc of high green swarth dropping gently into a cove of orchards. And above the ridgeline, the summit of the Templum. Dwell here for a while as it is a place where the *tylwyth teg* are known to congregate, being enclosed and unfrequented. Thereafter, follow the path across the meadow, through the gate, and past rows of young oaks until a straight and level trackway is gained. To the left, enclosed by a high fence, are the ancient oaks known as Gog and Magog.[2] Gog, the male tree, expired in 2001, its flensed corpse still extant but now pale as bone. The dead oak was subjected to a conflagration in 2017. Magog has also suffered the ravages of fire in 2009, yet blessedly clings to life. Knurled and protuberant, this time-worn sentinel is the last surviving exemplar of the Avalon Oaks. In stillness she has witnessed the turning of countless seasons. Her duramen long decayed and consumed, her crown retrenched, she remains a source of quiet wisdom for the duteous postulant. Alas, Magog has been perpetually burdened with clooties and trinkets proffered by witless pilgrims, even placed within her great hollow, although these are now removed. Her age is unknown. Some reckon a mere 500 years; others point to the 2,000 season-rings recorded after a companion-oak was felled in 1906. Yet her corporeal antiquity is irrelevant, as the orientation of both Gog and Magog towards the summer solstice sunrise attests to their immutable inner reality; they are

2 Although the origins of Gog and Magog are traditionally acknowledged as biblical – the eschatological enemies of the Messiah, Lethbridge argues at length for an alternative mythological and etymological root, namely that Magog is the Great Mother, the Earth Goddess; and Gog is her consort, the Sun. This is wholly appropriate given the fundamental roles of these atavistic powers in the metempsychotic cycle of the Avalonian Great Quest, reified in the arbors of the ceremonial Oaken Path, which is aligned to the summer solstice sunrise.

avatars and incarnations of the primordial arbors that comprise the ceremonial avenue leading to the Templum.

Congress with the ancient, indwelling genius of Magog may be attained via the methods described above. She is deeply maternal, an abiding wellspring of cunning. Her root-wisdom can be discerned in the runes of her bark, the simulacra and symbology of her deadwood, wherein whorls and burrs form triskeles, eyes and manifold physiognomia. Her roots, fastened in the native soil of the Island, are intermediaries for the ancestral dead and those who dwell in the piceous realms; her branches are wands and staves of celestial gnosis; her tumid trunk is the dwelling-place and sanctuary for myriad life; her seeds are the inheritors of, and successors to, her venerable Arte. When approaching Magog, use this salutation:

Mad llano mamm a'n dėrwin forð.

The phonetic spelling is:

Mad laano mamm an derwin forth.

Magog is the Arborial Queen of the Holy Island, being a beloved ally of the Sororitas Avalonis. As such, she may intercede on behalf of the catechumen in matters concerning the Great Quest, if entreated properly, and according to her judgement. Her advice may also be sought for, in conformity with the precepts of the Graal, it is freely given. Yet she is also a Daughter of Avalon, a servant of the Holy Island and the Magna Mater, being born of its earth and raised into fulsomeness by its nurturing beneficence.

Gog, although expired, provides a habitat for diverse spirits, which slumber in the depths of his trunk, coiled and obscured by leaves, soil and dead heartwood.

This orison may be spoken to Magog. Alternatively, the catechumen may extemporise:

Queen of the Holy Island's arbors;
Virid Daughter of Avalon;
I ask for your benison.
Give me fixity of purpose
Such that my wisdom grows as a taproot,

Becoming steadfast in the blessed soil of this Elysium,
And my ardour reaches as boughs
Towards the glittering thrones
Of the Undying Gods.

The Oaken Path is the *sacra via*, the sacred ceremonial road that leads from the shores of the Holy Island to the Templum itself. To apprehend the primordial path of the Inner Island, stand betwixt Gog and Magog, facing the Templum. Marshalling the Oculi Magicka, turn and observe that Gog is alive and verdant, still ancient but crowned with sylvan vigour. Look ahead and see an entire avenue of venerable oaks ascending Stone Down Hill towards the Tor. Their trunks are wide and kyphotic, cloaked in lichen. Crooked boughs arch overhead, the oaks' canopies vaulting the avenue. The pathway is dirt, exposed roots forming serpentine, moss-clad steps. Behind you the avenue extends for a distance, then terminates at an open sward. Beyond lies a wooden jetty flanked by reeds and, thereafter, the glistening expanse of the great inland sea. This is the place of disembarkation for those supplicants who would participate in Avalonian rites or ascend to the foot of the Templum to petition the Sororitas Avalonis.

Bow to both Gog and Magog, then depart. Pass through the gate leading to the base of Stone Down Hill and follow the path through that meadow, ascending a distance, then stop. In vision, see the Oaken Path rising with you to your right, following the contours of the land. Walk towards it and stand in its midst. From within the avenue of oaks, look down the hill. Leaves stir in the breeze; a number loosen and tumble to the ground. Sunlight dapples the asperous path. Below, a figure approaches along the avenue, adumbrated by the trees' shade. He stops. The figure is clad in a rough grey cassock and cowl. He is tall, thickset and large of frame, his face obscured behind a wide hood. He raises his head to look at you. Do not descend towards him. Instead, turn and continue your ascent of Stone Down Hill. The hooded figure is the Guardian of the *sacra via*, the *dėrwin forð*. He will not follow you.

At the brow of the hill, the Tor rises dramatically in its masculine, conical form. Continue walking until you meet the gate that leads to Paradise Lane. Modern field boundaries prevent further progress along the Oaken Path. Take the trackway towards Paradise Lane. To the right the trees part, revealing a glorious vista across the cove-shaped valley observed earlier.

The catechumen should frequently send forth the Umbra Animae to the

Oaken Path, always arriving first at its entranceway, the place of ingress. The Guardian is perpetually present. Although silent, his manner can be gruff and dismissive; he may bodily bar your way to prevent any ascent. At certain junctures in the Great Quest, the catechumen will be required to traverse the *sacra via* to the Adytum of the Temple, yet the Guardian will ultimately determine its timing. Spirit congress with Magog can be maintained although, if the Guardian bars access to the Oaken Path, such colloquies should take place at its furthest borders.

¶ THE RITES OF ADJURATION

The quaternity of goddesses, the Four Matronae, each govern a portion of the Holy Island. Being both incarnations of the Magna Mater yet in-and-of-themselves, their cooperation is essential to the success of the Great Quest. Therefore it behooves the catechumen to adjure and petition them in turn, from shrines located within each of their realms.

Wayfare the outer and inner precincts, identifying suitable locations for shrines within each of these moieties: a secluded grove or a lonely, uninhabited glebe are preferred. Close proximity to trees and shrubs is not recommended, as the use of candles and incense will be required. The four ritual spaces will be ordained by fate and determined by cunning. Call upon the spirits and presiding deity to assist in your search, and trust wholly in their telesis to direct you to suitable locations. Dowsing may also be employed, in conjunction with the Oculi Magicka. Abide in quietness in these places to intuit their character. Identifying any resistance or receptivity is key to determining their suitability.

Once a ritual locus has been established, commit its location to memory. The shrines themselves will be of utmost simplicity, being fashioned from the sacramentalia acquired previously. Take the appropriate items and place them upon the ground, preferably directly on the soil. Lustrate the surrounding area, which will become the ritual space, with fumigant herbs and resins. Then, pour waters from the Red and White Springs over the objects, pronouncing the following:

> *I anoint this shrine with the waters of the White Spring and the Red Spring in honour of the [Dark / Pale / Aureate / Roseate] Queen of the Holy Island.*

Repeat the above process until shrines have been established in each of the four Domains of the four Matronae. Hereafter, they may be used to further evoke, petition and work with individual goddesses. The sacramentalia may be adorned with flowers and other offerings from Nature. When not in use, the shrines may be occulted to avoid the attentions of others.

Under the hours of darkness, wayfare to the shrine within the Domain of the Dark Queen bearing a libation of red wine; be silent and equable of spirit. Upon arrival, become still in quiet observance until you are becalmed. If it is safe to do so, incense may be lit. Face towards the Templum and bow. Stir your volition and sensorium into absolute fixation, fully attending to the task at hand. Speak the following:

Mad llano mọr duɨwissa,
Bran-gwaladr, duβ rriyėn a'n llann.

The phonetic spelling is:

Mad laano meurr deuwyissa,
Bran-gwalader, doov reegan an lann.

Pour the libation upon the shrine, acknowledging that it is a sincere offering. Then declaim this panegyric, or extemporise. Poetry is beloved of the Four Matronae, being an expression of divine inspiration. Its rhapsodic and magickal word-weaving will rouse the Dark Queen:

When the moon's eye is closed
And trees tremble to the sound of seething wood
You are there O Dark Queen, ember-eyed,
As shadowed as the crooked path ere trod.
When the whetted words of truth are sought,
You are the long-sighted Raven of Boding,
The Ragged Rider between the Worlds.
And when the blood of our last evening is stilled,
You wait upon the threshold as Mother of Midnight,
To impart the deepest of Mysteries to our sundered selves.
Be with me now O Mistress of Shadow
And bless my earnest Quest.

Know that the Dark Queen, and other diverse spirits, have heard your appellation. She may be close at hand. Be still and hearken to any noises; be vigilant of *ostenta*, natural bodements, theophantic manifestations, or modulations in temperature. Be cognisant of thoughts, feeling, emotions, gnostic impulses or any such qualia. After a time, bow again to the Templum and depart in silence without glancing back.

Within the twilit hours of dawn, wayfare to the shrine within the Domain of the Pale Queen bearing a libation of mead. Face towards the Templum and bow. Speak the following:

Mad llano mọr duɨwissa,
Glʉr moruin, gwɨnn rriẏėn a'n llann.

The phonetic spelling is:

Mad laano meurr deuwyissa,
Gloor morooin, gweunn reegan an lann.

Pour the libation upon the shrine, acknowledging that it is a sincere offering. Then declaim this panegyric:

When the dawn is rimmed with gold
And new flesh awakens upon the glistening dew of morn,
You are there O Luminous Queen, within your argent grove,
Your breath like wind through the reeds.
When the milk-white host comes forth,
You are the Herald, the Mantled Maid;
Yours is the hand that anoints and tends with care.
And when the blood of our new life is stirred,
You are the Exalted Priestess, forever unknown,
Who sanctifies our crown and our foundation.
Be with me now O Mistress of Light
And bless my earnest Quest.

Be still. After a time, bow again to the Templum and depart in silence without glancing back.

Within the hours of daylight, wayfare to the shrine within the Domain of the Aureate Queen, bearing a libation of red wine. Face towards the Templum and bow. Speak the following:

Mad llano mọr duɨwissa,
Gwlad-llėβėrjad, berθ rriyėn a'n llann.

The phonetic spelling is:

Mad laano meurr deuwyissa,
Gwlad-lefferjad, berth reegan an lann.

Pour the libation upon the shrine, acknowledging that it is a sincere offering. Then declaim this panegyric:

When the chambers of the world
Tremble to the sound of laughter
You are there O Untamed Queen, emerald-eyed,
Stained with the blood and wine of conquest.
When the Eye that sees all is opened
Judgement descends upon us, your consorts;
Beneath your glare our spirit is tested.
And when dawn's blood is quickened unto flame
You stand sunwise in chains and rings of gold
To receive our whispered and sacred oaths.
Be with me now O Sovereign Mistress
And bless my earnest Quest.

Be still. After a time, bow again to the Templum and depart in silence without glancing back.

During the hour of sunset wayfare to the shrine within the Domain of the Roseate Queen, bearing a libation of mead. Face towards the Templum and bow. Speak the following:

Mad llano mọr duɨwissa,
Gwėlɨð mamm, rrʉð rriyėn a'n llann.

The phonetic spelling is:

Mad laano meurr deuwyissa,
Gweleuth mamm, rooth reegan an lann.

Pour the libation upon the shrine, acknowledging that it is a sincere offering. Then declaim this panegyric:

When the dusk is rimmed with pearl,
And the land swollen to maturity,
You are there O Prosperous Queen, fecund and proud,
Your blessings like a mantle upon the harvest.
When twilight's song tells of hard-won accord,
You are the fading regent's omen,
The mists beneath a darkling sky.
And when the wingéd words of ending are spoken
You are the Last Breath of Divine Wisdom;
The King-Taker's glistening edge.
Be with me now O Mistress of Balance
And bless my earnest Quest.

Be still. After a time, bow again to the Templum and depart in silence without glancing back.

Time should be spent at each shrine, in communion with the respective deity, rapture being your objective. Rest, pray, meditate, observe, sleep, sing, dance. Share meals and libations with the Goddess. Make offerings. Dwell and converse with her in the knowledge that she is present, and delights in your company. Note which of the Four are most receptive to your attentions.

the temple and the adytum

THE RITES OF LUSTRATION

Any ascent to the Tor Temple is a fateful endeavour. Yet it is necessary for the catechumen to do so frequently, in order to encounter and become familiar with the numen of the Adytum; to literally and metaphorically ascend. But also to conduct rites, to understand the eldritch geographies of the Holy Island, and to perceive the turning of the sorcerous cosmos.

Before any ascent commences, the catechumen must be ritually purified. Therefore, in preparation, take a quantity of sacred water drawn from the White Spring and anoint your head with it. Know that the water is charged with the virtues of the White Serpent. Speak these words:

I anoint my crown with the water of the White Spring,
fructified with the powers of the White Serpent.

Then take a quantity of sacred water drawn from the Red Spring and anoint the feet. Speak these words:

I anoint my foundation with the water of the Red Spring,
fructified with the powers of the Red Serpent.

In so doing, the catechumen is purified with the Waters of the Earth. Ensure this ritual affusion takes place prior to any physical ascent to the Templum.

In processing to the Tor Temple, the wayfarer should maintain a fixity of intent, being always mindful of the sacred nature of the destination. Embark upon the journey to the Templum, increasing in solemnity, from the Outer to the Inner Precincts. Cross the threshold from the Inner Precincts to the base of the Templum and follow the existing footpaths. Ascension should occur slowly but ceaselessly, one's gaze consumed wholly with the route ahead. The catechumen will sense a falling away and narrowing of the earth, and a rarefication or cooling of the subtle vapours of the air. When the summit of the Templum is gained, perambulate its threshold, walking deosil, bowing to the Domains of the four Queens in the northwest, northeast, southeast and southwest directions. Then perform a second circuit, and through the Oculi Magicka see the four Roads of the four Queens, each extending from its respective airt to the centre of the Templum. The roads will appear as linear channels of light fading to the very horizon at their extremities, and converging as a crossroads and a *crux decussata* at a fixed point upon the summit of the Holy Hill, an axis mundi known as the Gate of the Templum. Do this on the occasion of each ascent.

Take time to apprehend the exquisite views from this uniquely elevated vantage point. Breathe deeply. Allow your sensorium to revel in the knowledge that where you stand – the Tor summit – is the *sanctum sanctorum* of the Island, its axis mundi, central place and high temple. Once the domain of the few, its chora[1] may now be apprehended by the many. Truly it is 'the holyest erthe in Englande.'

Marshall the Oculi Magicka once more and study the surrounding landscape in every direction. Views extend to Wiltshire in the east, Dorset to the south, the Quantock Hills and Exmoor to the west, and the Bristol Channel to the northwest. The horizon is the finitor, the rim of the Graal, where the visible landscape of the middle world is a manifested congressum of life and death; a material expression of the aeonian cycle: of being, becoming and ceasing-to-be. See the Holy Island as a land of naught save rolling green swards, orchards and woodland. The Oaken Path stretches away and descends Stone Down Hill. No dwellings or tilled soil are to be seen. Girdled with estuarine waters, the inland sea is still and argent beneath the wide skies. It inundates the low-lying Levels from the northwest, where the island of Westmore can be clearly seen

1 Chora meaning, in this context, the subtle aspects of place; its inherent otherness, as opposed to the topos or physical features of a locale.

along with the local islands of Beckery, Godney, Martinsey, Andersey, Westhay, Meare and Panborough, which form the subastral constellation of Arthur's Wain. Beyond and to the north lie the great hills of the Mendips, extending to the horizon. To the east is the swell of land that is West Pennard, and to the southeast the isthmus connecting the Holy Island to the world-at-large, bisected by the linear earthwork of Pontis Vallum, which is water-bounded to the north and south. Beyond it lies a concave inlet, where the waters of the inland sea circle round to the west, demarcating a long peninsula bearing the Polden Hills. Wearyall Hill reaches out from the Holy Island towards this peninsula but does not meet it. A faint pilgrim path follows the spine of Wearyall and snakes towards the Templum. Be still and absorb the luminary reality of the Inner Island, acknowledging it as a spiritual refugium; a Fortunate Land and Blessed Isle of the Dead.

Upon the Templum, know that the tower of St Michael is not present, nor the modern compass rose. Instead, towards the northeast, see a large brazier, which is circular and raised upon four courses of dressed masonry. Within, heaped upon hot stones, lie diverse barks, herbs, grasses and resins. Their thick and pungent vapours suffumigate as a column of smoke, gyred by the wind. The brazier is perpetually lit, its divine fire maintained by a fellowship of adorants. Its purpose is to honour the deities of the Holy Island, confer their protection, and both lustrate and enchant the land. This is the Altar of the Templum.

Towards the centre of the Adytum is a circular turf door sunken into the soil of the Temple, its girth the same as the altar. Upon its face is carved a vesica piscis, the two points of the mandorla oriented to the northwest and the southeast, the directions of summer solstice sunset and winter solstice sunrise, aligned to the roads of the Dark Queen and the Aureate Queen. The Roads of the four Queens gather here. Stand upon the Gate, within the mandorla, and see the Roads as lines of light converge at chest height. The Gate is a nexus, an axis mundi. When located upon it, the catechumen becomes that nexus. The locus of convergence is both a Cartesian coordinate and a point within the breast of the catechumen.

Even though the outer, mundane reality of the Tor summit as a Temple has long since passed, it is still acknowledged as such by many (one objective of the Quest is re-enchantment and re-consecration.) Thus, the Tor is accessible to anyone and everyone, from those who honour its timeless sanctity, to the unenlightened who profane its face with refuse, or would even do it harm. All must be accepted by the catechumen, for a chief virtue of the Holy Island and its denizens is tolerance. Its guardians and deities will uphold the righteousness of the Tor and defend it from ill-doers. Nevertheless, an inescapable truth is that the Holy Hill is frequently populated and little can be done to assuage this. Therefore, when enacting rituals upon it, the catechumen must learn to ignore any distractions from these visitors, or choose quieter times of day or night.

Enfleshed pilgrimages to the Templum should now occur regularly, such that the Altar and the Gate, the water-girdled Holy Island, its salient features, and the Domains and Roads of the four Queens, can all be recalled instinctively and seen with clarity. The Quotidian Meditations are especially efficacious when performed upon the Tor summit. Sunrise and sunset should be observed, their points of congress with the horizon committed to memory. The catechumen should also abide upon the Templum in darkness, noting the phase of the moon and the presence of any planets or significant asterisms.

From the vantage point of the Tor summit, the locations of each of the shrines to the four goddesses should be identified and visualised as columns of light. Become intimately acquainted with the boundaries marking the thresholds of the four Domains of the four Queens. Meditate on the mysteries of these realms, specifically the underlying significance of those landscape features within the bounds of each demesne. There are many strata of correspondences to dwell upon, in particular the syzygies of the four domains:

- The route of the Red Serpent passes into and out from the elongated, recumbent, feminine face of the Tor, through the Domains of the Dark Queen and the Aureate Queen, the goddesses of chthonian darkness and death, sexuality and worldly lust – the lineaments of the sinistral path;

- The route of the White Serpent passes into and out from the narrow, conical, masculine face of the Tor, through the Domains of the Pale Queen and the Roseate Queen, the liminal goddesses of the thresholds, of purity, wisdom and virtue – the lineaments of the dextral path;

- Both ophidian currents arrive at the Tor via the domains associated with the solstitial sunrise, wherein dwell the two Graals whose elixirs impart otherworldly inspiration and divinely inspirited speech;

- Both currents depart via the domains associated with the solstitial sunset, wherein dwell the two Graals whose elixirs impart the powers of worldly renewal and affirmation;
- At the solstices, the only occasions in the solar year when the ecliptic crosses the Milky Way, at its rising and setting the Sun meets the Roads of the Four Queens, completing a circuit and opening the gates between worlds;
- The Domains of the Dark Queen and the Pale Queen, the stations of death and ascent, are homothetic with the summer solstice, its gates providing anabasis to the corporeal plane for the spirits and deities who dwell in the chthonic realms;
- The Domains of the Aureate Queen and the Roseate Queen, the stations of life and descent, are homothetic with the winter solstice, its gates providing katabasis to the corporeal plane for the spirits and deities who dwell in the celestial realms.

¶ THE OPHIDIAN RITE

Perform the Rites of Lustration and ascend to the Templum in peace and solemnity. Bow to the intercardinal directions, the Roads of the Four Queens. Stand within the mandorla of the vesica piscis, upon the Gate of the Templum. Know that this locus is the axis mundi of the Arte, the nexus of alchemical convergence for the middle, celestial and chthonic realms. It is both the crossroads and the *crux decussata*, the diagonal cross of sacrifice. It is where the dying and resurrected rays of solstitial sunrise and sunset converge, and from where the four roads of the goddesses diverge to meet the Celestial Gateways at the horizon; the crossing-point of the cosmic matrix.

Observe the finitor and turn towards the northwest, which is the Domain of the Dark Queen. Via the Oculi Magicka see a meandering artery of red light in the distance, rippling beneath the surface of the great inland sea. It is not a singular channel but a braid, bifurcating and reconnecting here and there, capillaries reaching out from a central coil. Follow its path as it meets the shores of the Holy Island; see it rise and penetrate the vegetal earth, following the swells and depressions of the land. This is the Red Serpent, the feminine telluric deity who journeys along the deep curves of the land, its rivers, wells and valleys. She is the geopsychic expression of the priestess, the Sophia, the river of menstrual ancestral blood which flows from the well of life. As her serpentine energy approaches the Templum, sense a reboance and a vibration of the ground itself. She passes beneath you, through the fabric of the Holy Hill, fructifying the aquifer of the Red Spring. Turn a half-circle towards the southeast, the Domain of the Aureate Queen, and see the same braid of energy pass from the Templum and depart the Holy Island, snaking into the distant waters.

Now turn towards the southwest, the Domain of the Roseate Queen, and see a serpentine artery of white light approach and pass into the Templum, fertilising the aquifer of the White Spring. This is the White Serpent, the masculine telluric deity who journeys along the highest hills and mounds, the ridges and spurs of Albion. He is the geopsychic expression of the priest, the Logos, the animating *semina*. Turn a half-circle and face the northeast, the Domain of the Pale Queen, and observe his departure from the Island.

The ophidian dance of these two atavistic currents is an undying flow; in kinship with the vesica piscis wherein you stand, their sacred marriage is a subastral and microcosmic expression of the *coincidentia oppositorum*, the union of opposites. Know too that the intertwining channels of the Red and White Serpents encompass the circumference of the earth entire; they are the ouroboros of the *Chrysopoeia*, the world-serpent that bites its tail and, in so doing, embodies eternal renewal.

Return to the northwest, with your sensorium wholly attuned to the directional flow of both currents, acknowledging their perpetual ingress to, congress with and egress from the Templum. Feel the immense, thunderous power of these two polarised telluric forces. Speak these words:

> *Dringid gwėlið nėdr-mamm.*

The phonetic spelling is:

> *Dreungeud gweleuth needr-mam.*

Now see a thin vein of red light, a mere thread, rise up from the primary channel in imitation of a rearing snake. Rather than pass into the fabric of the Tor, it ascends towards the summit, flowing over and above the contours of the hill. Its terminus gains the Adytum and slows, before passing into and through your breast. Feel the vitality of the Red Serpent. Its power flows into your body and descends through the Lapis Viridis to the Rubeus Lapis behind your umbilicus, igniting it with crimson fire. This is the *serpens ignis*. Face the southeast and see the vein of red energy pass out of your breast, declining the Holy Hill to rejoin its parent current.

Now turn to the southwest and speak these words:

Drɨngɨd gwėlɨð nėdr-tad.

The phonetic spelling is:

Dreungeud gweleuth needr-tad.

Perceive a vein of white light rise up, follow the contours of the Templum and gain the summit, whereupon it too passes into and through your breast. Feel the vitality of the White Serpent and see its power ascend through the Lapis Viridis to the Albus Lapis behind your brow, igniting it with argent fire. Face the northeast where the vein of white energy passes out from your chest and departs the Templum. Stand and discern the unbroken in-flowing and out-flowing of energies from the Red and White Serpents, and know that the centre of your corporeal self, in congruity with the Templum, is the *axis mundi* and crucible where the two currents intersect and become one.

Turn back to the northwest. Continue to feel the red energy of the Red Serpent resonate and flow through you. Now, arrest its progress and hold the current's power within you; feel your bodily frame suffuse with red light unto fullness; perceive the fires of the Rubeus Lapis blaze and the seed itself gleam with effulgence. Speak these words:

I admit unto fullness the in-flowing powers of the Red Serpent.

Turn to the southeast. After a moment and, in a singular act, cast loose the energy pent up within, such that it passes out through your breast. See it flow forth and descend the steep terraces of the Templum. Speak these words:

I deliver unto sparsity the out-pouring powers of the Red Serpent.

Face the southwest and repeat the process: arrest the flow of the White Serpent and contain it until your bodily frame is wholly saturated; see the Albus Lapis flame and blaze. Speak these words:

I admit unto fullness the in-flowing powers of the White Serpent.

Turn northeast and free the constrained energy through your breast. Speak these words:

I deliver unto sparsity the out-pouring powers of the White Serpent.

Stand for a moment, then perceive both veins of power fall slowly from the *axis mundi* of your chest and sink into the earth of the Templum, to rejoin their parent-currents flowing ceaselessly below, through the fabric of the Holy Hill. Energetic residuum may still be contained in your body, which should be dispersed through your feet into the ground. Walk freely around the Templum; meditate; sit and observe; contemplate for a time the symbolic apparatus of this rite, the confluence of theandry and directionality. Finally, bow to the four intercardinal directions and depart.

The consequences of this ritual are manifold and largely, but not wholly, ecstatic. It attunes both the *pneuma* and the corporeal body of the catechumen to the powers of the Red and White Serpents, by locating a portion of their virtue within the torso of the catechumen. Its many blessings include: an orientation to the systasis of each of the quadripartite realms – their virtues and qualities; it provides a synoptic insight into the ophidian flow in relation to the Holy Island; it facilitates the raising of power, energy or *mana*; finally, it ensorcels the initiand, thereby widening the gates of gnosis, engendering an osmotic understanding of the Holy Island's entire *prohairesis*, and furthering the cycle of personal transmutation. Thus, on one hand, the mysteries of the telluric currents' alchemical marriage are made intimate; on the other, it should be noted that any geotrauma conveyed by them will be profoundly felt.

The Ophidian Rite may be performed whenever the catechumen is needful of percipience during the ordeals of the Great Quest, whether bodily located upon the Templum or via the visionary faculties of the Umbra Animae and Oculi Magicka.

figure 5 The Cosmogram of the Holy Island.

¶ THE EPIPHANIC RITES

The Matronae, the four Queens of the Holy Island, invite parallels with the magicko-mythical tutelary spirits who preside over the four quarters of the earth. In particular, comparisons with the Four Heavenly Kings who reside on the lower slopes of the world-mountain Meru, the offspring of the Chinese foundation-deities Fuxi and Nuwa, and the *lares* of the thresholds and cross-roads, children of the chthonic aspect of the Magna Mater, are apposite. Yet the four Queens are greater than mere guardians. They actively govern their realms, and the inner and outer aspects of each Domain are inextricably intertwined with the delineation of their powers, qualities and intents. As such the four Queens should be additionally regarded as localised equivalents of the Morai or Parcae. A further parallel can be found in the Idaean Dactyls or *daimones* who dwelled upon Mount Ida in the service of the Magna Mater. Straddling the realms of the living and the dead, the Matronae can be understood as both *goēs* and psychopomps, escorting souls to and from the realm of the dead while also working their sorcerous Arte upon those souls in service to the Great Quest.

The catechumen should, in roaming the Holy Island, learn to discern the *hypokeimenon* of each domain, its essential character, as an expression of the will of the respective goddess. Further, their chora should be intuited where the threshold of one realm is crossed into another. Be attentive to moods, emotions, atmospheres, events, weather, energetic tides, *ostenta*, the behaviour of both humans and animals, and the appearance of natural forms. All phenomena of the Holy Island can be interpreted in this manner, no matter how seemingly insignificant. In particular, winds are an important signifier of the Matronae's disposition. For instance, during one undertaking of the Quest, the author regularly observed a significant increase in windspeed as he approached the shrine of the Dark Queen, rising in agitation while he dwelled there, only for it to subside upon his departure.

As mentioned previously, time should be spent in contemplation of the Holy Island's configuration with respect to its quadripartite nature, the Roads of the four Queens and their correlation with the solstitial directions, the in-flowing and out-flowing of the Red and White Serpents, and the location of salient landscape features. Thus, by illative means, a profound discernment of the Matronae's arcana will be acquired.

Through the Rites of Adjuration, libations have been made to the Four. You are known to them. Now is the occasion of their epiphania; a visionary apprehension of their eminence by means of evocation. It should be noted that no circle of Arte, nor banishment, is present in the rites outlined below, for the Island entire is charged with numinous power, and the presiding Matronae will go where they will without restriction; no such ward can bind or defend, nor is it needed. However, incense may be used to lustrate any ritual area.

It should also be noted that the delineations of the four Queens below are provided only in order to grant the catechumen an initial visionary portrait. Over time the goddesses will manifest in various guises: whirling, dancing entities; many-limbed beings; therianthropes; fulgid or tenebrous forms; or simply as women cowled and robed.

Therefore during the hours of night, walk in silence to the shrine of the Dark Queen. Sit before the shrine, become still and perform the Quotidian Meditations. Face towards the Templum and genuflect, with the shrine before you. Once becalmed, light a candle along with pleasing and fragrant incense, and place them both before the shrine. Call to your spirit allies and ask them to attend this rite. See them emerge from the darkness and gather at the threshold of the shrine. Thank them for their assembly, which gives testimony to your commitment and propinquity. Then pronounce the following:

Mad llano pedwar rriŷaneð.

The phonetic spelling is:

Mad laano pedwar reeganeth.

Hail to the Four, the Matronae of the Holy Island;
The Elder Ones who dwelled here before the dawn of thought,
The Ageless Ones whose years are beyond knowing,
The Timeless Ones whose deeds outstrip the first uttered prayer,
The Bornless Ones whose memories are without end.

Pour a libation of red wine upon the shrine beyond the candle flame. Utter the following petition:

I call upon the Dark Queen of the Holy Island,
She who stands beneath the Black Sun,
She who keeps the gates to the deepest catacombs,
She who walks their paths towards the fleshless mysteries,
And returns their poisons to her Graal.
Attend to me, Mistress of the Black Flame, Witch-Mother to the cloven company.

Wait patiently for her autophaneia, which will transpire only if she is so inclined. She will become unveiled from the night, as though illumined by the lunar sphere. Her countenance is proud and imperious. Her dark hair is long and fastened at the neck; she is sharp of feature, her eyes a piercing grey. Her habiliments are a black kirtle beneath a cloak of raven feathers. Around her throat are adornments of obsidian, bone and thorn. At her belt are many keys.

When she stands before you, beyond the candle, genuflect and give her thanks. Her mien may be disdainful, ominous, aloof, indifferent or welcoming. Converse with the Dark Queen, if she is willing. Explain your intentions. Request her assistance, namely to help you during the Great Quest and to impart whatever wisdom she deems necessary. She may ask you questions, or request something in return, or give you something. Once satisfied, she will turn and leave of her own accord. Bow when she does so. Extinguish the candle and incense carefully and leave swiftly.

During the hours of dawn, walk in silence to the shrine of the Pale Queen. Sit before the shrine, become still and perform the Quotidian Meditations. Face towards the Templum and genuflect, the shrine before you. Light a candle and incense, and place them both before the shrine. Call to your spirit allies and ask them to attend this rite. Thank them for their assembly. Then pronounce the following:

Mad llano pedwar rriyaneð.

The phonetic spelling is:

Mad laano pedwar reeganeth.

Hail to the Four, the Matronae of the Holy Island;
The Elder Ones who dwelled here before the dawn of thought,
The Ageless Ones whose years are beyond knowing,
The Timeless Ones whose deeds outstrip the first uttered prayer,
The Bornless Ones whose memories are without end.

Pour a libation of mead upon the shrine beyond the candle flame. Utter the following petition:

I call upon the Pale Queen of the Holy Island,
She who stands at the threshold of death and life,
She who keeps the Gate of Ascension,
She who walks the Oaken Path towards the rousing fire
And returns its dawning to her Graal.
Attend to me, Mistress of the Veiled Cosmos, Midwife to the kairotic breath.

If she deigns to attend, the White Mistress will arise attired in a white gown fastened with silver oak leaves. Her eyes are a pellucid blue, her pale hair tonsured in the draoidhean fashion. A sickle hangs from her braided belt. Her mien may be distant, otherworldly, peaceful or benign. Genuflect, give thanks and converse with her, explaining your intentions and asking for assistance. When she departs, bow again, extinguish the candle and incense carefully and leave swiftly.

During the hours of daylight, walk in silence to the shrine of the Aureate Queen. Sit before the shrine, become still and perform the Quotidian Meditations. Face towards the Templum and genuflect, the shrine before you. Light a candle and incense, and place them both before the shrine. Call to your spirit allies and ask them to attend this rite. Thank them for their assembly. Then pronounce the following:

Mad llano pedwar rriyaneð.

The phonetic spelling is:

Mad laano pedwar reeganeth.

Hail to the Four, the Matronae of the Holy Island;
The Elder Ones who dwelled here before the dawn of thought,
The Ageless Ones whose years are beyond knowing,
The Timeless Ones whose deeds outstrip the first uttered prayer,
The Bornless Ones whose memories are without end.

Pour a libation of red wine upon the shrine beyond the candle flame. Utter the following petition:

I call upon the Aureate Queen of the Holy Island,
She who stands beneath the Fulgid Sun,
She who keeps no gates or thresholds,
She who walks all paths towards the wanton world
And returns its carnage to her Graal.
Attend to me, Mistress of Unbound Glory, Witch-Lover to the fecund will.

Should the adorant behold her autophaneia, the Golden Mistress will appear barefoot, bounteous and radiant in her womanhood. Her vestures are a diaphanous kirtle inlaid with gold, loosely gathered at the waist. Long, red hair gyres freely. Her emerald eyes glisten. Her mien may be dismissive, languorous, capricious, or cordial. Genuflect, give thanks and converse with her, explaining your intentions and asking for assistance. When she departs, bow again, extinguish the candle and incense carefully and leave swiftly.

During the hour of sunset walk in silence to the shrine of the Roseate Queen. Sit before the shrine, become still and perform the Quotidian Meditations. Face towards the Templum and genuflect, the shrine before you. Light a candle and incense, and place them both before the shrine. Call to your spirit allies and ask them to attend this rite. Thank them for their assembly. Then pronounce the following:

Mad llano pedwar rriyaneð.

The phonetic spelling is:

Mad laano pedwar reeganeth.

Hail to the Four, the Matronae of the Holy Island;
The Elder Ones who dwelled here before the dawn of thought,
The Ageless Ones whose years are beyond knowing,
The Timeless Ones whose deeds outstrip the first uttered prayer,
The Bornless Ones whose memories are without end.

Pour a libation of mead upon the shrine beyond the candle flame. Utter the following petition:

I call upon the Roseate Queen of the Holy Island,
She who stands at the threshold of life and death,
She who keeps the Gate of Descension,
She who walks the paths through the Fields of Reckoning
And returns their gloaming to her Graal.
Attend to me, Mistress of Theandry, Breastplate of transfigured souls.

The advent of the Roseate Queen is marked by a swift epiphania. Her habiliments are a long embroidered russet gown gathered by a leather belt. Around her neck is a string of golden barley ears and a golden band bearing an emerald jewel. Her auburn hair is woven into a single braid; her brown eyes are stern and unwavering. Her mien may be forbidding, proud, resolute, custodial or melancholy. Genuflect, give thanks and converse with her, explaining your intentions and asking for assistance. When she departs, bow again, extinguish the candle and incense carefully and leave swiftly.

¶ INTERMISSIO: DIVINITY AND DUALITY

In purely reductionist terms, we can assign the following definitions to myth, religion and magick: myth recounts the separation of divine unity into opposites and its subsequent narratives; religion is concerned with the dogma of that dualism; and magick explores the manipulation of those polarised powers.[2] Magick in particular relies to some extent upon a semiosis of opposites, such as:

- Masculine and feminine
- Darkness and light
- Sperma and menses
- Sacred and profane
- Celestial and chthonic
- Creation and destruction
- Attraction and repulsion
- Form and chaos
- East and west, north and south
- Reason and intuition
- Objective and subjective
- Benevolence and malignancy
- Life and death
- Inner and outer; esoteric and exoteric
- Day and night, Sun and Moon
- Midwinter and midsummer
- Matter and spirit
- Past and future
- Sleep and wakefulness
- Motion and stasis
- Dextral and sinistral

The earliest mythologies originated in Africa approximately 150,000 years ago. In their migration across the planet, archaic hominids carried with them these ur-myths. Despite the accretions specific to emerging cultures and civilisations, myths do appear to possess a common precedent, their shared roots

2 Principles four and seven of the *Kybalion* are particularly relevant to this discourse.

explaining the high level of correspondences between world mythologies. The same mythemes – the fundamental components of mythic narrative – recur again and again, whether in relation to flood myths, trickster gods as cultural gatekeepers, the acquisition of fire, gods of death and resurrection, divine twins, or eschatology.

Specifically in relation to cosmological dualism – that is, the dualism of creation myths – the earliest examples originated from Asia or Eurasia approximately 40,000 to 20,000 years ago.[3] In these ur-cosmogonies, the first deity was divided into opposing powers in the form of primordial waters, which separated for the world to emerge as a hill or an egg (a motif echoed in later Orphism and alchemy.) Early Greek cosmogony posits that Gaia was born out of primal Chaos, a concept appropriated in Crowley's Gnostic Mass, where Babalon is cognate with Mother Gaia. Egyptian myth describes the initial bifurcating of divinity in terms of masculine and feminine principles: Father Heaven and Mother Earth; Geb and Nuit. Pythagorean philosophy tells of the Monad – the primordial first deity – becoming divided and yielding the Dyad. Thereafter, the gods multiplied and dwelled with humankind, each deity being associated with a physical location in the landscape. At some point a schism occurred and this Edenic state of heaven-on-earth became sundered, ushering in a time of withdrawal when the Days of the Gods ended; they abandoned the earth and retreated into the celestial realm (an act known as the *dei otiosus*), thereby drawing to a close a golden age of communion and providence.

These creation myths are not dissimilar to the models proposed by modern scientific cosmology and astrophysics, where the universe is fundamentally chaotic; a seething realm of violent stars and tortured planets, all subject to an unrelenting cycle of creation and destruction from forces of unimaginable ferocity. Earth as a place of fecundity and diversity is a consequence of the relative stability afforded to our portion of the galaxy, wherein complex life is able to evolve and flourish. The primal deities of modern cosmology are Chaos, the raw stuff of creation; and Providence, the benign conditions required for our existence.

The fundamentally chaotic nature of the universe is at odds with the cosmos – that is, the universe as perceived from Earth. The cosmos is ordered, harmonious and predictable: the same stars wheel overhead year on year; the

3 See White (2016), chapter 3.

Sun and Moon rise and set with constancy; the planets follow the path of the ecliptic; the solstices and equinoxes mark the seasons. As earth-bound creatures, the cosmos forms the basis of our entire worldview: it determines our methods of time-reckoning; navigation; our astrotheological systems of belief and religious observance; agriculture, augury; natural cycles of stasis and activity, abundance and scarcity; endogenous rhythms; and magickal practice. Humanity and the apparently harmonious rhythms of the cosmos are inextricable.

That myth, religion and magick are largely dualistic is a function of the cosmos: day and night are microcosms of the annual solar cycle, which is in turn a microcosm of human life, which is a microcosm of mythic time – the death and rebirth of the gods and of creation itself. These human-apprehended cosmic cycles also give rise to mythic geographies: certain gods and souls of the dead dwell in the pellucid celestial realm above; others reside in the darkness of the underworld below. The Sun, which along with the planets and certain asterisms, descends into the lower realm at sunset and re-ascends into the heavens at sunrise, is an ever-present allegory of the magicko-mythical cycles of life, death and rebirth. Cosmologically, the birth of stars gave rise to light and life across the universe. The root of humankind's existential terror is that the Sun will die and fail to rise – as one day it must – and we will be returned to the eternal, primordial darkness. That midwinter has historically been the locus of numerous seasonal religious festivals is testament to this preoccupation. The triumphant rebirth of the Sun at the winter solstice assuages our existential angst.

Though these semiotic correspondences are useful for endowing the cosmos with meaning, they become problematic when extended to value-systems, moralities and ethics. For example, theistic dualism posits the existence of a 'good' god of light and an 'evil' god of darkness. The good god and his avatars are associated with spirit, the heavens, the Sun, daytime, creation, benevolence, purity and order. The evil god and his legions are related to matter, the physical world, night, darkness, chaos, destruction, disobedience, uncleanliness and transgression. The attributes of the Devil, Satan, Beelzebub, Iblis, Ahriman, Samael, Angra Mainyu and others can be taken as a synoptic whole, and are typically seen as cognate with sinister deities such as Set, Chernobog, Adro, Cthulhu and Typhon. All can be characterised as forces in opposition to the cosmic order and the natural cycles of existence, where light is given primacy over darkness.

The simplistic black-and-white thinking of dualism gives rise to all manner of fallacies, leading to profound repercussions. For example, there is no question that humans – and indeed the vast majority of complex organisms – are creatures of light, inasmuch as the Sun is a prerequisite for life. Over millennia therefore, the Sun has accrued connotations of goodness. Yet, conversely, night is not inherently evil, even though it has become intractably conflated with adversarial aspects of deity, sometimes as a result of both orthodox and heterodox actors appropriating darkness and night as symbols of antinomianism. Yet night is as much a part of the natural order as day.

As a result of this binarism, 'black gods,' gods of death, the underworld and night have been absorbed into a general diabolic mélange and made synonymous with evil opposer-gods. Certain traditions have assisted in this obfuscation. In Talmudic lore, Satan is also the Angel of Death who exacts divine judgement on those deemed unworthy of life. Beelzebub is identified as lord of the underworld. Saturn is the black god of strife and toil. The Prince of Darkness is supposedly the ultimate left-hand deity. The chthonic Norse deity Hel has been etymologically subsumed into a dominant western mythos where the underworld is a realm of eternal suffering, damnation and evil. Yet the more complex reality, as evinced by numerous mythologies, is that not all gods of death, night and the underworld are malevolent or antagonistic; they are of a wholly different, more nuanced order compared to the evil opposer gods of theistic dualism; Osiris is a 'black god' by virtue of his death and resurrection; he embodies the end and the beginning. Thus, his 'blackness' represents mystery, initiation and transformation. In contrast, but by the same token, mythology recounts innumerable instances of co-called 'good' gods of light and order inflicting destruction, chaos, ruin and woe on the world.

Still more problematic is the gendering of divinity, which ultimately determines the vectors of mythic narrative and, in turn, the contours of theology, orthodoxy and society. A common trope of mythic cosmogenesis concerns the emergence of creation from a feminised void, nothingness or chaos, which is only made possible by a masculine deity subduing or inseminating the feminine. Over millennia, it is argued, this single act ultimately gave rise to theological dogmas of female oppression and exploitation, the rise of patriarchy, and the promulgation of mythic narratives designed to condone the subordination of female power. In relation to theistic dualism, the *argumentum ad absurdum* of gendered theistic dualism can be summed up in the doctrine of the Fall, which posits the entire world – and Nature – as inherently sinful, degraded and deficient; in gnosticism it is known as the Hysterema. The profound impact of this concept was twofold: firstly, it diabolised the earth and, to a lesser or greater extent, drove its exploitation; the logic being that if Nature is evil, then its maltreatment is morally justifiable. It is no coincidence that studies of colour in medieval culture indicate that green was associated with the supernatural, specifically faerie, and the Devil himself.[4] Secondly it demonised the feminine, both in terms of women as a sex (being the daughters of Eve, who brought about the Fall) and as the female-gendered Earth: Gaia, the Magna Mater. King Amangon's defilement of the Well Maidens brings these two impulses together in a metaphor encapsulating both misogynistic aggression and environmental exploitation.

In the modern era, the mythic root cause of the subordination of female power has been reassessed. Carol P. Christ, Monica Sjöö, Starhawk, Barbara Mor, Marija Gimbutas and others have proposed that humankind's earliest societies were matriarchal and matrifocal, venerating a great primordial goddess. In this model the ur-goddess-creatrix is not a mere vessel receiving the procreative male seed but a powerful creator in her own right. She is both the serpent and the egg, a nothingness that is pregnant with *potentia*, resisting insemination. She fertilises herself; the birth of the universe is parthenogenetic.

This contention shifted the gender dialectic of embodied cosmic powers, giving rise to the contemporary Goddess Spirituality movement, which is especially active upon the Holy Island of Glastonbury. Through a re-evaluation of the antecedents and correspondences of narratives dealing with polarised aspects of divinity, the masculine aspect is typified as phallocentric, solar-oriented, patriarchal, hierarchical, orthodox, rational, monotheistic, reactionary, repressive, misogynistic, aggressive, imperious, dogmatic, nihilistic, transcendent and anti-Nature. By contrast, the feminine aspect is characterised as lunar-oriented, peaceful, sexual, immanent, egalitarian, life-affirming, nature-loving, nurturing, progressive, sensual, polytheistic, spiritual, animistic, heteredox and celebratory.[5] A notable adjunct to this revisionism can be found in Kenneth Grant's Typhonian Order, emerging from the Thelemic tradition, which further subverts traditional notions of theistic dualism by proposing that all religions and cults have their origins in a single magickal

4 Huxtable, 332.

5 It might be argued that this example of theistic dualism is as flawed as the black-night-evil / white-day-good axis described previously.

organisation; an ur-religion worshipping a supreme goddess, venerating the stars rather than the Sun (specifically the stellar complex of Draco), and exalting the sacred powers of procreation and sexuality. Known as Typhon, the goddess is cognate with Chaos. She is the unmated mother, the *prima materia* who sired the universe parthenogenetically. Veneration of the primordial chaos-goddess occurred during the Aeon of Isis, when the Nowl-star was Thuban in the constellation of Draco, and Draconian powers descended into the subastral realms through this world-axis. Typhon's first son was Set, the adversary of Horus who embodies solar-phallic consciousness. Set represents raw sexuality and the concealed or repressed portions of the psyche. The Typhonian Order employs aspects of *vama marg*, the prohibited practices of Hinduism using female psycho-sexual secretions or *kalas*, as a means of spiritual attainment. Gnosis is also gained through the Averse Sephiroth, the hidden Tree of Life, from which all true magickal power supposedly originates, being an emanation of the primeval Typhonian current.

Grant's model is notable for its eliding of so-called left-hand aspects of theistic dualism with a goddess-centric model. He asserts that the cosmo-vulvic ur-religion of Typhon was antinomian by conventional standards. But the purpose of its apparent preoccupation with darkness, danger and the systematic, deliberate transgression of social and religious taboos was to highlight its core assertion: that the correspondences of moral and theistic duality are wholly relativistic. The illusion of duality, good and evil, light and darkness can and must be transcended. Coition therefore becomes a sacrament through its annihilation of this illusion and the possibility of attaining advaita vedanta or non-duality; in other words, mystical unity or a return to primal consciousness. Ironically, this is arguably the goal of 'right hand' magick.

Through these critiques of dominant patriarchal religious models and a subsequent discarding of their values, the diabolised feminine rather than the 'good' solar-phallic tyrant-god becomes the path to salvation. As part of this inversion, adversarial figures are transformed from the evil, degraded, malignant force of theistic dualism. The Devil of the witches, for example, becomes a green-hued champion of cunning-women and the spiritually emancipated female. He represents a rejection of orthodoxy, of the doctrine of a fallen world; a symbol of nature's spiritual immanence.

That the Great Quest, the initiatory cycle of Avalonian Mysteries, is concerned with the manipulation and unification of polarised aspects of divinity should by now be evident. What this discourse aims to illustrate is that cosmological dualism is context-specific but also unavoidable and, to some extent, necessary; not least as a means of constructing a semiotic framework within which the magician may operate. Yet the theory and practice of the Great Quest assigns equal significance to the manifold interstices between these polarities: the literal and symbolic liminalities of dawn and dusk, boundary and threshold. In the gender dialectics of magicko-mythical traditions these are reflected in, for example, the androgyny and gender-diversity of archaic shamanic cultures, and the *jálkr* of the Norse *seiðrmaðr*, of which Óðinn is an exemplar.[6]

Thus, the twin traps of ontological and moral dualism should be studiously avoided. All that can be said on the matter is this: binarism oversimplifies a more complex reality, and the values and correspondences ascribed to polarised aspects of cosmic powers are subjective, relativistic and fluid, determined by the belief-systems dominant at any time. In truth, dualities are not immutable principles but complementary forces that transform each other and transmute into one another in an eternal interchange. This is evident in natural processes. The powers will continue their eternal dance, and the wise will embrace them all with equal merit beyond any personal or cultural bias.

¶ THE STATIONS OF THE SUN

In the context of the Avalonian mythos, the Quest requires the catechumen to acknowledge the cosmic process as both a physical and spiritual phenomenon. The upper, lower and middle worlds and all things contained therein constitute an ever-unfolding drama of animate, intelligent entities. If myths are sacred narratives, the product of mystical engagement with directly apprehended divine powers, then the cosmic drama enshrined in myth provides a means to reconnect with the fundamental magickal realities of existence. The activity of the Sun, its annual pilgrimage through the twelve celestial houses of the zodiac, the solar stations of the solstices and equinoxes, the diurnal and annual waxing and waning of light and darkness, are all actions of divinity expressed through the agency of an inspirited cosmos. The sun's movements are not simply allegorical, they are the irrefutable cycles of life, death and rebirth embodied and enacted in the ever-turning orrery of the cosmos.

6 See Klæðskeri.

day

Every ancient culture venerated the Sun as a deity, the soul of the world and the literal heart of the macrocosm. The deific Sun is the supreme benefactor, provider of life and fecundity, consort to the Magna Mater, mighty Gaia. From Plato to Paracelsus and Agrippa, the Sun was understood to possess an exoteric and esoteric aspect. The terrestrial Sun gives light and warmth to earthly life; the invisible, eternal Sun, the light of the Logos, sustains the spirit with divine power. All who bathe in the light of the solar orb also absorb the virtues of the planets. It regulates their movements and channels their celestial powers towards the earth through its rays. It is the destination of the shaman, who 'flies through the Sun Door to the realm of eternally awakened consciousness ... the realm of the immortal ... The solar region beyond time and space.'[7] As the Sun's virtues sustain worldly life so, in return, humankind sustains the Sun through devotional acts. This symbiotic web of the cosmos, the exchange of power, is illustrated in Egyptian theology. The Sun god Ra's quotidian journey into the underworld and his subsequent rising is guaranteed by the conduct of the regent and the populace at large, a force of balance embodied in the goddess Ma'at. If the king failed to perform the necessary rites and sacrifices, the Sun would no longer rise but instead collapse into chaos and darkness. Thus, as an embodiment of balance and order through sovereignty, the Sun is represented by the orb atop the sceptre and the golden rays of the regnal crown.

As a solar trinity of sunrise, zenith and sunset, encapsulated in the Egyptian deities Khepera, Ra and Atum, the Sun represents the stations of growth, maturity, and decline. Its fourth hidden, unmanifest station is the Sol Niger of the underworld. These four stations correspond to the four alchemical stages of Albedo, Citrinas, Rubedo and Nigredo. Alchemically, every animate and inanimate thing is said to contain a seed of gold, which is the metal of the Sun. This is symbolic of earthly life's omnipresent indwelling divinity; the universal daemon, which is stimulated by the Sun's energy. Just as flora consumes solar light in order to flourish, so the alchemist undertakes the Great Work to encourage the growth, unfolding and flowering of the divine seed.

The sorcerous landscape of the Holy Island provides an interface between human and divinity, earth and cosmos, microcosm and macrocosm. The

7 See Halifax.

initiatory circuit of the Great Quest is an expression of this symbiosis and, through conscious engagement, provides a means to bring its opposing powers into unity. Therefore, when the Sun approaches its zenith, ascend to the Templum and bow to the cross-cardinal directions, which correspond to the four Roads of the Matronae. Face towards the Sun. Stand in stillness and close your eyes. Feel its heat and light upon you. Meditate on the mysteries of this communion; through its vigour, the Sun reaches out across the unfathomable distances of the cosmos in intimacy to caress and warm your skin. It has done so unfailingly for every day of your life, and for all the days of every life you have lived. Through its causata, this most loyal and beloved of stars, ineffably potent in its beauty and remorselessness, has granted life to your ancestral line, and to you.

Rouse and attend to the Umbra Animae. As described previously, focus your sensorium wholly on the etheric double's receipt of the Sun's emanations, such that its constant benisons are intuited as golden motes, untold in number, settling onto the subtle body's contours and absorbed in an endless cycle. Despite the Sun's great distance, feel a profound ardour and proximity as your subtle body receives its auratic virtues and becomes filled with light, even unto nimiety; see the three lapides glitter, reflecting and refracting its brilliance. In receiving its succour, know that the astrum's source is divine, the world's eternal and supreme benefactor. Speak these words:

Hail to thee O Aureate King;
Praise be unto thee Sustainer of all Life.
Thou art the distant Torch-Bearer;
Thou art the radiant Eye of the World.
From thy rising unto thy setting
Thou art within me and within all things.
Far-reaching and mighty is thy blessed lustre!

sunset and dusk

On an evening when the sky is free of cloud, watching the sunset from the Tor is a popular convention. As a temple and stellar observatory, it provides a wholly appropriate vantage point. From the Tor the boundary of the horizon, the rim of the Graal, is visible in every direction. Thus the position of the Sun's rising and setting in relation to specific landscape features across the solar year can be observed. At the summer solstice, the longest day, the points of rising and setting are at their northerly extremes; at the equinoxes, when day and night are of equal length, the Sun rises due east and sets due west; at winter solstice, the shortest day, the Sun makes a brief transit from its southerly rising to southerly setting.

As the watchers upon the Templum of the Tor observe the fulsome Sun's descent to meet the horizon, a sorcerous transformation occurs; the world briefly enters into a state of liminality, a twice-occurring station of the day that is neither light nor dark, but a porous commingling of the two. Sunset is the marriage of day and night, the mandorla formed by the intersection of two opposing states. In Gnostic tradition it is the Horos, the threshold between the Pleroma, the fullness of God above, and the darkness below. The horizon is a contested land, a partition between the supernal and chthonic. The tutelary spirits of the Gates of the Sun grant transit across its borderlands. Despite our modern understanding of the solar system's machinery, a visceral blend of awe and anxiety still accompanies the observation of sunset. Bearing witness to the temporary death of our star provokes an atavistic, existential tremor; we know this rite of transition presages the ineluctable drawing in of the darkness. Yet this is a learned response imparted by cultural and societal mores. For earlier northern European cultures, sunset marked the commencement of the day.

As already discussed, in certain mythologies access to the underworld is gained via the boundary of the sky, particularly during solstitial sunrise and sunset. While the horizon performs the role of cosmic portal, the Sun functions as a vehicle carrying souls, spirits and deities into and out from the underworld. The conjunction of the two is a place of emergence, a cosmic hypnogogia where otherworldly energies seep into the corporeal realm, just as the unconsciousness of sleep bleeds into wakefulness.

Therefore, let the catechumen ascend to the Adytum before sunset and stand in quiet contemplation. As the Sun's radiance turns to a mild gold in its descent, become attuned to the subtle changes in phenomena: the lengthening of shadows, the cooling of the air, the quietening of nature. Reach out to the Sun as you did before. Feel its warmth and light failing, its vigour waning. Take note of your feelings and emotions. In intimate correspondence with the dying god, speak these words:

Hail to thee O Rubeate Lord;
Praise be unto thee Flame of Twilight.
May this prayer sustain thee in thy voyage
To the lintel of the Western Gate,
And thence to the deepest regions.
May the nadir of thy journey
Forever be the prelude to thy rising!

When the Sun meets the horizon, know that the Gate of Descension, the road into the underworld, is briefly opened. Remain in quiet attentiveness until the last rays of the Sun's disk have completed their katabasis. Now stand and perceive the unlit earth. It has entered a state of nigrescence. Again, attend to the changing modulations of this sunless world. Breathe deeply and be calm of body. Wander the borders of the Templum as the crepuscular netherworld darkens further unto night.

night

Night is the last wilderness. Through the Sun's absence the world is transfigured into something other and untamed. This assertion is simple to test: walk a familiar but remote route free from modern artificial lighting by day, then walk it again in darkness. The land occupies the same Cartesian coordinates, and exists in the same Euclidian space, but it is different; contradistinctive and defined by its own qualities. For the majority of humans the secret country of night remains unknown and unexplored. It persists in the collective memory as a taboo realm, a phantasmagoria where malignancy lurks in the dark, waiting to do harm. Historically, Nature was considered fearful and chaotic, moreso at night; the farm, the homestead, the village were islands of civilisation amidst a sea of threat. It is no coincidence that the majority of folklore sprang from rural rather than urban communities. Tales of wandering revenants and infernal hounds encountered on a darkling and lonely path have stayed with us over the centuries.

That night has become a fearful place of otherness is in part a consequence of our perceptual limitations. The human eye uses cone cells by day. At night rod cells are employed, which are more sensitive to light but respond to a narrower spectrum of wavelengths. Colour vision is absent while peripheral vision is enhanced (this may explain the propensity for seeing movement at the edge of one's vision, giving rise to certain occult ideas concerning perception of the eldritch.) In essence, during the night hours, we see with a different eye, albeit one which is rarely used. This in itself should intrigue the magician.

One persistent, atavistic anxiety concerning the night is this: it is a realm over which humankind has no dominion. Despite attempts to keep it at bay, to illuminate and, in so doing, reclaim and govern it, the darkness remains irrepressible. Night prevails and exerts itself and, in response, humanity relents and withdraws. Just as the airborne creatures of day make way for the bat and the owl, so too do humans desert the tenebrous world. That the night is so profoundly distinct to day is an asset for the magician. The sky becomes a bejewelled register of myths where gods and heroes are visible in their celestial abode. The Moon, our closest celestial body, rises and falls as the Sun, yet also waxes and wanes, imparting no heat and little radiance. Spiritous denizens rouse and come forth to hold sway in the darkness. There is a reversal of occupation and the land becomes the domain of the unseen host: the dead; the *tylwyth teg*; the land wights; the deities of hill, hedge and stream. In this sense night is an inversion of day although, as discussed previously, the moralities of black-and-white dualism are, at best, unhelpful and, at worst, wholly false.

The sepulchral qualities of night and its associated rituals of preparing for sleep draw obvious comparisons with death and the afterlife. Some, but certainly not all, underworlds are described as places of darkness: shadowy, sombre and bleak, being chthonic in nature. The Sun descends below the horizon of the mortal world, ushering in night, and in turn brings an enfeebled light to the realm of the dead. In opposition the Moon rises, drawing the powers of the otherworld into the realm of the living; its rising heralds the unseen's dominion over the hours of darkness. Meanwhile, creatures of day withdraw into the oblivion of sleep. If the body is a microcosm of the cosmos, sleep provides a quotidian preparation for the long repose of death. The conscious self descends into a state of unknowing; the body stills, cools, becomes dormant. Just as the soul departs the body at the point of physical extinction, so too may the incorporeal self, the Umbra Animae, wander free of its mortal shackles amidst Sleep's Acre, journeying to the otherworld or into the night to carouse with spirits of meadow and wood. Similarly the witch goes forth in spirit, in nocturnal pilgrimage to the sabbat. Thus, sleep rehearses the inevitable crossing of the threshold from life to death, a phenomenon that may be traumatic but is wholly natural and essential to the evolution of the self.

As a living microcosm, the body of the magician contains both day and night, light and darkness. The goal of the Great Quest is to know, to understand, and ultimately to reconcile these polarities. Therefore an intimacy with the nocturnal realm is essential, it being a refugium for, and gateway to, the otherworld. It is also the most suitable time to perform magick, as we read in the second century CE *Apologia* of Apuleius: magic 'needs as a rule night-watches and concealing darkness, solitude absolute and murmured incantations.'

By day the Holy Island is a realm of uncanny atmospheres and topographies, and this is only accentuated at night. In darkness the land is transfigured, becoming a mythic and otherworldly *verendum*. Therefore, on a cloudless night, dwell upon the Templum in darkness. Use no artificial light. Feel the land settle into a dark peacefulness. A dissolution takes place. The iron grip of daylight consensus gives way to abstruseness and nuance, and the tyranny of photopic vision is shrouded with an ungovernable mantle of dubiety. Straight becomes crooked; the mundane becomes numinous. The imagination stirs and dilates. It is the world's long exhale; a time for quiet communion.

As by day, focus on the Umbra Animae and know that, in the darkness, the Bodily Retinue will receive no succour from the Sun. Turn to the north and feel the Sun's absence, knowing it is now located beneath you, in the depths of the netherworld. Sense a loosening of the subtle body, as though it desires the freedom of the night. Descend the Templum, letting the Umbra Animae guide you along the hidden pathways of this darkling Elysium. Wayfare the unlit lanes without fear. Be jocund and revel in the silence and stillness, the silvered limpidity of moonlight, the roborant scents, the reduction in visual acuity. With your sensorium sharpened and imagination expatiated, these are the optimum conditions for spirit-apprehension. Know that they see you and surround you. Acknowledge them. Acknowledge that the night is theirs, in accordance with long-held covenants. Welcome any nocturnal encounters with otherworldly agents; they have chosen to reveal themselves because you have yielded wholly to the night.

dawn and sunrise

The secret rites and pageants of night are concluded when the eastern horizon receives its first light; in concert the unseen host begins its withdrawal into the Holy Island's mists. This is the limbus of dawn, the same liminal time as dusk, when day and night are briefly united in a celestial mandorla.

Stand upon the Templum even while the canopy of stars remains visible. Face towards the direction of sunrise and attend to the horizon, where first light heralds the sun's return from its travails through the underworld. Observe the sky transform to a deep azure. Discern the familiarities and differences to dusk: a similar liminality, but a reversal of energies. Now, the otherworldly powers are divesting their night-time sovereignty. With each passing moment, it becomes the domain of day. The air freshens. A bird's call heralds the world's ascent from the unconscious depths of sleep towards wakefulness. It is a time of renewal, even while the memories of night's still and silent mysteries persist. The Hadean glow of sunset is replaced with the amaranthine bloom of sunrise. As the triumphant Sun climbs towards the Gate of the East and slowly crests the horizon, in acknowledgement of this rite of emergence, stand and welcome the light of the new Sun. Feel its distant emanations upon the contours of your body and, through the Umbra Animae, draw them into the Bodily Retinue. Attend to the qualities of these sensate rays, which are products of the vivified Sun's emergence. Then speak these words:

Hail to thee O Pale Prince;
Praise be unto thee Flame of the Dawn.
Thou whom none can resist,
Whom Nature adores,
Hast gained the Lintel of the Eastern Gate.
Bring forth thy Unfailing Fire;
Raise thy crown above the dew of morn!

Perform this fourfold rite of meditation and prayer daily during the remainder of the Great Quest.

❧ *the great quest*

¶ CONSECRATION OF THE GRAAL HYPOSTASIS

Take the bowl or cup you chose prior to commencement of the Great Quest and perform the Rites of Lustration. Ascend the Templum in daylight hours bearing the vessel and water from the Red and White Springs. Bow towards the Domains of the four Queens and acknowledge the four Roads, then stand within the mandorla of the vesica piscis upon the Gate of the Templum. Perform the Quotidian Meditations until wholly calmed. Via the Oculi Magicka see four figures standing upon the threshold of the Templum in perfect stillness, one located at each of the stations of the intercardinal directions. Each figure is clad in a grey cassock and long cowl, face obscured behind a wide hood, habiliments redolent of those worn by the guardian of the Oaken Path. Additionally, each bears a decorated bronze bowl, held at chest height. Perform the Ophidian Rite, seeing veins of red and white light rise up to the brow of the Templum and converge upon your breast, where they intersect and flow through you before declining the Holy Hill in the opposing airts. On this occasion however, see the braid of red light from the Red Serpent first flow into the breast of the cowled figure in the northwest, then into the vessel he bears, before passing through you to reach the vessel held by the figure in the southeast, then the bearer itself, before it descends. Similarly, see the braid of white light from the White Serpent first flow into the breast of the cowled figure in the southwest, then into the vessel he bears, before passing through you to reach the vessel held by the figure in the northeast, then the bearer itself.

Rotate through the compass points a number of times until this configuration is committed to vision and clearly discerned by the Oculi Magicka. Now, walk towards the figure in the northwest, which is the domain of the Dark Queen. Pour water drawn from the Red Spring into your cup and raise it before you to chest height, such that it occupies the same space as the bronze bowl held by the cowled figure. Speak these words:

> *I lustrate, sanctify and ensorcel this vessel with the in-flowing waters of the Red Spring, fructified by the powers of the Red Serpent.*

Turn and walk through the axis of the vesica piscis towards the figure in the southeast, which is the Domain of the Aureate Queen. Hold your cup at chest height and speak these words:

> *I lustrate, sanctify and ensorcel this vessel with the out-pouring waters of the Red Spring, fructified by the powers of the Red Serpent.*

Pour the spring water from your cup onto the ground. Repeat the process, attending to the figure in the southwest, which is the Domain of the Roseate Queen. Pour water drawn from the White Spring, hold your cup at chest height, and speak these words:

> *I lustrate, sanctify and ensorcel this vessel with the in-flowing waters of the White Spring, fructified by the powers of the White Serpent.*

Walk to the figure in the northeast, which is the Domain of the Pale Queen, and speak these words:

> *I lustrate, sanctify and ensorcel this vessel with the out-pouring waters of the White Spring, fructified by the powers of the White Serpent.*

Pour the spring water from your cup onto the ground. Return to the central mandorla upon the Gate of the Templum. See the braids of red and white light retreat and sink into the earth of the Holy Hill. Walk to each of the four figures in turn, genuflecting and offering thanks. Each will nod and depart. Take your vessel, which is now hallowed as a ritual sacramentalia. Enfold it in virgin fabric and use it for no purpose beyond that which is specified herein.

¶ THE FIRST STATION

Gather your hallowed vessel and water from the Red and White Springs. During the hours of night, walk in silence to the shrine of the Dark Queen. Sit before it, become still and perform the relevant Quotidian Meditations. Face towards the Templum and genuflect, the shrine before you. Once calm, light a candle along with pleasing and fragrant incense. Call to your spirit allies and ask them to attend this rite. Unveil your sacramental vessel, fill it with water from the Red Spring, then pronounce the following:

Mad llano pedwar rriẏaneð;
Mad llano mọr duiwissa,
Bran-gwaladr, duβ rriẏėn a'n llann.

The phonetic spelling is:

Mad laano pedwar reeganeth;
Mad laano meurr deuwyissa,
Bran-gwalader, doov reegan an lann.

Pour a libation of red wine upon the shrine beyond the candle flame. Utter the following petition:

Hail to the Four, the Matronae of the Holy Island.
I call upon the Dark Queen,
She who bears the Graal of Spirit, charged with the gift of Quiescence.
Grant me a draught,
That I may become the Corpus Noctis.
Attend to me, Mistress of the Black Flame, Witch-Mother to the cloven company!

If she deigns to appear, it will be in a form bearing the bronze bowl wielded by the cowled figure who stood upon the Templum in the northwest. Hold your cup such that it occupies the same space as the Dark Queen's Graal. She may speak to, or question you, before breathing onto or placing something into the Graal's elixir; it may be her finger, her tongue, an object upon her person, or something else. Pause for a moment until you are given a signal to drink, then lift your cup to your lips and drain its contents. Give thanks to the

Dark Queen, who may abide with you a while, or simply withdraw. Once she has departed, extinguish the candle and incense and leave. Pay close attention to bodily sensations, emotions and dreams as the ensorcelled elixir interpenetrates the Bodily Retinue.

Having performed the Rites of Lustration, on a following day as the hour wanes towards sunset, ascend to the Templum in the knowledge that the rites of katabasis and anabasis, the *terma* of the Holy Island, will shortly commence. Bow towards the Domains of the four Queens and acknowledge the four Roads. Then sit with eyes closed in silent meditation upon the banks of the Templum, facing toward the Sun. Speak the Orison of Sunset and contemplate its words. During its descent to meet the reddening horizon, draw the dying Sun's rays into your Bodily Retinue and raise energy by stoking the central Lapis Viridis with controlled breathing, as previously described. When the Lapis Viridis is fulgent with the in-flowing auratic virtues of the setting sun, stand upon the Gate of the Templum and turn towards the Road of the Roseate Queen. If she has previously granted you any words, phrases, symbols, signs or objects, make use of them now. Send a swell of energy from the Lapis Viridis through the Road of the Roseate Queen to the far horizon; in tandem, call to the Imperatrix and turn your velleity into heartfelt entreaties.

Via the Oculi Magicka, see a white snake winding through the grass of the Holy Hill, its alabaster skin glistening in the evening. Above, a heron tilts its head gracefully. It dives, plucks the snake from the hill and climbs, the white serpent writhing in its beak.

Now, use a needle to prick a finger such that a single drop of your blood falls onto the earth of the Holy Hill, and is absorbed into it. This is your modest *sphagia*.

Still the mind and body further until the physical self becomes wholly serene and dormant. Orient your attention towards the Umbra Animae and stir it into limerence. The Sun approaches the lintel of the horizon. Know that your etheric double trembles with exstasis at the imminent inumbration of the earth. At this point of liminality in the cycle of the day, you feel a sudden and profound alterity as the Sun rests upon the threshold. The tutelary spirits of the Celestial Gates grant the Sun transit across its borderlands into the underworld; in microcosm, the Gate of Decension is also opened, dissolving the partition between the supernal and chthonic upon the banks of the Templum. Commit to memory the position of sunset upon the horizon.

Marshalling the Oculi Magicka once more, look here and there along the

Tor's reddening terraces until the epiphania of the Roseate Queen is observed. Regal in her mantled sovereignty, she will approach and beckon for you to stand. In response, the body of flesh will remain in stasis. But the Umbra Animae, as the bridge between the corporeal and metaphysical, will rise. Being irresistibly drawn from its enfleshed self, your locus of consciousness is now resident within its etheric double. Take time to turn and observe your dormant physical body, which appears pale and devoid of life, and then follow the Roseate Queen as she guides you. In the crepuscular light, she will halt before a particular place oriented to the Sun's setting, whereupon a small aperture in the Tor's grassy bank will be unveiled. No wider than your torso, and with a rudely fashioned stone lintel at its base, it is an unprepossessing portal. The Roseate Queen gestures for you to crawl inside. You genuflect, as the heron lands nearby and stabs the threshing serpent, its dagger-beak tearing strings of ophidian flesh.

Enduring dank earth, darkness and claustrophobia, you drag yourself along the dun and earthen tunnel. It widens into a passageway until, passing through an archway, you are deposited into a souterrain, where a plain gravestone is embedded in the floor and two archways are located in opposite walls. You have passed through one of them. You follow a narrow spiral of steps that descend to meet a wider stepped passage. It is dark, but faintly lit by an unknown source. The rupestrian, dripping walls rise to form a low vault. The steps are wide and rough-hewn, curving in a slow spiral. You descend, each sound provoking an echoing antiphon. In time the simple staircase meets a level passage of stone flags and beyond, a glimpse of light. Before a stone arch stands a cowled figure attired in the manner of the Graal guardians upon the Adytum of the Tor. As you approach, the sentinel observes you but does not move. Once you are close, the figure appraises you carefully and finally moves aside. You step through the arch into an uncanny ill-lit vista: before you is open countryside absent of fence or field; only rocky heathland sweeping down towards a wide valley, where a thin mist gathers around a winding river. The valley side is cleaved by a vigorous brook; spring water cascades down a rugged channel towards the distant river below. Upon the river's far bank, great circular earthen mounds are spread across the valley floor. The season here is in opposition to the place from which you departed. Studying the mounds, you discern their variety: all vary in dimensions; some are moated; others are ringed with trees or surrounded by circles of stone uprights. You begin the journey towards them. During your descent, you look back to the archway and observe that it is flanked by a cluster of tightly-packed trees of impossible girth and height, their mighty boughs shrouding the hill's summit in shadow and rising to meet the clouds. And beyond this dark arboreal fortress is the Sun, breaching a blanket of cloud above and staining it a deeper red than any sunset you have witnessed. There is an eldritch aspect to the light and a feeling of embodied sentience to the land, even though it appears to be empty of life. A bird flies from the archway and glides overhead towards a particular mound. It is the heron, the long shafts of its notched wingtips splayed wide.

You continue, and do not look back again until you have crossed a narrow bridge and reached the borders of the heron's destination: a great mound circumscribed by an outer earthen bank and deep inner ditch. Before you, a single processional way leads to the interior where a ring of tall wooden posts is linked by a catena of heavy, drooping chains. A patterned bronze door is sunk into the scrub of the mound, which looms high and redoubtable. Before the door stands a tall figure, its entire body tightly bound in black linen and masked with a deer skull. Mist thickens as the figure beckons you forward, inspects you, then leans into the heavy bronze door, which opens with a reboant groan. The Sun has now descended further, hanging in the twilit sky like a lambent coal. Its glow is enfeebled and you discern another darkly radiant body accompanying it, emitting its abyssal luminance with ever-greater vigour, even as the blood-red Sun weakens.

Within the confines of the great mound is a timber-vaulted, circular chamber, lit by guttering rushes. The door through which you entered is only one of nine set into the chamber's walls, although these were not visible from the mound's exterior. The floor is the colour of ash and the air is thick and sulphurous. In its centre is a raised altar upon which rests a bell and a skull. A red serpent winds its body through the skull's eye sockets. The heron sits upon a high plinth. As you observe it, the bird begins to moult. Feathers spin and cascade to the ashen ground, as new black feathers sprout from its body. At the completion of this transformation, the heron has become a raven. It descends from its plinth and alights upon the altar, where it attacks and mutilates the red snake with great vigour.

You ring the bell and one of the nine doors opens. You pass through and enter a darkened tunnel. The tunnel opens into a wide, flat plateau, seemingly raised high above the valley. Here, the Sun is impossibly monumental, its last vestiges faded almost to naught. Instead, in its place, a vast nigrescent orb hangs low in the Hadean sky. And below it, bathed in its chthonic light, a woman aloof and imperious; she who stands beneath the Black Sun. The Dark Queen. She is barefoot and wears nothing save for a long black kirtle and a headdress of black feathers. Her arms are stained to the elbows with black ash. A stiff wind buffets her long, dark hair. The raven flies out from the tunnel exit and wheels overhead. Genuflect, walk towards her and speak these words:

> *The Corpus Noctis is before you, Mistress of the Black Flame. You have found me amidst the mausolea of the Mother. Now, reveal my bones to the black raven, to the Sun of midnight.*

The Mortifer takes your hands and draws you towards her. She places her blackened fingers upon your shoulders, your chest, your face and your crown. Her thumbs conjoin over your brow and you feel a pressure there, a concentration and transfer of power. She turns you abruptly to face the black sun and propels you forwards in the direction of the precipice's edge. Before the full glare of its dark radiance, the Sol Niger begins the work of Nigredo.

Attend to your breathing. And with each breath, draw the dark sun's incandescence into your subtle body, as though receiving a million motes of black light. Feel the Lapis Viridis within your chest begin to blacken and see this *mortificatio* disperse throughout the Umbra Animae until all three of the lapides are atrophied and fuliginous. There is no pain, even as the *soma pneumatikon* is entirely consumed in black flame, its fire charring and withering until only a desiccated husk remains. Yet the single mote of pellucid, golden light at the centre of the Lapis Viridis remains undimmed, and the solar wind of the black sun does not winnow your fragile self. With tongues of black flame still wreathed upon you, you look towards the Dark Queen, but she and the raven are no longer present. You are alone. Beneath the glare of the silent, gaping, aphotic star, you proceed back towards the tunnel. At this juncture, something may emerge and attempt to prevent your departure. You must attend to this matter alone.

Retrace your steps through the chamber of the great mound and exit towards the bridge across the river. Ascend the valley-side in the direction of the knot of colossal arbors, beyond which the black sun now grazes the horizon. Do not stop until you have gained the archway. Ascend the stairwell. You emerge in the vaulted souterrain. Here, the main stairwell ends but a narrower spiral of steps ascends further. You climb these and meet a circular oaken trapdoor, which is unlocked. Hoisting this open and climbing through, you emerge into the clear night upon the Adytum of the Tor, beneath a mantle of stars. You have passed through the Gate of the Templum. Breathe the nocturnal air; feel the wind upon you. Then traverse the Tor summit, walking towards your recumbent body until you are reunited. Remain still, while you are still wreathed in the black flame of the Sol Niger until the fire is spent. Open your eyes. Attend to your feelings and emotions. You may depart the Holy Hill, or remain upon it until dawn.

¶ INTERMISSIO: THE SOL NIGER

The Black Sun is the geoneiric sun of the underworld, the realm of Annwn and the abode of the *tylwyth teg*. It is not wholly in opposition to the 'vulgar' Sun of the corporeal world but rather an unmanifest twin that emerges when its sibling descends below the horizon and weakens to the point of death, at the nadir of its diurnal journey. In turn, the Sol Niger is revealed as the sun behind the sun; in the chthonic realms of spirit, the hidden sun is made manifest.

The Black Sun exposes that which is hidden, suppressed and buried. Through a descent into the psychic soil of the earth, the catechumen is exposed to its brilliant darkness and, in turn, to an ineluctable unveiling of, and confrontation with, the things repressed and imprisoned in the subconscious. This does not *eo ipso* result in exposure to existential peril: insanity, trauma, pain, dissolution, agony, chaos or annihilation, but to the fear of these things; the eidola of ontological emptiness. The perpetual threat of despair engenders terror, yet this is an illusion of life which the Black Sun seeks to rectify. The Dark Queen is the power that liberates the self from its psychic prison. She works with the Sol Niger to effect the process of Nigredo, which destroys all that is obstructive to the soul's development; in combination, they ruthlessly dispose of whatever is no longer useful or truthful. Nigredo describes an apprehension of the Sol Niger as part of a process of self overcoming. The light within the darkness is known as the Lumen Naturae, the inner living light of primordial, ever-present, non-dual awareness; the light of Nature perpetually illuminating the whole of creation. To see the light that is hidden in the darkness is to gain gnosis, which frees the spirit hidden and trapped inside the transient world of egocentric reality. The burning away of the Eleusinian eidolon reveals the daemon. This is part of the initiatory process, just as the mystery religions have for centuries used the tools of existential terror to illuminate and transfigure, and ultimately extinguish an initiate's fear of death. It is cognate with the sacral king's dismemberment by Set during the rituals of Heb Sed, and with Shiva's fierce purification upon Mount Arunachala, where anything inessential to the evolution of the self is rooted out and burnt to a cinder in his fires.

In certain traditions the Black Sun is cognate with Saturn. But Saturn imparts its harsh lessons through the terrestrial sun, albeit its esoteric aspect, which regulates the planets' movements and, through its rays, channels their powers towards the earth. Trauma, pain, dissolution and agony already exist in the world. These are the mundane, brute facts of existence, endured by millions. War does not wait for the mantle of darkness to commit its atrocities; they take place under the full glare of the midday Sun. In contrast, the Black Sun is transcendent otherness, the light of the lower regions that shines perpetually in the darkness. It is Sirius-B, the hidden child, the heavy star from which transmission of the initiatory current is derived. The star system transmits vast and potent energies to Earth, which influence its energetic tides in ways both profound and disruptive. In Egyptian lore, Sirius lies in the region of Duat, the portion of the cosmos where, during the rites of Heb Sed, the Egyptian regent ascended via an axis mundi from his stellar temple, located upon a stepped dias in imitation of the primordial mound. There is also an explicit relationship between Sirius and the rites of death and rebirth: the time when Sirius is invisible each year due to its proximity to the rising sun, a period which numbers seventy days, corresponds to the amount of time traditionally given to rites of embalming. Along with Set, Sirius is associated with Isis, the beneficent mother goddess and queen of the underworld, whose feminine creative power enabled the resurrection of Osiris and his subsequent immortality. As Nu-Isis she is cognate with the primal goddess of the north and Typhon. Thus, through its correspondences with Set and Isis, the Sirius system is associated with the subconscious, the rites and mysteries of the hidden land or underworld, and the initiatory traditions of *neheh* – the primacy of the soul and its survival via the metempsychotic cycle of life, death and rebirth.

More broadly, Sirius is woven into the initiatory rites of numerous mystery cults, not least those of Eleusis, which are concerned with the agrarian seasonal cycle as a death-and-resurrection metaphor, and paralleled in symbols of katabasis and anabasis – the soul's descent into, and return from, the underworld. Thus, Sirius is unequivocally the star of spiritual awakening and initiation.[1]

The phrase 'Osiris is a black god' was reputedly whispered in the ear of each neophyte at the culmination of their initiation into the Mysteries, indicating that, in life, Osiris contained death; he had endured destruction but been reborn by virtue of the magick of Isis, who is analogous with Sirius. Osiris might therefore be said to contain the black star of Sirius, which is also associated with Set, his nemesis. In the words of Crowley, 'since the end must beget the beginning... blackness is also attributed to the sun.'[2] Thus, the Black Sun (the sun-behind-the-sun that is Sirius) represents life through death, beginning through ending. It might be argued that exposure to the initiatory luminous darkness of the Sol Niger, the process of Nigredo, is cognate with the notorious but unknowable Black Rite of the Mysteries.

Something must be said of the dichotomy presented in the Sol Niger's uncanny union of light and dark: its black light and dark brilliance. These contradictory terms can be understood as illustrative of the limitations of language, which breaks down when attempting to describe the ineffable; the point where intellect gives way to affectus. The philosopher and mystic Pseudo-Dionysius the Areopagite alludes to the mysteries of God as a 'brilliant darkness.' Similarly, The black light of Sufism sets the mystic's being on fire, destroying the apparatus of the human organism. In Gnosticism, both the lowest regions of the Pleroma – the physical world – and the highest – the primordial divine void – are closest to darkness. This is an expression of the divine darkness from which we are born and to which we will return. The void, the deep silence of eternal chaos can only be experienced via a falling away of knowledge, language, intellect and selfhood. To comprehend it requires cataphatic amnesia, where the knowable is emptied from the mind. This again is cognate with the black sun, which is equated with transcendence through a nullification of the ego.

As the sun of Elphame and the mound-dwelling Fair Folk, Sirius connects the race of fey with their stellar origins and the pre-schism Draconian Aeon.

1 The role of Sirius in the Mysteries is likely related to its status as the chief star in the Bennu asterism. The Bennu bird is cognate with the Phoenix, the emblem of the solar god reborn from the underworld of Amenta and linked to both Osiris and Horus. See Massey, 493.

2 Crowley, 118.

In that era the primordial Goddess was venerated in her earthly incarnation as the Magna Mater, when the covenant between flesh and spirit, the mundane earth and Annwn, self and nature, regent and land, was intact. Nigredo is therefore the first step towards the restoration of that covenant through a reconciliation of the self. It is the initial station of the Great Quest, which leads to the attainment of the Graal, the *lapis exilis*; the *coincidentia oppositorum* and the reunification of the primordial self. Nigredo imparts a psychic death, mortification and rebirth, because to know the psyche requires a descent to the underworld. In Annwn, a deconstruction and reconstitution takes place. The Sol Niger burns and blackens the old, giving rise to new flesh; a new vessel for the new self purified by the dark radiance of illumination.

¶ THE SECOND STATION

During the hours of dawn, walk in silence to the shrine of the Pale Queen. Sit before it, become still and perform the relevant Quotidian Meditations. Face towards the Templum and genuflect, the shrine before you. Once settled, light a candle along with pleasing and fragrant incense. Call to your spirit allies and ask them to attend this rite. Unveil your sacramental vessel, fill it with water from the White Spring, then pronounce the following:

Mađ llano pedwar rriyaneð;
Mađ llano mọr duɨwissa,
Glʉr moruin, gwɨnn rriyėn a'n llann.

The phonetic spelling is:

Mad laano pedwar reeganeth;
Mad laano meurr deuwyissa,
Gloor morooin, gweunn reegan an lann.

Pour a libation of mead upon the shrine beyond the candle flame. Utter the following petition:

Hail to the Four, the Matronae of the Holy Island.
I call upon the Pale Queen,

She who bears the Graal of Admittance, charged with the Gift of Anamnesis.
Grant me a draught,
That I may become the Corpus Aurora.
Attend to me, Mistress of the Veiled Cosmos, Midwife to the kairotic breath!

If she deigns to appear, it will be in a form bearing the bronze bowl held by the cowled figure who stood upon the Templum in the northwest. Hold your cup such that it occupies the same space as the Pale Queen's Graal. She may speak to or question you before breathing onto or placing something into the Graal's elixir; it may be her finger, her tongue, or another an object upon her person, or something else. Pause for a moment until you are given the signal to drink, then lift your cup to your lips and drain its contents. Give thanks to the Pale Queen, who may abide with you a while, or simply withdraw. Once she has departed, extinguish the candle and incense and leave. Pay close attention to your bodily sensations, emotions and dreams as the ensorcelled elixir interpenetrates the Bodily Retinue.

Subsequently, before the night sky has succumbed to dawn's twilight, ascend to the Templum, having performed the Rites of Lustration. Bow towards the Domains of the four Queens and acknowledge the four Roads, then sit with eyes closed in silent meditation upon the banks of the Holy Hill, facing toward the eastern Gate of the Sun. Rouse the Umbra Animae, which even now remains withered and fuliginous from the process of Nigredo. Discern the single mote of golden light at the centre of the Lapis Viridis and its faint glow. Your locus of consciousness now firmly resident within the subtle body, by willed vision becomes disarticulated from the corporeal self. Climb to the summit of the Adytum and proceed towards the circular turf door sunken into the soil of the Hill, upon which the vesica piscis is writ. A cowled guardian is present, but he does not detain you. Rather, he opens the door of the Gate of the Templum and beckons for you to climb through. You do so and descend the stone stairwell to the souterrain, and thence to the wider staircase that leads to the hidden lands beneath the mound. In time, the cold, dank decline meets the level corridor leading to the stone arch, once again guarded by the cowled sentinel who grants you passage into the open heathland beyond. The vista is as before. Now hanging in the starless sky above the opposite horizon, the Sun rises towards the kyphotic bank of cloud. The brilliant darkness of the Sol Niger still radiates across the untilled land, yet a warm and golden apricity also emanates from its heart, growing in vigour and enflaming the clouds into a deep bronze.

In the valley below, amongst the many great tumuli there, lies a moated, turfed mound girded by a ring of hazels, which are briefly illumined by the Sun. You descend through the brush and sward towards it, crossing the bridge over the river running through the valley bottom and then traversing a simple array of timbers spanning the mound's moat. Before the tumulus, shaded by the trees, is an ornately patterned copper door that opens soundlessly when approached. Within is a square limestone narthex, its circular ceiling open to the elements. Before you, steps lead down to a deep pool which spans the full width of the room, save for a pillar upon a plinth at either side. Beyond, steps lead from the pool to a far door set into an arch. Sitting upon the pool's edge is a pale-skinned woman; barefoot, her long tresses curling over simple vestments. Bearing an amphora, you recognise her as a Well Maiden, an undine of the springs. A moon is reflected in the still, aphotic pool, which the Maiden gestures for you to enter. You do so, each step marking a slow descent into its cool waters. Knees, waist, chest and neck meet the pool's glistening lamina; finally, your head becomes fully submerged, the algid waters pressing against and flowing into the Umbra Animae. Suspended in the inky depths, the Waters of Ablution begin to dissolve the pitch-coloured husk of your charred and blackened body, lifting away the ashen chaff like so much sediment. You remain immersed until the *soma pneumatikon* is wholly cleansed and purified. The three lapides now emit a radiant limpidity, illuminating the well-waters. Indeed, your whole etheric body glows with a gentle, white light. You emerge from the pool and ascend the far steps. As you do so, moonlight is briefly refracted across your wet body, transforming it into a luminescent display of the colours of the rainbow. The well-waters have turned to a milky white. You bow to the Maiden and proceed towards the far copper door, which opens as you approach. Passing through, you enter a limestone, domed naos. At the centre of the room is a raised silver sepulchre upon which lies the Pale Queen, who slumbers beneath a long white veil of silk tulle. Perched atop a high column is the raven of the Dark Queen, the corpse of a white serpent before it. As before, the bird begins to moult, shedding black feathers that collect as a dark stain at the column's base. White feathers come forth in abundance and the raven is transformed into a swan. Around its neck is a gold chain and a bell. In its agitation, the bell chimes.

Genuflect towards the recumbent Goddess and speak these words:

> *The Corpus Aurora is before you, Mistress of the Veiled Cosmos. You have found me amidst the depths of the waters. Now guide my nativity, beneath the pure-white swan, towards the world's dawning.*

But the Pale Queen does not stir. The swan flies through the door across the room. You follow and find yourself deposited at the mound's entrance, where you first gained ingress. Retrace your steps along the valley towards the fortress of colossal arbors and the portal into the Holy Hill. The Sun, now fulgid and golden, rests high in the sky, grazing the cloudbank above it. You pass through the archway and ascend the dank stairwell. In time the rupestrian walls glisten; countless beads of water glow as bright as diamonds. The stairwell brightens further as you approach the light-source. Entering the souterrain, the Pale Queen stands before you in the centre of the vaulted room. Still obscured by her long veil, she is aflame with argent light. Walk towards her. She presses her hands to your belly and you sense a commutation of power. Then, she gestures for you to proceed through one of the souterrain's two archways. You do so. The passage darkens and narrows, becoming an earthen tunnel. You crawl along the loam until reaching an aperture. Drawing your body through it, you emerge onto the grassed terraces of the Tor, facing the dawn. It is the cusp of sunrise. You stand and observe that the Altar of the Templum, the great brazier upon the summit of the Holy Hill, is ablaze; the smoke from its divine fire gyres high into the morning sky. The Pale Queen, the Lucifer, is now beside you, her veiled head inclined towards the horizon and the Gates of the Sun. As the reborn Sun meets the threshold of the borderlands and rouses the world to wakefulness, she is revealed as the Virgin of Nature; the Ever-Living Flame of Rebirth and the Veiled Light of the Lumen Naturae. Your shadow-self, the purified Umbra Animae, becomes filled with limerence. Close your eyes and utter the Orison of Sunrise, drawing the virtues of the new sun into your Bodily Retinue. When you open your eyes, the Pale Queen is gone; only her white veil remains, discarded upon the Hill. A bell sounds and the swan alights nearby, a writhing white snake in its bill, which it lowers onto the ground. The serpent disappears into the safety of the grass. The swan then plucks the Pale Queen's veil and takes flight, climbing above the Holy Island towards the great inland sea.

Commit to memory the position of sunrise upon the horizon. Then proceed towards your recumbent corporeal body and become reunited with it. Attend carefully to your emotional, psychic and physical sensorium, as their aetiology will be affected by the process of Albedo you have undergone. A timidity, guilelessness and detachment should be expected.

¶ THE THIRD STATION

During the hours of daylight, walk in silence to the shrine of the Aureate Queen. Sit before it, become still and perform the relevant Quotidian Meditations. Face towards the Templum and genuflect, the shrine before you. Once stilled, light a candle along with pleasing and fragrant incense. Call to your spirit allies and ask them to attend this rite. Unveil your sacramental vessel, fill it with water from the Red Spring, then pronounce the following:

Mad llano pedwar rriyaneð;
Mad llano mọr duɨwissa,
Gwlad-lléβérjad, berθ rriyén a'n llann.

The phonetic spelling is:

Mad laano pedwar reeganeth;
Mad laano meurr deuwyissa,
Gwlad-lefferjad, berth reegan an lann.

Pour a libation of red wine upon the shrine beyond the candle flame. Utter the following petition:

Hail to the Four, the Matronae of the Holy Island.
I call upon the Aureate Queen,
She who bears the Graal of Flesh, charged with the Gift of Volition.
Grant me a draught,
That I may become the Corpus Lux.
Attend to me, Mistress of Unbound Glory, Witch-Lover to the fecund will!

If she deigns to appear, it will be in a form bearing the bronze bowl wielded by the cowled figure who stood upon the Templum in the northwest. Hold your cup such that it occupies the same space as the Aureate Queen's Graal. She may speak to or question you before breathing onto or placing something into the Graal's elixir; it may be her finger, her tongue, an object upon her person, or something else. Pause for a moment until you are given a signal to drink, then lift your cup to your lips and drain its contents. Give thanks to the Aureate Queen, who may abide with you a while, or simply withdraw. Once she has departed extinguish the candle and incense, and leave. Pay close attention to bodily sensations, emotions and dreams as the ensorcelled elixir interpenetrates the Bodily Retinue.

Thenceforth, perform the Rites of Lustration and ascend to the Templum when the Sun climbs towards its zenith. Bow to the Domains of the four Queens and acknowledge the four Roads. Then sit with eyes closed in silent meditation upon a quiet portion of the Holy Hill, facing toward the Sun. Perform the Quotidian Meditations and acknowledge it by speaking the Orison of Day. In particular, draw the blessings of the fulsome Sun into the subtle body, raising energy by stoking the central Lapis Viridis with controlled breathing, as described previously. When it is fiercely incandescent with the Sun's in-flowing auratic virtues, stand upon the Gate of the Templum and turn towards the Road of the Aureate Queen. If she has previously granted you any words, phrases, symbols, signs or objects, make use of them now. Send a pulse of energy from the Lapis Viridis through the Road of the Aureate Queen to the horizon; in tandem, call to the Goddess of Glory and make heartfelt entreaties to her, for the perlocutionary effect of your petitions will be her coming forth.

Marshalling the Oculi Magicka, look here and there along the Tor's terraces. You see a swan at rest upon the grass and, as you observe it, the bird begins to moult, shedding white feathers that collect as a white nest around it. Brown mottled feathers spring forth and the swan is transformed into an eagle, which lifts its great wings, spreads them wide and takes to the air.

Look across the summit of the Tor once more. In time, you will be granted an autophaneia of the Aureate Queen. Stand and await her as she comes forth, then bow. Radiant in her concupiscence, she approaches barefoot, adorned in gold, with long red hair gyring freely. Her pellucid emerald eyes are fixed upon you. In them you see both percipience and resolve; beneath the sun of the alchemical process of Citrinas, nothing is hidden from her gaze. Speak these words:

> *The Corpus Lux is before you, Mistress of Unbound Glory. You have found me beneath the vulgar star. Now, seize my becoming as the eagle might, upon the altar of your resolve.*

She circles you a number of times, then draws closer. Attend to the Umbra Animae and observe how it is stirred into afflatus by the proximity of the Aureate Queen. Through the Oculi Magicka, attend to the details of her allurements: her vestments and countenance. Feel her eyes upon you as she continues her circuits, always drawing closer. The etheric self will become roused to a heightened state of limerence, which is reflected in the Aureate Queen's own mien. She will cease her pacing and come to a halt behind you. Do not turn but, instead, become aware of her propinquity: the sound of her breathing; the sensation of her exhalation upon you; her bodily perfume. Whisper these words:

> *My Queen, I petition you:*
> *Liberate and intoxicate your adorant;*
> *Receive my pietistic embrace;*
> *Accept this connubial vessel so that*
> *Through your glory I may become transfigured;*
> *Through your mettle I may be made sovereign;*
> *Through your fervour I may learn True Will.*
> *Receive my agape O Queen*
> *And lead me into the wanton world.*

The Aureate Queen will draw yet closer still, such that she becomes united with your self; Goddess and catechumen occupying the same Cartesian space. This is theandry; a form of transvocation as opposed to possession; the Aureate Queen is not in command of your faculties. Rather, it is a temporary concrescence, a marriage of spirit during which an intimate co-existence takes place, a sharing of consciousness and an exchange of selfhood through the theophany of the Aureate Queen within the body of the catechumen. For the duration of this alligation, the Goddess becomes part of the Bodily Retinue and the catechumen becomes briefly deified.

Focus your sensorium wholly on her presence within the borders of your Bodily Retinue and attend to any alterations in mood, emotion, character, thought, memory or impulse. The catechumen should expect changes to their ipseity, whether subtle or profound. Aesthesis may be heightened or altered.

To test this, physically depart the Holy Hill in unity with the Goddess of Glory and wayfare the Inner and Outer Precincts, paying close attention to the chora of the land; the behaviour of birds and other animals; the weather and winds; the play of sunlight and shadow; the subtle signals of trees and plants. Discern the Inner Island through the Oculi Magicka and observe the actions of its spiritous denizens in response to your alterity. Visit the abodes of your spirit allies: the Holy Island's autochthons and tutelary *genii*. Call them forth and note their reaction to you, and their responsiveness to your enquiries. Summon the ancestors of Avalon; perform divination; feel the ophidian dance of the Red and White Serpents beneath your feet; acknowledge any increased sensitivity to energetic tides and foci of telluric energy. In short, test the consequences of your invocation by communing wholeheartedly with the numen of the Holy Island. They will be highly receptive to your assumption of the Aureate Queen's godform.

As you begin to acclimatise to your theandry, focus upon and refine your interoception; that is, the ability to identify, understand, and respond to the internal signals exchanged between the Umbra Animae and the Aureate Queen. In the same way the former may direct and guide the perceptions of the conscious self, so too may the latter, if given license. This can manifest as an internal susurrus; a sensory tremor, or as a surge of gnosis, inspiration or psychagogy. Be open and receptive to these prompts.

Take your purified but nascent self, the body renewed through the process of Albedo, and go forth into the world at large. Be drawn to places of human occupation. Walk, observe and delight in the spirit of community, the manifold energies of the populace; converse with others and do not discriminate. Note the people you are drawn to and their reaction to you. Similarly, observe those who fix your gaze and acknowledge you; those who give you a wide berth and those who you attract. Your auratic alterity will be discerned by others, whether consciously or not. Those who are alerted to it will be worthy of your attention, should they desire it. Then, eat, drink and laugh; play or listen to music; dance and be roused to euphoria; revel in your physicality; consume intoxicants if you wish. Be carefree and uninhibited, unburdened of consequence. Do those things you would otherwise shun. Become a voluptuary; dissolute, sensual and subversive. Courageously embrace the world in its totality, for the Goddess of Glory delights in such acts of zeal.[3]

3 It should be self-evident that you avoid situations of personal jeopardy.

Thus, the illuminant, transfigured into a unified whole, must sacrifice the innocence of the Corpus Aurora upon the Aureate Queen's altar of experience. This is the nature of Magistery: change; transmutation; an eternal act of becoming. Sovereignty of the self is attained through True Will, which is in turn a consequence of absolute liberty. By developing a fearless and exalted lust for life, the catechumen manifests the gift of Volition, granted by the Graal of Flesh. Thereafter, the forces of opposition are unified and brought into the service of one another: the spirit works through the flesh to witness the wasteland's transformation into a virid realm, which in turn nourishes the spirit. As a result of this alchemical *conjunctio* of flesh and spirit, red and white, sulphur and mercury, the charged Graal is stirred into manifestation.

Once you are sated, return to the Adytum of the Tor. Remaining utterly attuned to the presence and intimate proximity of the Goddess, whisper these words:

My Queen, I petition you:
Withdraw and depart your adorant;
Decline my pietistic embrace
And forsake this connubial vessel.
Through your glory I have become transfigured;
Through your mettle I have be made sovereign;
Through your fervour I have tasted True Will.
I lead myself from the wanton world
And complete my Quest alone,
As it must be.

The Aureate Queen withdraws from the borders of your body and stands behind you. Turn and genuflect, acknowledging the subtle intimation in her emerald gaze. Once the Goddess has departed, sit upon the turf of the Holy Hill and reflect on what has passed. Attend to your emotional, psychic and physical sensorium now that your Bodily Retinue is no longer graced with deity. Via the Oculi Magicka, see an eagle alighting nearby, a red snake in its hooked beak, which it lowers onto the ground. The serpent is alive and slides promptly into the grass. The eagle looks towards you, emits a shrill cry, and launches itself from the Holy Hill into the wide skies.

¶ THE FOURTH STATION

During the hour of sunset, walk in silence to the shrine of the Roseate Queen. Sit before it, become still and perform the relevant Quotidian Meditations. Face towards the Templum and genuflect, the shrine before you. Once stilled, light a candle along with pleasing and fragrant incense. Call to your spirit allies and ask them to attend this rite. Unveil your sacramental vessel, fill it with water from the White Spring, then pronounce the following:

Mad llano pedwar rriyaneð;
Mad llano mọr duɨwissa,
Gwėlɨð mamm, rrʉð rriyėn a'n llann.

The phonetic spelling is:

Mad laano pedwar reeganeth;
Mad laano meurr deuwyissa,
Gweleuth mamm, rooth reegan an lann.

Pour a libation of mead upon the shrine beyond the candle flame. Utter the following petition:

Hail to the Four, the Matronae of the Holy Island.
I call upon the Roseate Queen,
She who bears the Graal of Egression, charged with the Gift of Utterance.
Grant me a draught
That I may become the Corpus Tenebris.
Attend to me, Mistress of Theandry, Breastplate of transfigured souls!

If she deigns to appear, it will be in a form bearing the bronze bowl wielded by the cowled figure who stood upon the Templum in the northwest. Hold your cup such that it occupies the same space as the Roseate Queen's Graal. She may speak to or question you before breathing onto or placing something into the Graal's elixir; it may be her finger, her tongue, or another an object upon her person, or something else. Pause for a moment until you are given the signal to drink, then lift your cup to your lips and drain its contents. Give thanks to the Roseate Queen, who may abide with you a while, or simply withdraw. Once she has departed extinguish the candle and incense, and leave. Pay close attention to bodily sensations, emotions and dreams as the ensorcelled elixir interpenetrates the Bodily Retinue.

Thereafter, as the Sun wanes, perform the Rites of Lustration and ascend to the Templum. Bow towards the Domains of the four Queens and acknowledge the Four Roads. Stand with eyes closed in silent meditation upon the banks of the Templum, facing toward the Sun. Speak the Orison of Sunset and contemplate its words. During its descent to meet the reddening horizon, draw the Sun's rays into your Bodily Retinue and raise energy by stoking the central Lapis Viridis with controlled breathing. When the Lapis Viridis is fulgent with the Sun's in-flowing virtues, stand upon the Gate of the Templum and turn towards the Road of the Roseate Queen. If she has previously granted you any words, phrases, symbols, signs or objects, make use of them now. Send a pulse of energy from the Lapis Viridis through the Road of the Roseate Queen to the very horizon; in tandem, call to and entreat the Imperatrix.

Rouse the Umbra Animae and become disarticulated from your enfleshed self. Your locus of consciousness now resident within its etheric double, via the Oculi Magicka, see an eagle wheel above the Holy Hill, the shafts of its great wings splayed. The eagle lands nearby and immediately begins to shed its feathers, which are borne away upon a sudden breeze. In their place, cinereal feathers come forth and the eagle is transformed into a heron. The bird preens itself and you are transfixed for a time. The heron then extends its heavy wings and takes flight. You recall that the heron is cognate with the legendary Phoenix, symbol of the alchemical process of Rubedo and an ancient constellation in which Sirius was the chief star.[4] Within the great terrestrial zodiac spread across the Somerset Levels to the south of the Tor, the station of Aquarius centred on Glastonbury is depicted as a Phoenix.

A subtle bodement tells you to turn around, whereupon you are confronted with a manifestation of the Roseate Queen. She stands staring fixedly at you. Then she approaches, her custodial mien replaced with a melancholic air. She

4 See Massey, 340. The Bennu constellation is cognate with the Phoenix and is associated with the commencement of the Sothic year, coinciding with Heliacal rising of Sirius. The lifespan of the Phoenix is claimed to be identical to the Egyptian Great Year, a period of one complete cycle of the equinoxes around the ecliptic, or roughly 25,868 years. A 'Phoenix Cycle' is one week of the Great Year i.e. 500 years and in certain texts is also reputedly the Phoenix's lifespan.

appears weary and burdened. Nevertheless, she smiles at you with kindness, as mother to progeny. Speak the following:

> *The Corpus Tenebris is before you, Mistress of Theandry. You have found me upon the mandorla: the gate and the point. Now, grant me the song of the lustrous bird, the wisdom of the Androgyne.*

With a hand upon your arm she guides you around the perimeter of the Adytum, gesturing for you to survey the Holy Island below, the lands and the great inland sea beyond to the far horizon. Note your temperament, and the phainomenon of the inner landscape: the direction of the wind; the scudding of clouds; the movement of birds and the limpidity of the Sun. The Mistress of Balance halts before the Altar of the Templum, the great brazier of the Holy Hill. Its pungent vapours rise and billow as black coils. She holds aloft a rock of red-hued substance, presses it to your breast and encloses her hand around it. You experience a brief sensation of energetic exiguity. Then she throws the rock into the divine fires of the Altar. The flames crack and spit. Three columns of smoke rise and gyre in the breeze: one red, one white, one green, becoming rarified as they climb into the ouranian realm of the Holy Island, and finally succumbing to evanescence.

The Queen observes you, as though in waiting. The day wanes; shadows lengthen. There is a profound stillness upon the Isle of Avalon. Above, a heron wheels in the reddening sky. Soon, the Sun will meet the lintel of the horizon and the Gate of Decension will open once more. You stand at a threshold of completion and commencement. The metempsychotic cycle of the Great Quest, the pursuit of personal and worldly transfiguration, is a perennial journey of renewal; an eternal act of giving, receiving and becoming. The process of refining and unifying the prima materia into the *ultima materia* is eternal. The Graal cannot be attained so easily. Nor can the wasteland, the covenant that was broken, be restored so soon. Yet even now there is a returning to wholeness, balance, harmony, mastery; a restoration of natural order; an incubation and an inheritance.

You bow towards the Roseate Queen and return to your corporeal self. When you have opened your eyes, she has departed. Rise and perambulate the borders of the Adytum once more. Be heedful of the Holy Island's homeostasis, its *natura naturans*, which is governed by the Goddess herself, and influenced by others. Stop at each of its intercardinal stations and speak;

extemporise a short utterance to the denizens of that place, conveying whatever message you feel compelled to make at that moment. But speak it as a recipient of gnosis and inspiration, and with authority.

The Great Quest is an odyssey of the spirit and the body. You have traversed its four stations. Yet there is one other to be undertaken.

¶ THE GREAT SYNAXIS

Depart the Holy Island and wayfare to a place encompassed by Nature, uninhabited and secluded from the attention of humankind. Dowsing may be employed to find a particularly propitious location; one from which the Tor of Glastonbury can be viewed. Confirm with its *genii locorum* that rites may be enacted within their demesne. Make to them an offering of honey or alcohol. Establish a locus upon the earth which will become the ritual centre. Then determine the cardinal and intercardinal directions and place a candle at each of those eight points approximately six feet from the centre (the diameter of the Circle of Arte is therefore approximately twelve feet.) Place a ninth candle at the centre of the circle, along with your consecrated vessel and water from the Red and White Springs.

Sit in silence and become attuned to the chora and haecceity of your surroundings. Perform the Quotidian Rites. At sunset, asperge the boundary of the circle widdershins, first with water from the Red Spring, then with water from the White Spring. The waters should be borne in your consecrated vessel. Combined, they form an uninterrupted ring of blue flame. Speak the following during its two-fold circumambulation:

> *I lustrate, sanctify and ensorcel this Circle of Arte in the name of the Matrona; the Queen of the Holy Island; the Goddess herself. May it be a bane and bulwark against all malign and destructive powers.*

Light all nine candles. Sit in the centre of the circle and close your eyes. Purify and attune the circle and its vicinity with fumigant herbs and resins, and perform the Rites of Lustration.

Call on your spirit allies to attend and witness this rite. Rouse the Umbra Animae and become dislocated from your corporeal body. The etheric double stands and walks a distance until reaching a place where the land meets the shores of the great inland sea. Drawn up onto the grass is a small almond-shaped barge, with a raised prow, which you climb into and sit at its bow. The barge is pushed into the waters and its weight shifts as someone climbs onboard. At no point should you turn around to observe your companion, who begins to row. This journey is your *immram*, the sea-bound crossing to the otherworld. Here, the Sun has begun its descent. You look at the wide and glistening waters before you. A skein of geese raise their wings as they descend and come to rest, while scores of gulls rest upon its expanse. Your destination lies ahead: the Hieronesos, the Isle of Avalon, its temple rising like a ziggurat from the surrounding orchards; and from the summit, a thin column of smoke reaches into the sky. Estuarine winds bring a freshening air; behind you are the sounds of an oar rising from and dipping back into to the water. The Holy Island draws closer and is briefly darkened by cloud, for a moment transformed into a daunting citadel brooding over a vitreous sea. Your unknown pilot guides the barge towards a wooden jetty flanked by wide reed-beds, which girdle the island's shores. When the barge's prow nudges its timber posts, you disembark and, without looking back, step from the jetty onto the earth of Avalon, the terrestrial Elysium. Your sensorium quickly acknowledges this country as a place of otherness and special sanctity; a haunted island wherein profane feet are forbidden to tread. Even at this juncture, there is a feeling of embodied sentience to the land; a profound and irresistible sense of being observed.

You walk through the green meads toward an avenue of gnarled and kyphotic oaks, which ascend the hill beyond towards the great terraced Temple at the heart of the island. A figure emerges from the trees. Clad in a rough grey cassock and cowl, he is tall, thickset and large of frame, his face obscured behind a wide hood. The guardian of the Oaken Path appraises you carefully, then nods and gestures for you to follow the ceremonial road. You do so, entering into a sun-dappled canopy of trees. The pathway is all dirt and pebbles; exposed roots form serpentine steps. Shortly before the *sacra via* inclines sharply, two oaks, one either side of the avenue, draw your attention. They are stooped in their senescence, but verdant nonetheless. You acknowledge both.

The Oaken Path now climbs. The Sun turns the virid vault above you to an iridescent mosaic. In time the path levels and a portion of the Holy Hill is glimpsed through the approaching outlet. The vista beyond the leaf-rimmed arch shimmers, as though barely visible creatures move here and there. Finally, you emerge from the arboreal road into a wide meadow. Orchards extend around the hill like a green collar. The ceremonial path continues towards the grass-clad Tor before you: the Templum of the Holy Island. You begin to climb once more. In time, tree and sward fall away, replaced by wind and air. The pathway narrows. Then, the hill's summit comes into view, looming with each step. A buffeting crosswind signals your arrival upon the Adytum; the elevated *sanctum sanctorum* of the Island; its axis mundi, central place and high temple.

Perambulate its borders, walking widdershins, bowing to the Domains of the four Queens in the northwest, northeast, southeast and southwest. Then perform a second circuit, and see the four Roads of the four Queens, each extending from its respective airt to the Gate of the Templum, where they converge. See the still inland sea that girdles the Holy Island, and all the lands to the far horizon, which is the finitor, the rim of the Graal, and the threshold between the upper and lower worlds. Stand upon the mandorla of the vesica piscis, carved upon the face of the Gate of the Templum. See the thick and pungent vapours from the Altar of the Templum gyre and rise into the wide skies. Be still. Breathe deeply. The brisk winds now become calm.

From within your circle, pour a draught of water from both the Red Spring and the White Spring into your consecrated vessel. During the ritual proper, your corporeal self will not be recumbent. Rather, it will be wholly congruent with the etheric self, using visionary autoscopy to move and speak in tandem.

Now, as the Umbra Animae stands upon the Gate of the Templum, know that it is the locus of the Arte; the axis mundi and nexus of alchemical convergence for the middle, celestial and chthonic realms. It is the crossroads and the *crux decussata*, the diagonal cross of sacrifice. It is where the dying and resurrected rays of solstitial sunrise and sunset converge, and from where the roads of the goddesses diverge. It is the crossing-point of the cosmic matrix where life begins and ends. On this occasion, you witness eight Roads rather than four, each extending beyond the rim of the horizon.

Your sensorium trembling with afflatus, turn to the east and utter these words, thence to the south-east and all the stations thereafter comprising the eight airts:

I call to the Queen of the East: Domina Spiritus;
Sword-wielder;
You who witness sunrise
When the year is poised in symmetry;
Open the gates and paths of your domain;
Come forth and reveal yourself.

I call to the Aureate Queen: Domina Lux;
Graal Keeper; sovereignty-giver;
You who witness sunrise
Upon the cusp of its strengthening;
Open the gates and paths of your domain;
Come forth and reveal yourself.

I call to the Queen of the South: Domina Vulcanus;
Spear-wielder;
You who witness the fulgid Sun
When the world is incandescent;
Open the gates and paths of your domain;
Come forth and reveal yourself.

I call to the Roseate Queen: Domina Tenebris;
Graal Keeper; sovereignty-taker;
You who witness sunset
Upon the cusp of its strengthening;
Open the gates and paths of your domain;
Come forth and reveal yourself.

I call to the Queen of the West: Domina Undina;
Cauldron-bearer;
You who witness sunset
When the year is poised in symmetry;
Open the gates and paths of your domain;
Come forth and reveal yourself.

I call to the Dark Queen: Domina Noctis;
Graal Keeper; psychopomp;
You who witness sunset
Upon the cusp of its weakening;
Open the gates and paths of your domain;
Come forth and reveal yourself.

I call to the Queen of the North: Domina Chthonios;
Stone-bearer;

You who witness the sunless realms
When the world falls into shadow;
Open the gates and paths of your domain;
Come forth and reveal yourself.

I call to the Pale Queen: Domina Aurora;
Graal Keeper; psychopomp;
You who witness sunrise
Upon the cusp of its weakening;
Open the gates and paths of your domain;
Come forth and reveal yourself.

Now, bend to touch the earth and, with your eyes fixed upon it, utter these words:

I call to the Matrona; the Queen of the Holy Island; the Goddess herself.
The Elder One who dwelled here before the dawn of thought;
The Timeless One whose deeds outstrip the first uttered prayer;
The Ageless One whose years are beyond knowing;
The Bornless One whose memories are without end.
Come forth and reveal yourself.

Turn through the airts and, in time, you will witness the autophaneia of the four initiatory goddesses, the Graal Keepers. Each rises from her respective direction, ascending the banks of the Tor. They approach as one, followed by a cowled Graal guardian. These four hooded figures assume positions upon the threshold of the Templum in perfect stillness at each of the stations of the intercardinal directions. They each bear a decorated bronze bowl, held at chest height, facing towards you. The four goddesses grow near, but halt before their respective candle upon the ground, one of eight forming the circle of Arte. Four further women ascend to the Templum's summit, emerging from the cardinal directions. Dressed in habiliments of wool; simple, long tunics, they too converge upon the candle-lit circle. All eight face towards you. From your central position, turn and bow to each in turn: the four initiatory Queens, with who you have developed a propinquity, and the four women who are new to you. Their eyes are upon you even though their mien may differ. Some may appear aloof and averse; others benign and welcoming.

Regardless of their demeanour, know that they attend in service to you, the initiand; and you attend in service to them.

You observe a ninth figure outside the circle, completing the ennead, slowly walking the threshold of the Adytum. She wears a simple gown gathered by a leather belt, beneath a woollen cloak. Bearing a golden vessel, she visits each of the four distant Graal guardians in turn, who pour a quantity of their elixir into her bowl. Then she approaches from the north, passing into the circle and standing before you. Genuflect in response, for you are graced with the presence of the Matrona herself, the Magna Mater and *prima inter pares* of the assembled Sororitas Avalonis, the nine sorcerer-maidens of the Holy Isle of Avalon. Speak the following to the Goddess:

Judge me according to my deeds Great Queen.
I come here, now, in all humility,
Having walked the precincts of this Holy Island;
Honoured its spirits, ancestors and guardians;
Drawn the sacred waters,
Performed lustrations, made offerings;
And raised shrines to the Four.

The Matrona smiles at you enigmatically. She may speak and ask you questions. Once she is satisfied, utter the following:

Upon this holy cynosure
I have been transfigured;
In the Sun's wake, descending to darkness and returning;
Fulfilling the sacral rites of renewal
And the eternal process of becoming.

Upon this holy cynosure
I have been transmuted;
Through gifts imparted by the Graals' elixirs,
A chrysopoeia upon my self
Has honoured cosmic conformity.
Upon this holy cynosure
I have been reconciled;
Red and white; solar and ophidian;

I am become verdant, and made sovereign,
Over the forces of opposition
Within the Retinue of the Body.

The Matrona breathes into her Graal, which is lined with silver but is otherwise all gold, and hands it to you. Hold your consecrated cup such that it occupies the same space as her vessel. Pause for a moment until you are given a signal to drink, then lift your cup to your lips and drain its contents. Give thanks and place your vessel upon the earth. Speak these words, facing towards the northwest:

By the Graal of Spirit, charged with the Gift of Quiescence, I became the Corpus Noctis and found Inspiration in the darkness.

And towards the northeast:

By the Graal of Admittance, charged with the Gift of Anamnesis, I became the Corpus Aurora and found Renewal in dawn's twilight.

And towards the southeast:

By the Graal of Flesh, charged with the Gift of Volition, I became the Corpus Lux and tasted True Will beneath the fulgid Sun.

And towards the southwest:

By the Graal of Egression, charged with the Gift of Utterance, I became the Corpus Tenebris and found Authority in the twilight of dusk.

And towards the Matrona in the north:

Now, by the Graal of the Matrona, I bring all things into unity under this Great Synaxis.

Perform the Ophidian Rite, seeing veins of red and white light rise up to the brow of the Templum and converge upon your breast, where they intersect and flow through you before declining the Holy Hill in the opposing airts. See the braid of red light from the Red Serpent first flow into the breast of the cowled figure in the northwest, then into the vessel he bears, before passing into the Dark Queen, through you to the Aureate Queen, thence to the vessel held by the figure in the southeast, and the bearer itself, before it descends. Similarly, see the braid of white light from the White Serpent first flow into the breast of the cowled figure in the southwest, then into the vessel he bears, before passing into the Roseate Queen, then through you and into the Pale Queen, passing into the vessel held by the figure in the northeast, and finally the bearer itself, before the braid descends the Templum.

Even while the ophidian energies flow through you, face north where, regardless of the time of day, the nowl star Polaris is visible in the eldritch skies. Rotating around it are the constellations of Ursa Minor, Draconis and Ursa Major. See these asterisms gleam and nictate brightly as a lucent column of white light descends from the heavens, passes through your crown and the three lapides, and through the mandorla upon the Gate of the Templum into the Holy Hill. In tandem, a column of red light from the deepest abyss of the underworld passes up through the hill, through your feet, through the three lapides and departs through your crown before ascending into the highest celestial realms. The Lapis Viridis within your chest is the nexus of convergence for these energies; it is the crucible where all are unified through their intersection. Draw these energies from the emerald jewel, blazing with argent fire, into the Bodily Retinue, even unto nimiety. When the vessel of your body radiates in its foison, and the three lapides gleam with effulgence, disperse the energies along the eight roads of the eight queens, towards where the celestial and chthonic realms meet at the liminal, cosmic boundary of the horizon. Speak these words:

I am the wasteland;
I am the Graal;
I am the Covenant that was broken;
And its restoration.

Stand for a moment, then perceive both veins of power descend slowly from the axis mundi of your chest and sink into the earth of the Templum, to rejoin their parent currents. Observe also the two columns of light withdraw to their respective domains. Any energetic residuum still contained in your body should be dispersed through your feet into the ground.

Turn to each of the eight sorcerer-queens in succession. Step forward. Each will place a hand upon either your brow, your breast or your navel. Some will do so swiftly with delight. Others will be hesitant or even give an impression of distaste. Regardless, on each occasion genuflect and step back. Finally, the Matrona will do the same. She may speak to you once more and place certain prohibitions upon you, which must be obeyed. At this moment of anagnorisis, bow to her in the knowledge that all nine of the ennead are one, merging and separating; refracting and reflecting according to the divine impetus.

If you desire it, you may ask the Goddess for admission to a rare synomosy; a *casus foederis* protecting and upholding the Avalonian *prohairesis*. If she grants you membership, you will be bound to the Holy Island.

You stand and watch the assembly depart, even as you spy three distant figures upon the Holy Hill, who also turn away in time. When the Adytum has emptied, descend from the Templum, following your route along the Oaken Path. Acknowledge the guardian if he is present, then climb into the barge still moored to the jetty amongst the reed beds. Presently your pilot embarks, and casting off, rows you to the shores of your ritual space. Do not look back at any point, even after disembarking. Walk towards the candle-lit circle and return to your corporeal body. Open your eyes, stand, thank your spirit allies and the *genii locorum*, giving the former license to depart, then close down the circle, extinguish the candles and incense. Ring your bell or chime as you did at the commencement of the Great Quest, and retreat from that place, leaving no trace of your presence.

¶ POST SACRA

The percipient initiate will acknowledge that the completion of the Great Quest marks the commencement of a deeper and more expansive engagement in the spiritual communitas of Avalon. There are many doors to pass through and realms to explore. These include further portals to Annwn, especially those in proximity to the Red and White Springs. Decension via these gates will reveal wholly new and different netherworldly domains to those previously experienced.

frìth

Frith or Celtic divination may be performed on the summit of the Tor; an appropriate location given that prognostication was typically conducted upon a templum, where a quadrangular open area was used for augural observation. While traditional *frìth* incorporated a panoply of omens, Avalonian *frìth* is particularly efficacious when restricted to ornithomancy and, specifically, the birds associated, or in kinship with, each of the four Queens.[5] It can be regarded as a reflex of the draoidhean practice of predicting the future by observing the flight and calls of birds. To conduct the Avalonian *frìth*, ascend the Tor, acknowledge the Domains and Roads of the four Queens, and make an offering of alcohol or honey. Stand upon the mandorla, the Gate of the Templum, and meditate upon the question to be asked. Then, perambulate the borders of the summit and observe the avian activities both near and far. Being otherworldly creatures capable of traversing the upper, middle and lower worlds, they are bearers of numinous knowledge and therefore worthy of attention. Using wisdom and cunning to examine the presence and flight of birds, their interactions, their height and position, their numbers and movements, and their encroachments in relation to the quadripartite division of the lands into four Domains corresponding to the four Queens, the auspice may be determined. When satisfied, give thanks and depart. While corvids – crows and magpies – may appear to dominate the Tor, it has not always been thus. Their presence may be interpreted as the waxing influence of the Dark Queen, which is dependent on time of day and seasonality. Yet buzzards, kestrels and kites, the totem-birds of the Aureate Queen, are also commonplace, as are wood pigeons and collared doves.

solstitial rites

The two solstices should also be considered in relation to the Holy Island's cosmology and astrotheology. As previously elucidated, certain alignments and orientations of landscape features correspond to solstitial sunrise and sunset, highlighting the significance of these liminal events as a means of synchronising the subastral world with the machinery of the cosmos. At winter

5 See Nichols for a short overview of traditional *frìth*.

and summer solstice when the Sun is respectively at its weakest and strongest, its points of rising and setting on the horizon, which mark the intersection of the ecliptic and the Milky Way, coincides with the Roads of the four Queens. Careful consideration should be given to the consequences of this liminal nexus, particularly in relation to the Gates of the Sun, which provide ingress for souls descending from the upper world at midsummer, and egress for the dead from the lower and middle worlds at midwinter. The enlightened initiate will conceive appropriate rituals in acknowledgement of, and participation in, these cosmic dramas. Through visionary aesthesis, they will witness a wondrous Magistery. Furthermore, know that, during the summer solstice, the sovereign ennead leads the Midsummer Sabbat across the Holy Island, where all those who honour the Great Queen become celebrants, participating in her otherworldly revels. Conversely, at the winter solstice, Arawn, Arthur and Merlin – the British Woden – lead the Wild Hunt, drawing Annwn's souls forth and aloft into Avalon's roiling skies.

imbas

Experimentation with the techniques of inspired or mantic poetry is encouraged, for the initiate has been blessed with its extasis. The spark of otherworldy inspiration gifted by the Dark Queen, and thereafter informed by Innocence and Experience, finally evolves into the gift of poetic speech; the rhapsodic, eloquent and transcendent Arte of magickal word-weaving granted by the Roseate Queen. The significance of this bequest should not be underestimated as, in Celtic tradition, poetic utterance is explictly linked to truth, authority and judgement, its source being the Sun. Through a synchronisation of their behaviour with the predictable movements of the Sun, regents were granted poetic prowess, the truest form of speech and an expression of their legitmacy and sovereignty. In short, divinely inspired poetry is the means by which the initiate may both obtain and articulate gnosis.

If Druids functioned as mediators between the physical world and the otherworld, maintaining good relations by advising monarchs and ensuring the proper ritual enactment of seasonal myths, Ovates navigated a path for the community through the ever-living cycles of myth via seership and healing, and Bards both retold the true myths of the people and conversed with the denizens of the otherworld. In Ireland in particular, the *filid* or poet-class occupied a higher status than Bards and were accorded the special status of *nemed* – a rank meaning 'sacred' and 'privileged,' granting them rights similar to those of a regent. The reason for this lay in the power the *filid* wielded. Firstly, they were the source of truth in a world not dependent on the written word, where all social and legal contracts existed only as memories or as spoken oaths. As bearers of the community's collective mind, all statements made by a poet were required to be true; if a poet failed in this task, the community's myths and memory became tainted with falsehood, leading inexorably to societal collapse. Secondly, through their truthful word-weaving – granted by special knowledge obtained via inspiration – the *filid* were able to ward or curse: on one hand they could protect a king from sorcery simply by remaining in his presence; on the other they could 'rhyme to death' men and animals – an act recorded by English sources up to the sixteenth century.

An additional power of the poet was prophecy and thus related to the seership of the Ovates. Poets divined knowledge of the future via three methods: *imbas forasnai* or 'encompassing knowledge which illuminates'; *teinm láeda* or 'breaking of marrow'; and *díchetal di chennaib* or 'chanting from heads.' The latter may relate to the divinatory abilities of oracular severed heads; the meaning of 'breaking of marrow' is disputed. Of the three, *imbas forasnai* is most clearly understood, being a technique for obtaining otherworldy insight through the consumption of flesh, chanting, and mantic sleep, or by the deliberate consumption of fairie-food. In support of the latter method, Yeats alluded to poets' special relationship with the fey, suggestive of a shaman's relationship with the spirits. The parallels with shamanism extend to the etymology of the Gaelic word *aí*, which is linked to the Welsh *awen*. In this context *awen*, translated as 'inspiration,' has the connotation of 'breathing in,' which is related to the power of the nine maidens' breath and, potentially, a form of breathwork; Gerald of Wales noted a shamanistic and ecstatic trance state among the Welsh poets, observing that their bodies were taken over by a force which apparently spoke through them.[6]

Therefore, the initiand should charge their hallowed vessel, invoke the four goddesses using the panegyrics contained herein or, better yet, extemporise. Then, in a calm and meditative state, with one's mind unburdened by extraneous thought, feel a stirring and quickening, and begin to chant, speak

6 The above paragraphs attempt to summarise aspects of Kramer's insightful paper, specifically Part II.

or write, without giving heed to the content of the verse. This method of channeling and automatic writing is well-attested as a technique for divining the will of the Goddess of Avalon.[7]

One scholar has suggested that Britain was an early centre of prophetic poetry, being the country from which early Irish mantic poets acquired their *imbas*.[8] We may go yet further in this supposition and declare Avalon as the nexus, the preeminent wellspring of poetic inspiration in Albion's mythopoetic unveiling.

discessus

For those who do not permanently dwell upon or near the Holy Island, the four shrines of the four Queens may be closed down and the sacramentalia removed for use in personal praxis. A small quantity of earth from beneath the shrine may also be taken – no more than a teaspoon-full is needed. The earth can prove efficacious in the pursuit of ongoing rapprochment. Make offerings to the tutelary Queen and *genii locorum* as part of this process.

The Great Quest should be repeated annually, to renew the bonds and covenants between initiate and the Island's numinous coterie. Each initiatory circuit undertaken will be deeper and more profound than the last, resulting in ever-greater personal transmutation and propinquity.

The Lamen of the Holy Island may be carried upon the body of the initiate. Further, a personal map-sigil should be crafted (see the example below), which comprises:

- The distal ring, showing the position of the sun upon the horizon during katabasis, when the western Gate of Descension was revealed; and the position of the sun upon the horizon during anabasis, when the eastern Gate of Ascension was revealed.

- The approximate locations in relation to the Templum marking the points where each of the sacramentalia were unveiled.

7 Taylor (2010), 109; 240–242.
8 See Chadwick.

- The approximate locations in relation to the Templum marking the points where each of the four shrines were established; the places of the sacramentalia's unveiling are joined to the shrines by vincula in the form of straight lines.

- The abodes of any significant spirit allies, marked with an '+'.

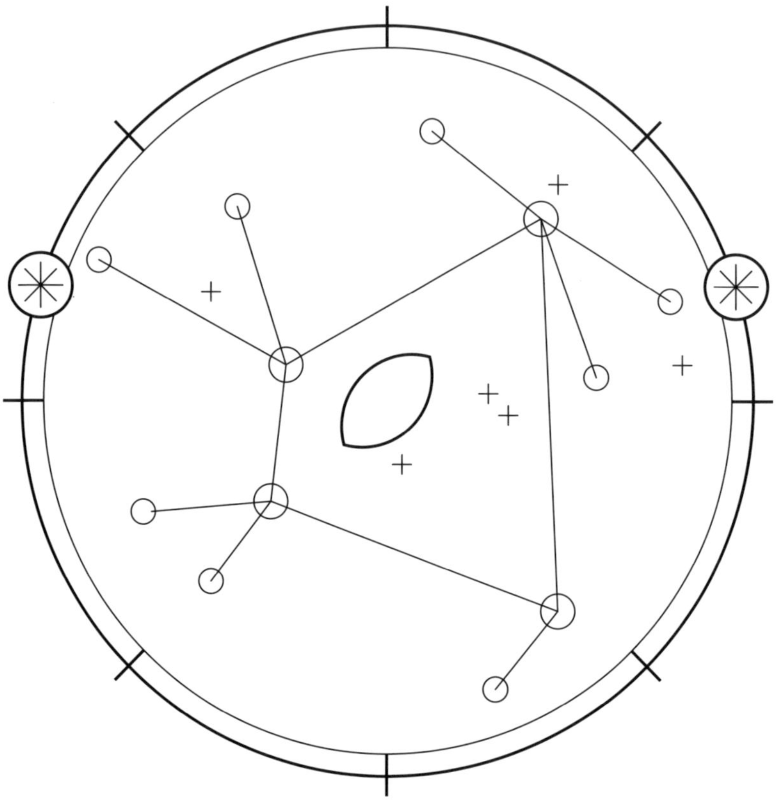

figure 6 An example of the map-sigil.

The procedures outlined as part of the rites of the Great Synaxis may be employed in personal practice to banish or invoke, cast a circle and raise energy:

- The Quotidian Meditations may be used to still the mind and focus attention prior to any ritual undertaking.

- The procedure to draw the virtues of the Sun into the body of the initiate via the Lapis Viridis may be used to raise energy.

- The Ophidian Rite may be used in combination with the Roads of the four Queens and the celestial / chthonic axis to centre and focus the initiate, and to raise energy.

- The eight goddesses of the Sororitas Avalonis may be invoked as protection, or as part of the preparation for establishing a ritual space. They will circumscribe the initiate and face outwards; the goddesses of the intercardinal directions each hold a bronze Graal; the goddesses of the cardinal directions possess the following: the figure in the north holds a disk of stone; in the east a gleaming leaf-bladed sword; in the south a great spear; and in the west is a decorated cauldron. The initiate stands at the centre of the circle upon the mandorla of the vesica piscis.

- A circle may be cast using the initiate's personal consecrated Graal, either by visualising lustrating light cascading from it, or by asperging.

- The sacramentalia and the earth of the shrines should be placed within the circle in an arrangement consonant with the initiate's personal map-sigil, such that the centre of the circle whereupon the initiate stands is the Gate of the Templum and the axis mundi of the Holy Island.

The initiate's personal Graal has been lustrated, consecrated and ensorcelled; blessed by each of the four queens and the Matrona herself, and fructified by their elixirs. As a reflex of the one true hierophanic Graal it is a powerful *famulus*, *verendum* and *vas magicum*, holding within it the virtues of the Holy Island. The water it bears may be employed in manifold contexts. For example, as a divinatory (e.g. scrying) tool; to heal, cleanse, purify, banish and exorcise; to fructify and make productive; as part of pietistic devotions (e.g. offerings); in acts of theurgy and *nekyia*; in spagyric procedures; or to impart inspiration, vitality, courage and volition, utterance and authority. The initiate should construct appropriate rituals in support of these acts of luminary telesis.

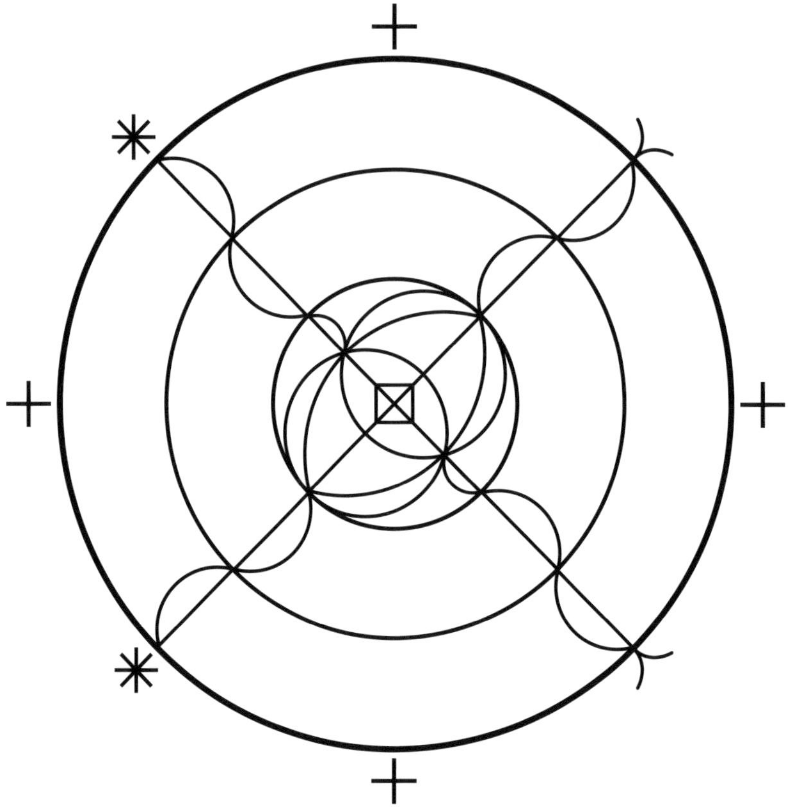

figure 7 The Lamen of the Holy Island.

postscribo

An understanding of Avalon's deepest arcana requires a different way of seeing and being; a rejection of the disenchantment of modern western materialism and an adoption of a fundamentally magickal worldview. Magick is as old as humankind, bound up with the mysteries of life and addressing a perennial deep-seated desire to understand the world rather than merely exist within it. Until recently, western culture excluded magick from its narrative of humankind's evolution. Yet alongside innovations in astronomy, agriculture, animal domestication and husbandry, medicine, engineering, art and government, magick also evolved as an extraordinary series of experiments with the cosmos, mediated by human psychology, intellect, action and emotion.[1]

Life for early hominids was no doubt, as the cliché goes, nasty, brutish and short. Exposed to the predations of Nature, which itself is, in many respects, nasty and brutish, a logical ancestral preoccupation was to rise out of a state of extreme vulnerability; to defend itself against the privations of their environment. But this did not preclude a recognition of the ever evolving and subtle web of interactions between humans, the land, and the wider cosmos. It is probable that the consciousness of our early ancestors perceived no distinction between self and non-self, inner and outer, humankind and Nature. Nor were the earliest magicks understood as specific disciplines segregated from culture, enacted by ritual specialists. Rather, they were part of the fabric of survival, based on an acknowledgement of the need for kinship and 'right

1 See Gosden for a notable introduction to the history of magick.

relation' with all things, whether living or inorganic, physical or incorporeal.

From our vantage point in the modern west, we can see that this sense of reciprocity with, and obligation to, Nature is lost. Our present condition is depressingly summarised in the famous biblical exhortation to 'be fruitful and multiply, and fill the earth and subdue it; and have dominion over the fish of the sea and over the birds of the air and over every living thing that moves upon the earth.' Furthermore, despoiling of the land is not a recent phenomenon; in fact it has a long and ignoble history. For example, extensive deforestation of Britain occurred throughout the Mesolithic and Neolithic. And in Roman-era Europe, the soil fertility of agricultural land became largely exhausted due to over-farming.[2] Yet, even through periods of disenchantment (which is marked not by a gradual decline over millennia but rather a set of peaks and troughs influenced by myriad complex factors),[3] humans maintained an intimate connection to the earth, to its deep mysteries, and to the more-than-human worlds with which it intersected.

The last few hundred years of industrial culture have wholly exsanguinated the body of enchantment however, such that it is now broadly perceived, in the modern west at least, as a curious novelty rather than a viable way-of-seeing-and-being. Arguably, coeval with that transition, any remnants of a fragile balance were lost when industrialisation required an unsustainable, exponential exploitation of resources; when control wholly descended into subjugation. To execute the industrial project required a total de-sacralisation of Nature, accompanied by mass human displacement from the land, marking the most profound of schisms. Only now, at the end of things, is the error realised.

In our current age of crisis, and in contrast to the biblical prohibitions that have for generations comprised the bedrock of western society, humankind's greatest sins are no longer carousing, divorce and effeminacy. Instead, our sins are those committed against the Earth, against Terra Mater. As an understanding of animal sentience evolves, our current treatment of intensively farmed livestock will one day be considered truly evil.

Magick therefore provides a path to re-enchantment. It inculcates a worldview and a mode of action based on an acknowledgement of the weave of cause-and-effect, negotiated by ideas of correct behaviour and of recip-

2 Palmer, 58–59.

3 See https://www.ecosophia.net/tag/disenchantment/ where John Michael Greer provides an excellent overview of this expansive topic.

rocal relationships with Nature. It reveals a reality where all things are alive with agency, possessed of spirit; and where society extends to non-corporeal realms. Avalon, the Holy Island, is a legominism; a symbol within which a path to re-enchantment is embedded. It remains a place of both sanctity and magickal possibility, its spiritous denizens waiting patiently for our arrival and participation. They invite us to don the discarded mantle of sovereignty and stewardship, to enact the perennial rites of exchange and reciprocity, which are essential to the wellbeing of the entire communitas. But such an undertaking is profound and irreversible, requiring a deconstruction of the socially conditioned and poisoned self. In occult tradition this is brought about by the initiatory process: a sundering; a dissolution and dissipation, leading to a reconstitution and transfiguration. Therefore, to the penitent pilgrim, the Holy Island of Avalon offers a great and terrible dispensation: sacrifice upon the verdant altar of Albion's preeminent magickal locus and vessel of power.

It should now be understood by the reader that this work is largely concerned with initiation by the divine ennead, the Sororitas Avalonis, who dwell upon the Holy Island; a recension of the nine maidens cult consanguineous with the earliest myths. Eight are guardians of the directions, four of whom are threshold deities and goddesses of initiation. All are aspects of the ninth, the Matrona, an incarnation of the Magna Mater. Arthurian myth attests to their role as healers when a barge brings the dying Arthur to the shores of Avalon. The great mystery of the healing process lies in the druidic doctrine of metempsychosis, which requires the eternal soul to descend to the underworld as part of the cycle of rejuvenation. This is why certain traditions allude to Arthur's dwelling-place as Annwn, the country beneath the hill where he continues to rest.

The nine maidens cult describes a *hieronesos*, a sacred island or high place, as their residence. In an Avalonian context this is the Templum, the Holy Hill. Upon the Tor, they preside over the entrance and exit-routes to Annwn; as such, their role as healers becomes cognate with the psychopomp – they guide the wounded souls into the earth, that they may be made whole once more. Thus, Avalon's status as an earthly Elysium becomes clear: it is the place where souls commence and complete the metempsychotic cycle of renewal. It is no coincidence that the sign of Aquarius in Maltwood's Temple of the Stars, which is centred on Glastonbury, is represented by the Phoenix – symbol of rebirth and renewal. The Graal contributes to this process, being a healing vessel cognate with the alchemical lapis exilis, attainable at the conclusion of the Great Work, which is concerned with wholeness, with refining and unifying the base metals of the self.

This renewal of the self can be understood as a healing of the inner wasteland, which must be resolved before the outer wasteland is addressed. By assuming the role of a solar hypostasis, the initiate temporarily wears the mantle of the sacral regent who, by virtue of that status, is required to perform the metempsychotic rites, in maintenance of cosmic balance and, therefore, of the land's fecundity. The wasteland is upon us at a planetary level, but it is not distributed evenly across the Earth. Even in this poisoned epoch of crisis, upheaval and trauma, reconciliation and healing are possible. By completing the Great Quest, the Avalon Working, through your deeds the earth is re-enchanted and fecundated. And the manifold forces of opposition – flesh and spirt, red and white, sun and earth – are united in a new compact.

Clouds scud alongside
As sheep scull a ragged line,
Ripping at the slope.
It is the limbus of dawn,
And only mist remains,
And hands upon Earth,
And air.

Mist weaves rhynes into the Levels;
Birds spin and chant over the Hides;
Enchantment makes knots in the blood,
And all is well upon the Hill.

In Dewtime they meet in silent conclave;
In Dreamtime they genuflect
To the sun and moon, the eight airts, the numen.

Blue gives way to gold as footfalls unspool, one below the other,
Descending a track called Paradise,
Towards the oaken and wilding Earth;
The lowing meadows, where time and space will take root again.

But not yet.

Not
Yet.

Clouds scud overhead
As cattle, moored in the pale light,
Curl tongues at level ground.
Then, in the nimbus of dawn, life falls away.
And only leaves remain,
And sun on leaves,
And breath.
And all is well beneath the Hill.

In Elysium.

IN ELYSIUM

the outer precincts

previous The Hieronesos, the Holy Island, known in this era as Glastonbury, has not wholly been an island in recent geological time. It was once a peninsula, linked to higher ground by an isthmus to the east. However, from the west Glastonbury would have appeared as an island, with water on three sides. / © Niklas Weiss.

above Glastonbury Tor viewed from the linear earthwork known as Ponter's Ball, at the eastern boundary of the Holy Island, which may have functioned as a *cordon sanitaire* against the profane world beyond.

A stone marking the location of Bride's Well beside the River Brue. In 1887 Dr John Arthur Goodchild underwent a visionary experience and was commanded to bury an apparently ancient blue glass bowl in its waters.

The view from Bride's Well looking east. Bride's Mound, the site of Beckery Chapel, sits beneath the Tor to the left. Wearyall Hill rises to the right.

The view southeast towards the Tor from Edmund Hill. At winter solstice dawn the rising sun appears to roll up its steep northern flank on the left; the sun's ascent, at an angle of 26°, is matched by the angle of the slope of the Tor.

The Glastonbury Thorn which, in legend, sprung from Joseph of Arimathea's staff when he placed it upon Wearyall Hill. The tree suffered multiple attacks over the years and was completely removed in 2019.

The imposing view of the mighty Tor from Wearyall Hill, which formed a point of ingress to the Holy Island for pilgrims, its spine a processional route to the interior. A monastery of holy virgins was located on Wearyall Hill's summit.

the inner precincts

The Tor embodies myriad cosmological and magicko-religious functions: as a world hill it is located at the centre of the Avalonian ritual landscape; as an axis mundi it is the point of coition between a chthonic well of souls – the underworld of Annwn – and the celestial realm; it is Mount Abiegnus, the Rosicrucian Mountain of Initiation or Hill of Vision; it is the dwelling-place of the nine witch-maidens of myth; and it is a reflex of the seven-tiered temple of antiquity, conforming to the strict definition of a templum.

Three paths ascend to the Holy Hill of the Tor:
Stonedown Lane, Paradise Lane and Maidencroft Lane.

Paradise Lane is especially lovely, running along the ridgeway of Stonedown Hill with views over a sweeping arc of high green swarth, dropping gently into a cove of orchards below.

Looking towards the Tor from the summit of Stonedown Hill.
The Tor's narrow, symmetrical 'masculine' aspect is evident.

Magog, the Arborial Queen of the Holy Island. This time-worn sentinel is the last surviving exemplar of the Avalon Oaks. Some reckon her age a mere 500 years; others point to the 2,000 season-rings recorded after a companion-oak was felled in 1906.

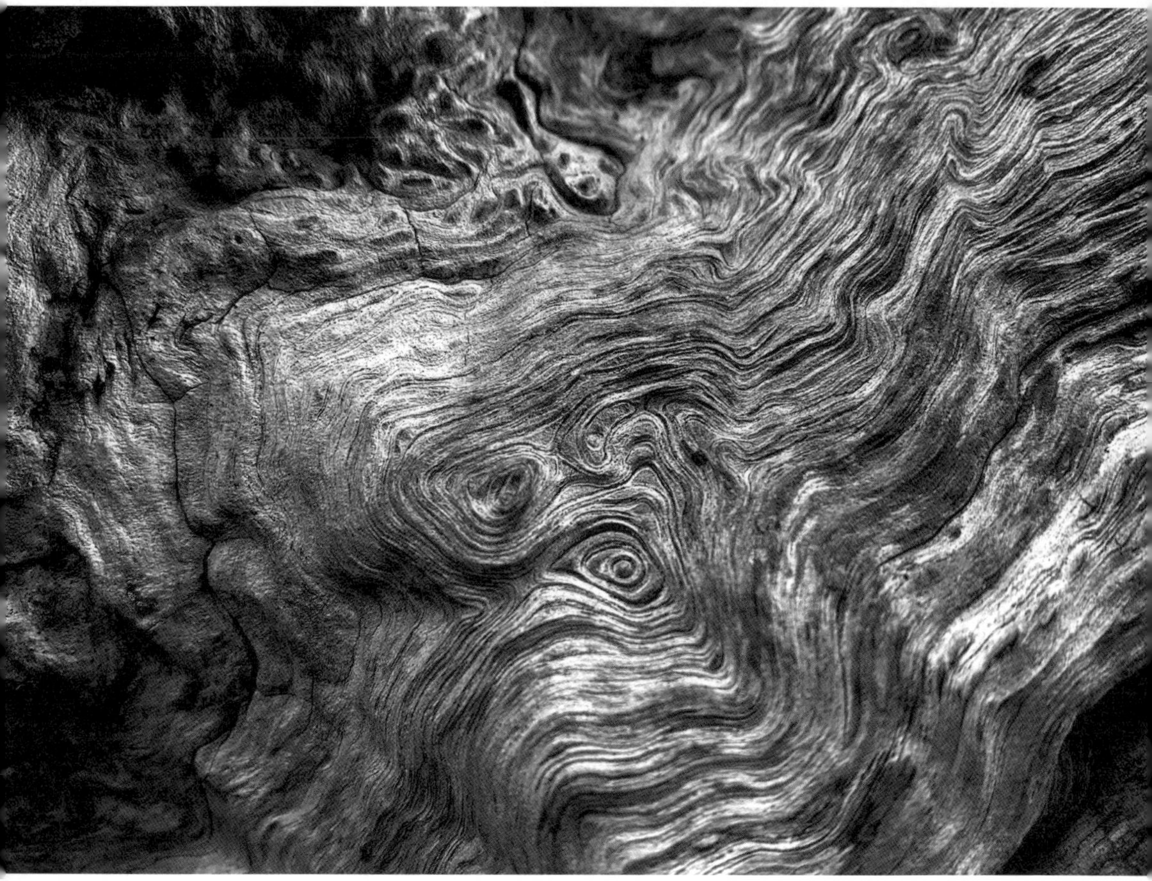

Magog's root-wisdom can be discerned in the runes of her bark, the simulacra and symbology of her deadwood, wherein whorls and burrs form triskeles, eyes and manifold physiognomia.

Gog, the male tree of the two, expired in 2001, its flensed corpse still extant but now pale as bone. Together, Gog and Magog mark the route of the Oaken Path, the ceremonial avenue leading to the precincts of the Tor.

The source of the Holy Island's abiding sanctity is the congressum of three natural landscape features: the great terraced hill of the Tor, and two freshwater springs, one red and one white, which rise at its base. The Red Spring shown here is located in Chalice Well gardens.

Excavations at Chalice Well in 1961 revealed flints and Roman pottery, and the stump of a Roman-era yew tree implying a long tradition of sanctity. High levels of iron oxide impart a reddish hue to the waters. Pilgrims drink the healing waters from this lion-head fountain.

The famous Chalice Well lid, incorporating the vesica piscis symbol of wrought iron and oak, was designed by Bligh Bond at the invitation of Alice Mary Buckton, then owner of Chalice Well.

Prior to the erection of a pump house in 1872, the White Spring emerged from a cave system beneath the Tor and flowed through a series of lime-encrusted dropping-wells. Now, the calcium-rich waters cascade down modern variants.

The temple of the White Spring within Victorian Well House invites pilgrimage. The dank, candle-lit interior housing pools and shrines is a true sanctum; a hypogeum with its own quadripartite layout in which the Avalonian Mysteries may be deeply discerned. © Jo Pritchard.

A shrine within the temple of the White Spring to the masculine aspect of the Avalonian powers, embodied here in the figure of Arawn / Gwyn ap Nudd. © Jo Pritchard.

(prev.) A shrine within the temple of the White Spring to Bríg / St Brigid. © Jo Pritchard.

St Joseph's heraldic shield, designed by Abbot Richard Bere and found as medieval stained-glass at St John's Church, Glastonbury. It depicts heavenly dew descending onto the red and white cruets of Joseph of Arimathea, which flank a cross of green thorn. Its imagery echoes the prophesy of the sixth century CE bard Melkin, who declared that 'neither water nor heavenly dew will be lacking for the inhabitants of the Holy Isle.'

Glastonbury Abbey is reputedly the site of England's first church, the Vetusta Ecclesia, established by Joseph of Arimathea in approximately 63 CE. According to legend, it is also the final resting place of King Arthur and Queen Guinevere.

The tower of St Michael's church upon the summit of the Tor rears up behind the ruins of Glastonbury Abbey. Its abbot, Dunstan, was said to have diverted the waters from the Red and White Springs to the abbey for use in alchemical experiments.

An egg-shaped Tor burr, formed by the natural erosion of sandstone, located within the grounds of Glastonbury Abbey. It has been speculated that these were employed as *omphaloi*, cult-stones marking the centre-point or navel of a sacred landscape.

Of the many orchards scattered throughout the Holy Island, Avalon Orchard upon the banks of the Tor is especially numinous, and well-loved by pilgrims.

Spirits of the orchards' apple trees are particularly active in spring, when the Holy Island is adorned with fragrant blossom.

Many of the Holy Island's apple trees are thick with mistletoe. Its abundance is an indication of Avalon's status as an earthly Elysium and terrestrial otherworld.

A celestial gift, mistletoe is unrooted from soil, relying on its host-tree for vitality. Thus, being aloof from and untainted by the profane earth, its sanctity remains intact.

The Tor's elongated 'feminine' aspect, as viewed from the northwest. Its terracing is clearly visible.

the temple and the adytum

An aerial view of the Tor fully reveals its terracing, which some believe was deliberately cut in order to describe a three-dimensional maze, based on the classical Cretan labyrinth, or the Welsh *caerdroia*. Others propose different theories. / © Marc Wolf.

The Bridey Bell at the foot of the Tor, one of nine limestone waymarkers with inset bronze bells. Designed by sculptor Barry Cooper and musician and artist Laurence Parnell, the nine 'syrens' mark a pilgrimage route between Wells and Glastonbury. Each bell produces a different musical note.

The Egg Stone or Dragon Egg, located on the Tor's southern slope. A Tor burr or omphalos stone, this venerated example serves as a shrine and place of meditation.

Offerings laid upon the Dragon Egg.

Shrines adorned with flowers can be found around the terraces of the Holy Hill.

A shrine with offerings of flowers and fruit.

At certain times of the year, pilgrims camp at the base of the Tor, amongst its trees and copses.

Campfires provide further evidence of seasonal habitation around the base of the Tor.

The morning sun casts a shadow of the Tor over meadows below Chalice Hill, the alleged resting-place of the Graal. The Red and White Springs rise in the valley between the Tor and Chalice Hill.

The Adytum, the summit of the Holy Hill, is marked in this era by the presence of the ruined tower of the church of St Michael.

the avalonian counterculture

At weekends, Glastonbury High Street is often thronged with pilgrims, buskers, traders, tourists, nomads and mystics.

The public proselytizing of social or spiritual messages, and the presence of street oracles, is commonplace in the town centre.

Pro-Goddess graffiti inscribed upon the pavements of Glastonbury.

selected bibliography & further reading

Adams, Peter Mark (2019). *Mystai: Dancing out the mysteries of Dionysos.* London, UK: Scarlet Imprint.
Allen, Richard Hinckley (1899). *Star-Names and their Meanings.* NewYork: G. E. Stechert.
Anonymous / Three Initiates (1912). *The Kybalion: A Study of the Hermetic Philosophy of Ancient Egypt and Greece.* Chicago: The Yogi Publication Society Masonic Temple.
Acher, Frater, and Sabogal, José Gabriel Alegría (2021). *Clavis Goëtica: Keys to Chthonic Sorcery.* Hadean Press.
Ashe, Geoffrey (1957). *King Arthur's Avalon: The Story of Glastonbury.* London: Collins.
Baring-Gould (1996). *Sabine: Myths of the Middle Ages.* London: Blandford.
Berg, Wendy (2010). *Red Tree, White Tree: Faeries and Humans in Partnership.* Cheltenham: Skylight Press.
Besant, Annie (2011). *The Ancient Wisdom.* Aziloth Books. Originally published in 1897.
Blavatsky, H.P. (2019). *The Secret Doctrine, the Synthesis of Science, Religion and Philosophy Vol II: Anthropogenesis.* The Theosophical Publishing Company Ltd.
—— (2003 ed). *Collected Writings of H. P. Blavatsky,* Vol.14: *Miscellaneous.* The Theosophical Publishing Company Ltd.
Bond, Frederick Bligh (1914). The 'Egg Stone' at Glastonbury Abbey. *Proceedings of the Somersetshire Archaeological & Natural History Society* 59, 64–73.
—— & George E. Mantle (2018). *Recent Discoveries at Glastonbury Abbey: An Account of the Excavations Undertaken by Mr. F. Bligh Bond, With his Notes Upon the Discoveries: Together With a Short History of the Abbey.* Franklin Classics.
De Boron, Robert (2005). *Merlin and the Grail: Joseph of Arimathea, Merlin, Perceval. The Trilogy of Arthurian Prose Romances attributed to Robert de Boron.* Translated by Nigel Bryant. Martlesham: D S Brewer.
Bowman, Marion (2014). Restoring / Restorying Arthur and Bridget: Vernacular Religion and Contemporary Spirituality in Glastonbury. *Vernacular Religion in Everyday Life:*

Expressions of Belief. Edited by Marion Bowman and Ülo Valk. London: Routledge.
Broadhurst, Paul & Miller, Hamish (1991). *The Sun and the Serpent.* Launceston: Pendragon Press.
Budge, E. A. Wallis (1904). *The Gods of the Egyptians.* London: Methuen.
Campbell, J. F. (2020). *The Celtic Dragon Myth.* Alpha Editions.
Carroll, Peter J. (1987). *Liber Null and Psychonaut.* Newburyport: Red Wheel/Weiser.
Castagnoli, Ferdinando (1967). *Orthogonal Town Planning in Antiquity.* Cambridge, MA: MIT Press.
Chadwick, Nora K. (1935). Imbas Forosnai. *Scottish Gaelic Studies* 4(2), 97–135. Oxford University Press.
Chumbley, Andrew D. (2014). *The Dragon-Book of Essex: Grimorium Synomosia Dracotaos.* Xoanon.
Collins, Andrew (2008). *The Cygnus Mystery.* London: Watkins Publishing.
Colquhoun, Ithell (2017). *The Living Stones.* London: Peter Owen.
—— (2017 ed). *The Crying of the Wind.* London: Peter Owen.
Coon, Robert (2008). *Voyage to Avalon: The Magick of Glastonbury: Heart Chakra of the World.* UK: Robert Coon.
—— (2008). *The Rainbow Serpent and the Holy Grail: Uluru and the Planetary Chakras.* UK: Robert Coon.
Cottrell-Boyce, Aidan (2021). British Israelism. *Critical Dictionary of Apocalyptic and Millenarian Movements.*
Crowley, Aleister (1981). *The Book of Thoth.* New York: Samuel Weiser, Inc.
—— & Skinner, Stephen (ed) (2021 ed). *Aleister Crowley's Four Books of Magick.* London: Watkins.
Cuncliffe, Barry (2010). *Druids: A Very Short Introduction.* Oxford: Oxford University Press.
Darrah, John (1997). Paganism in Arthurian Romance. Martlesham: Boydell Press.
Deacon, Richard (1968). *John Dee: Scientist, Geographer, Astrologer and Secret Agent to Elizabeth I.* London: Muller.
Deane, John Bathurst (1833). *The Worship of the Serpent.* London: J. G. & F. Rivington.
Doxtater, Dennis (2009 draft paper). Yggdrasil as Map: Precedents for a large-scale Eliadian cross structure in prehistoric Scandinavia and probabilities of integration with locations of largest mounds.
Eliade, Mircea (1988). *Shamanism: Archaic Techniques of Ecstasy.* London: Arkana.
Von Eschenbach, Wolfram, A T Hatto (trans) (1980 ed). *Parzival.* London: Penguin.
Enright, Michael J. (2006). *The Sutton Hoo Sceptre and the Roots of Celtic Kingship.* Dublin: Four Courts Press Ltd.
Evans-Wentz, W. Y. (2009). *The Fairy-Faith in Celtic Countries.* BiblioLife.
Fortune, Dion (1987). *Esoteric Orders and their Work.* Wellingborough: Aquarian Books.
—— (1995). *Glastonbury: Avalon of the Heart.* New York: Weiser Books.
—— (2000). *The Cosmic Doctrine.* New York: Samuel Weiser Inc.
—— (2012). *The Magical Battle of Britain: The War Letters of Dion Fortune.* Cheltenham: Skylight Press.

——, Margaret Lumley Brown, Gareth Knight (2006). *The Arthurian Formula.* Thoth Publications.

Frazer, James George (1900). *The Golden Bough: A Study in Religion and Magic.* London: MacMillan and Co. Limited.

Frisvold, Nicholaj De Mattos (2021). *Trollrún, A Discourse on Trolldom and Runes in the Northern Tradition.* Hadean Press.

Fulford, Michael (2021). *Silchester Revealed: The Iron Age and Roman Town of Calleva.* Windgather Press.

Furlong, David (2007, paper). *Egyptian Temple Orientation: Astronomical Alignments in the Temples of Egypt.*

Gantz, Jeffrey (trans.) (1976). *The Mabinogion.* London: Penguin.

Garland, Nicky (2012). Ritual Landscapes of Pre-Roman Britain. *TRAC 2012: Proceedings of the Twenty-Second Annual Theoretical Roman Archaeology Conference, Frankfurt 2012.* Edited by Annabel Bokern, Marion Bolder-Boos, Stefan Krmnicek, Dominik Maschek and Sven Page. Oxford: Oxbow Books.

Garrard, Bruce (1986). *Greenlands Farm.* UK: Unique Publications.

—— (2014). *Free State: Glastonbury's alternative community, 1970 to 2000 and beyond.* UK: Unique Publications.

Gary, Gemma (2014). *Traditional Witchcraft: A Cornish Book of Ways.* UK: Troy Books.

Geoffrey of Monmouth (2011). *Geoffrey of Monmouth's Life of Merlin: A New Verse Translation.* Translated by Mark Walker. Amberley Publishing.

Geoffrey of Monmouth (1973). *The History of the Kings of Britain.* Translated by Lewis Thorpe. London: Penguin.

Goddard, David (1999). *The Tower of Alchemy: An Advanced Guide to the Great Work.* New York: Samuel Weiser.

Goodchild, John (2018). *The Light of the West.* Edited & introduced by Sara Craig Lanier and Roland Spottiswoode. Ardrigh Books.

Goodrich, Peter H. (2004). *Merlin: A Casebook.* London: Taylor & Francis.

Godwin, Joscelyn (1994). *The Chemical Wedding of Christian Rosenkreutz.* US: Phanes Press.

Gosden, Chris (2021). *The History of Magic: From Alchemy to Witchcraft, from the Ice Age to the Present.* London: Penguin.

Grant, Kenneth (1994). *Nightside of Eden.* London: Skoob Books Publishing.

Grant, Kenneth (2015). *The Magical Revival.* London: Starfire Publishing.

Greene, Wendy Tibbetts (1987). 'Malory's Merlin: An Ambiguous Magician?' *Arthurian Interpretations* 1(2), 56–63.

Greer, John Michael (2003). *Phallic Religion in the Druid Revival.* Third Mount Haemus Lecture: https://druidry.org/wp-content/uploads/2020/01/THIRD-MT-HAEMUS-LECTURE-.pdf. Accessed 29 March 2024.

Grigsby, John (2003). *Warriors of the Wasteland: A Quest for the Pagan Sacrificial Cult Behind the Grail Legends.* London: Watkins Publishing.

Hale, Amy (2011). John Michell, Radical Traditionalism, and the Emerging Politics of the Pagan New Right. *The Pomegranate* 13(1), 77–97.

Halifax, Joan (1982). *Shaman: The Wounded Healer.* London: Thames & Hudson.
Hall, Manly P. (2011). *The Secret Teachings of All Ages: An Encyclopedic Outline of Masonic, Hermetic, Qabbalistic and Rosicrucian Symbolical Philosophy.* Dover Publications. Originally published in 1928 by the Philosophical Research Society.
Hardcastle, F. (1990). *The Chalice Well Glastonbury, Somerset, England: A Short History.* Glastonbury: The Chalice Well Trust.
Heinz, Sabine (2010). Afterlife and Celtic Concepts of the Otherworld. *Thise Stories Beren Witnesse. The Landscape of the Afterlife in Medieval and Post-medieval Imagination. Medieval English Mirror* 7. Edited by Liliana Sikorska. Frankfurt am Main: Peter Lang.
Hickman, Louise (2014). The Nature of the Self and the Contemplation of Nature: Ecotheology and the History of the Soul. *The Concept of the Soul: Scientific and Religious Perspectives.* Cambridge Scholars Publishing.
Hopkinson-Ball, Tim (2007). *The Rediscovery of Glastonbury: Frederick Bligh Bond: Architect of the New Age.* The History Press.
Hughes, Jonathan (2012). *The Rise of Alchemy in Fourteenth-Century England.* London: Bloomsbury.
Huxtable, M. J. (2008). *Colour, Seeing and Seeing Colour in Medieval Literature.* Doctoral thesis, Durham University.
Kassell, Lauren (2000). Reading for the Philosopher's Stone. Marina Frasca-Spada and Nick Jardine (eds), *Books and the Sciences in History*, 132–150. Cambridge: Cambridge University Press.
Kimball, Samuel Arthur (1975). Merlin's Miscreation and Repetition Compulsion in Malory's *Morte D'arthur. Literature and Psychology* 25.
Hutton, Ronald (2015). *Pagan Britain.* New Haven: Yale University Press.
Jung, Carl G. (1964). *Man and his Symbols.* Garden City, NY: Anchor Press.
—— (2014) *The Collected Works, Vol. 5: Symbols of Transformation.* London: Routledge & Kegan Paul Ltd.
Klæðskeri, Markku (2019). *The Autumn King: Ivar the Boneless, Edmund of East Anglia and the Cult of Yngvi-freyr.* Nemglan Press.
Knight, Stephen (2009). *Merlin, Knowledge and Power Through the Ages.* Ithaca, NY: Cornell University Press.
Knight, Gareth (2011). *Merlin and the Grail Tradition.* Cheltenham: Skylight Press.
—— (2020). *Dion Fortune and the Lost Secrets of the West.* Cheltenham: Skylight Press.
Kramer, William E. (2010). *Filid, Fairies and Faith: The Effects of Gaelic Culture, Religious Conflict and the Dynamics of Dual Confessionalisation on the Suppression of Witchcraft Accusations and Witch-Hunts in Early Modern Ireland, 1533–1670.*
Latura, George Beke (2013). Plato's Cosmic X: Heavenly Gates at the Celestial Crossroads. *Ancient Cosmologies and Ancient Prophets: Anthropological Notebooks* (Slovene Anthropological Society, 2013) – SEAC XX Conference Proceedings.
Leitch, Yuri (ed.) (2013). *Signs and Secrets of the Glastonbury Zodiac.* Glastonbury: Avalonian Aeon Publications.
Lethbridge, Thomas Charles (1975). *Gogmagog: The Buried Gods.* London: Routledge.

Littlejohn, Scott C., Malcor, Linda A. (2013). *From Scythia to Camelot: A Radical Reassessment of the Legends of King Arthur, the Knights of the Round Table, and the Holy Grail.* London: Taylor & Francis.
Loomis, R. S. (1992). *The Grail: From Celtic Myth to Christian Symbol.* Constable.
Lucan, Marcus Annaeus (2014). *Pharsalia.* Translated by A. S. Kline.
Macalister, R. A. Stewart (1908). *Eachtra an Mhadra Mhaoil; Eaċtra Macaoim-an-iolar.* The Irish Texts Society.
Mackay, Jonangus (ed.) (2010). *Michellany: A John Michell Reader.* London: Michellany Editions.
MacKillop, James (2004). *A Dictionary of Celtic Mythology.* Oxford: Oxford University Press.
MacPherson, George (2016). *The Old Grey Magician: A Scottish Fionn Cycle.* Luath Press Ltd.
Maier, Bernhard (2000) *Dictionary of Celtic Religion and Culture.* Translated by Cyril Edwards. Martlesham: The Boydell Press.
Malcor, Linda A. (2000). Merlin and the Pendragon: King Arthur's 'Draconarius.' *Arthuriana* 10(1), *Essays on Merlin*, 3–13.
Malory, Thomas, Cooper, Helen (ed.) (2008). *Le Morte D'arthur.* Oxford: Oxford University Press.
Mann, Nicholas R. (2004). *Energy Secrets of Glastonbury Tor.* Green Magic.
—— & Philippa Glasson (2007). *The Star Temple of Avalon.* UK: The Temple Publications.
—— (2010). *The Red and White Springs of Avalon.* UK: The Temple Publications.
Marinatos, Nanno (2010). Light and Darkness and Ancient Greek Cosmography. *Light and Darkness in Ancient Greek Myth and Religion.* Lexington, MA: Lexington Books.
Marlan, Stanton (2008). *The Black Sun: The Alchemy and Art of Darkness.* Texas: A&M University Press.
Martirosyan, Hamlet (2013). *The Land of the Celestial Gates, from Lion Character in the Petrogliphs of Syuniq and the Ancient World.* Edit Print Publishing.
Massey, Gerald (1883). *The Natural Genesis* Vol II. London: Williams & Norgate.
Matthews, Caitlín & John Matthews (2019). *The Lost Book of the Grail: The Sevenfold Path of the Grail and the Restoration of the Faery Accord.* New York: Inner Traditions.
Matthews, John (ed.) (1984). *At the Table of the Grail.* London: Arcana.
Mathisen, David Warner (2014). *The Undying Stars.* Beowulf Books.
McCarthy, Josephine (2017). *The Book of Gates: A Magical Translation.* Quareia Publishing.
McHardy, Stuart (2002). *The Quest for the Nine Maidens.* Luath Press Ltd.
Mela, Pomponius, F E Romer (trans.) (1998). *Pomponius Mela's Description of the World.* University of Michigan.
Michell, John (1990). *New Light on the Ancient Mystery of Glastonbury.* Gothic Image.
—— (2008). *Dimensions of Paradise: Sacred Geometry, Ancient Science, and the Heavenly Order on Earth.* Rochester, VT: Inner Traditions.
—— (2013). *The New View Over Atlantis: The Essential Guide to Megalithic Science, Earth Mysteries, and Sacred Geometry.* New York: Red Wheel.
—— & Christine Rhone (2008). *Twelve-Tribe Nations: Sacred Number and the Golden Age.* Rochester, VT: Inner Traditions.

Monaghan, Patricia (2004). *The Encyclopaedia of Celtic Mythology and Folklore.* Facts on File.
Mortimer, Nigel (2005). *John Lydgate's* Fall of Princes: *Narrative Tragedy in Its Literary and Political Contexts.* Oxford, Oxford University Press.
Natawidjaja, D. H., A. Bachtiar, B. Endar, M. R. Daryono & A. S. Subandrio (2018). Evidences of Large pyramid-like structure predating 10,000 Year BP at Mount Padang, West Java, Indonesia: Applications of geological-geophysical methods to explore buried large archeological site.
Nennius (2000) *History of the Britons* (*Historia Brittonum*). Edited by J. A. Giles. In Parentheses Publications.
Nichols, Kelsey (2020). *Frith: An Authentic Celtic Divination Guide.* Hadean Press.
North, Richard (1997). *Heathen Gods in Old English Literature.* Cambridge University Press.
Oesterdiekhoff, Georg. (2008). Magic and animism in old religions: The relevance of sun cults in the world-view of traditional societies. *Croatian Journal of Ethnology and Folklore Research* 45, 43–66.
Palmer, Martin (2012). *Sacred Land: Decoding Britain's extraordinary past through its towns, villages and countryside.* Piatkus.
Partridge, Christopher (2016). Aleister Crowley on Drugs. *International Journal for the Study of New Religions* 7(2), 125–151.
Pearson, Nigel G. (2021). *A Ring Around The Moon: Witch Rites Revisited.* Troy Books.
Pennick, Nigel & Paul Devereux (1989). *Lines on the Landscape: Leys and Other Linear Enigmas.* Robert Hale Limited.
Pollington, Stephen (2011). *The Elder Gods: The Otherworld of Early England.* Anglo-Saxon Books.
Poultney, James Wilson (1959). *Bronze Tables of Iguvium.* Baltimore: American Philological Association.
Powys, John Cowper (2007). *A Glastonbury Romance.* London: Gerald Duckworth & Co.
Prince, Ruth & David Riches (2001). *The New Age in Glastonbury: The Construction of Religious Movements.* Berghahn Books.
Pyle, Howard (1913). *The Story of the Grail and the Passing of Arthur.* New York: Charles Scribner's Sons.
Ratz, Philip & Lorna Watts (2003). *Glastonbury: Myth & Archaeology.* Tempus Publishing.
Reedijk, Lenie (2018). *Sirius, the Star of the Maltese Temples.* Malet Books.
Reiche, Harald A. T. (1993). Heraclides' Three Soul-Gates: Plato Revised. *Transactions of the American Philological Association* (1974–2014) Vol. 123, 161–80. The Johns Hopkins University Press.
Richardson, Alan (2009). *Aleister Crowley and Dion Fortune: The Logos of the Aeon and the Shakti of the Age.* Llewellyn Publications.
Richmond, M. (1997). *Temple: Sirius.* Manasadeva Press.
Rebisse, Christian (2005). *Rosicrucian History and Mysteries.* Supreme Grand Lodge of the Ancient and Mystical Order Rosae Crucis.
Robb, Graham (2013). *The Ancient Paths.* London: Picador.
Roberts, Anthony (1977). *Atlantean Traditions in Ancient Britain.* London: Rider & Co.

—— (ed.) (1992). *Glastonbury: Ancient Avalon, New Jerusalem.* London: Rider & Co.
—— (1990) *From Atlantis to Avalon and Beyond: A Collection of Memorabilia.* Zodiac House Publications.
Robinson, M. (2009). Ardua et Astra: On the Calculation of the Dates of the Rising and Setting of Stars. *Classical Philology* 104(3), 354–375.
Ross, Anne (1967). *Pagan Celtic Britain: Studies in Iconography and Tradition.* London: Routledge and Keegan Paul.
Ruggles, Clive (2005). *Ancient Astronomy: An Encyclopedia of Cosmologies and Myth.* ABC-CLIO.
Salayová, Andrea (2018). Aspects of Temporality in Greek Magical Papyri. *Graeco-Latina Brunensia* 23(1), 181–194.
Schlemmer, Phyllis V. & Palden Jenkins (1996). *The Only Planet of Choice: Essential Briefings from Deep Space.* Gateway Books.
Scott, John (1981). '*An Early History of Glastonbury: An Edition, Translation and Study of William of Malmesbury's 'De Antiquitate Glastonie Ecclesie.*' Boydell Press.
Selby, John (2008). *Dion Fortune and her Inner Plane Contacts: Intermediaries in the Western Esoteric Tradition.* PhD thesis, University of Exeter.
Selling, Kim (1998). The Locus of the Sacred in the Celtic Otherworld. *Sydney Studies in Religion.*
Sjöö, Monica & Barbara Mor (1991). *The Great Cosmic Mother: Rediscovering the Religion of the Earth.* HarperCollins.
Slavin, Bridgette (2008). The Irish Birdman: Kingship and Liminality in *Buile Suibhne. Text and Transmission in Medieval Europe*, 17–45.
Spence, Lewis (1970). *The Mysteries of Britain.* London: Rider & Co.
Stahl, William Harris (trans.) (1990). *Macrobius: Commentary on the Dream of Scipio.* Columbia University Press.
Stewart, R. J. (2007). *The Well of Light: From Faery Healing to Earth Healing.* R. J. Stewart Books.
Stock, Lorraine Kochanske (2002). Civilization and Its Discontents: Cultural Primitivism and Merlin as a Wild Man in the 'Roman de Silence.' *Arthuriana* 12(1).
Strabo (1854). *The Geography of Strabo.* Translated by H. C. Hamilton & W. Falconer. London: Henry G Bohn.
Stratton-Kent, Jake (2010). *Geosophia: The Argo of Magic.* London: Scarlet Imprint.
Stukeley, William (1743). Abury, A Temple of the British Druids, With Some Others, Described. London: W. Innys, R. Manby, B. Dod, J. Brindley.
Sulistyowati, Dian & Aldo W. Foe (2021). Indonesia's Own 'Pyramid': The Imagined Past and Nationalism of Gunung Padang. *International Review of Humanities Studies* 6 (1), 125–137.
Tacitus Cornelius (1942). *The Annals.* Translated by Alfred John Church & William Jackson Brodribb, edited by Sara Bryant. New York: Random House Inc.
Taylor, Barry (2010). *A Pilgrim in Glastonbury.* Glastonbury: Abbey Press.
Taylor, Jeremy & Mark Taylor (2020). *A Ritual Landscape Considered: Cosmography and Anglo-Saxon Ship Burials.* https://arcanelandscape.com/arcane/wp-content/up-

loads/2020/12/A-Ritual-Landscape-Considered-J-Taylor-M-Taylor-v2-WEB.pdf
Taylor, Thomas (trans) (1917). *On the Cave of the Nymphs in the Thirteenth Book of the Odyssey; From the Greek of Porphyry.* London: John M. Watkins.
Tolkien, J. R. R. (1979). *Tree and Leaf; Smith of Wootton Major; The Homecoming of Beorhtnoth Beorhthelm's Son.* London: George Allen & Unwin.
Troyes, Chrétien (1991). *Arthurian Romances.* Translated by Carleton Caroll & William Kibler. London: Penguin.
Various (1991). *The East Yorkshire Village Book.* Countryside Books.
Voronov, Victor (ed) (2013). *Liber Nigri Solis.* Theion Publishing.
Waddell, John (2015). *Archaeology and Celtic Myth: An Exploration.* Dublin: Four Courts Press.
—— (2018). *Myth and Materiality.* Oxford: Oxbow Books.
Warren, William F. (2022). *Paradise Found: The Cradle of the Human Race at the North Pole.* Amsterdam: Fredonia Books.
Watts, Dorothy: Religion in Late Roman Britain: Forces of Change; Taylor & Francis (2002)
Weston, Jesse L. (2011). *From Ritual to Romance: Folklore, Magic and The Holy Grail.* Dover Publications.
Weston, Paul (2010). *Avalonian Aeon.* Glastonbury: Avalonian Aeon Publications.
White, Gordon (2016). *Star.Ships: A Prehistory of the Spirits.* London: Scarlet Imprint.
—— (2022). *Ani.Mystic: Encounters with a Living Cosmos.* London: Scarlet Imprint.
Wilbert, Johannes (2004). The Order of Dark Shamans among the Warao. *In Darkness and Secrecy: The Anthropology of Assault Sorcery and Witchcraft in Amazonia*, Edited by Neil L. Whitehead & Robin Wright. Durham NC: Duke University Press.
Williams, John & Iolo Morganwg. (2004). *Barddas: A Collection of Original Documents, Illustrative of the Theology Wisdom, and Usages of the Bardo-Druidic Systems of the Isle of Britain.* Boston, MA: Weiser Books.
Williams, Mary (1990). *Glastonbury and Britain: A Study in Patterns.* Research into Lost Knowledge Organisation Trust.
Williams, Rowan (2020). *The Book of Taliesin: Poems of Warfare and Praise in an Enchanted Britain.* Penguin.
Wilson, Robert Anton (1991). *Cosmic Trigger 1: The Final Secret of The Illuminati.* Scottsdale, AZ: New Falcon Publications.
Withrington, John Kenneth Brookes (1991). *The Death of King Arthur and the Legend of his Survival in Sir Thomas Malory's 'Le Morte Darthur' and other Late Medieval Texts of the Fifteenth Century.* PhD thesis, University of York.
Woodward, Roger D. (2006). *Indo-European Sacred Space: Vedic and Roman Cult.* Champaign IL: University of Illinois Press.
Woolley, Benjamin (2002). *The Queen's Conjuror.* London: Flamingo.
Worthen, T. D. (1995). The Pleiades and Hesperides: Finding parity with an astronomical key. *Vistas in Astronomy* 39(4), 539–545.
Young, Francis (2022). *Magic in Merlin's Realm: A History of Occult Politics in Britain.* Cambridge: Cambridge University Press.

index

Æcerbot ritual 37

A

Abiegnus, Mount 112, 228
Adoil 32
Adytum 43, 91, 94, 112, 113, 133, 140, 145, 147, 151, 169, 179, 182, 186, 193, 196, 199, 202, 205, 262
Akhet 42, 87
Albedo 77, 99, 104, 167, 189, 192
Albertus Magnus 58
Albus Lapis 115, 118, 120, 136, 151, 152
Alchemy xiii, 17, 28, 33, 58, 67, 68, 70, 81, 161
Alliterative *Morte Arthure* 86
alterity 95, 96, 123, 178, 192
Amangon, King 30, 31, 33, 34, 75, 78, 83, 85, 164
anabasis 43, 149, 178, 183, 209
ancestral dead 129, 138
Andania xiv
Anglesey 58, 61, 111
Annwn 43, 47, 49, 50, 51, 53, 55, 56, 57, 60, 64, 65, 76, 84, 86, 92, 98, 99, 102, 103, 112, 115, 123, 182, 185, 205, 207, 215, 228
Antares 47
Apuleius 172
  Apologia 172
Arawn 31, 47, 48, 51, 55, 57, 60, 64, 79, 92, 129, 207, 240
Arcturus 49, 57
Artemidorus 63, 64
Arthurian tradition 5, 14, 48, 67, 78, 102, 127
Arthur, King 5, 11, 12, 13, 14, 15, 19, 48, 49, 55, 57, 64, 78, 79, 80, 81, 82, 84, 85, 86, 92, 97, 125, 126, 127, 133, 147, 207, 215, 223, 244
Ashmole, Elias 33
Athelstan, King 33
Atiedian Brethren 38
Atlantis xiii, 18, 19, 20, 31, 39, 57
awen 70, 98, 102, 208

B

ba 87
bandruí 64, 95
Beckery 14, 49, 126, 147, 224
Bede 59
  Historia ecclesiastica gentis Anglorum 59
Belinus, King 39
Bere, Richard (Abbot) 30, 243
Bernard of Treviso 28
Blake, William 17
Blavatsky, Helena Petrovna 58, 71
Bond, Frederick Bligh xviii, 6, 92
Book of Gates, The 42
Book of Taliesin 12, 55
Book of the Dun Cow 31
Boötes 49

Brewant-rriyén 99
Bride's Hill 126
Bride's Well 126, 127, 223, 224
Brigid 16, 95
Brigid, Saint 14, 59, 65, 126, 243
Bronze Age 41, 48
Buckton, Alice Mary 5, 238

C

caduceus 23, 46, 70
caerdroia 10, 253
Canis Major 47
Caradoc of Llancarfan 12
Cartimandua xvii
Celtic Christianity xiii, 8, 16
Celtic culture xiii, xv, xvii, 37, 41, 49
Celtic religion xvii, xiii, 16, 53, 62, 207
Chaldean Oracles 24
Chalice Hill 10, 24, 46, 47, 67, 127, 133, 261
Chalice Well 5, 7, 8, 71, 127, 134, 236, 237, 238
Chapel Perilous xii, 14
chora 146, 154, 192, 197
Christ 5, 18, 49, 67, 68, 164
Christianity xiii, 10, 16, 18, 65, 127
Chrysopoeia 150
Circe 42, 74, 111
Citrinas 77, 100, 104, 167, 190
Clavis Inferni 40
Collen, Saint 54, 55
Collyer, Alison 6
Colquhoun, Ithell 24, 26
Compitalia 41
Coon, Robert 17, 24
Corpus Aurora 99, 100, 104, 186, 188, 193, 203
Corpus Lux 100, 104, 189, 191, 203
Corpus Noctis 98, 103, 177, 181, 203
Corpus Tenebris 101, 104, 194, 196, 203
Crowley, Aleister xiv, xix, 50, 87, 161, 184
Cyprian, Saint 40

D

Dactyls 42, 66, 154
Dame du Lac 81, 83, 84
De Boron, Robert 79
  Estoire de Merlin 79
Dee, John xiii, 5, 33, 49, 68, 81
dei otiosus 161
Delphinas, Nicolas Barnaud 28
Devil 162, 164, 165
Diodorus Siculus 62
directionality 25, 35, 36, 39, 40, 46, 91, 112, 152
divination 38, 61, 64, 192, 206
  ornithomancy 38, 206
Dod Lane 24
Domsteinene stone circle 35
dowsing xvi, 121, 128, 134, 140, 197
Draco 19, 30, 45, 46, 48, 50, 51, 69, 83, 165
dracontia 58
Dragon Meridians 25, 26
Druidry xiii, 11, 16, 18, 19, 47, 58, 59, 60, 62, 63, 72
Druids xiii, xvii, 7, 17, 18, 58, 59, 60, 61, 62, 63, 71, 80, 207
Dunstan, Abbot xiii, 13, 33, 245

E

Eachtra an Mhadra Mhaoil 84
Egypt 16, 18, 32, 36, 50
Egyptian Great Year 51, 195
Egyptian theology 25, 40, 49, 54, 72, 87, 161, 167
Eireks Saga Víðförla 57
Eiríks saga rauða 65
Eleusis xiv, xix, 60, 183
Elucidation 30, 31, 34, 78, 83, 85
ennead xv, 64, 65, 92, 94, 96, 97, 202, 205, 207, 215
entheogens xix
  fly agaric xix
  soma xix, 69, 115, 181, 187
Ephorus of Cyme 38
Epidaurus 33
Estoire del Saint Graal 30
Excalibur 11, 69, 84, 125

F

Faerie 31, 51, 53, 54, 55, 56, 80, 81, 82, 85, 86, 164
Fall 57, 86, 163, 164
Fear Doirich 82
feathers 62, 134, 156, 180, 181, 187, 190, 195

fey 52, 53, 55, 56, 92, 94, 115, 129, 184, 208
filid 207, 208
Fionn mac Cumhail 86
Fjölsvinnsmál 65
Fortune, Dion 5, 6, 18, 47, 51, 58, 70, 78, 80, 81, 83, 92, 93, 102, 112, 133
The Arthurian Formula 78
The Cosmic Doctrine 6
Fraternity of the Inner Light 6, 78
frith 206
Fuxi 23, 25, 28, 40, 154
fylgia 116, 117

G

Gaia xii, xvi, 66, 161, 164, 167
Gajamo-rriyén 98
gallisenae 64
genii locorum 41, 92, 96, 128, 130, 197, 205, 209
Geoffrey of Monmouth 5, 11, 64, 79, 86
Historia regum Britanniae 11
Vita Merlini 64, 79, 80
Geomancy xiii, xvi, xviii, 14, 19, 25, 28, 32
Gerald of Wales 12, 79, 208
Gildas 12, 80
Gipsy Lane 133
Glastonbury Abbey xviii, 10, 13, 18, 19, 24, 125, 127, 244, 245, 246
St Mary's chapel xviii, 19
Glastonbury Zodiac xviii, 20
Goddess spirituality 78
Gog 13, 47, 99, 128, 137, 138, 139, 235
Golden Dawn 72
Goodchild, Dr John Arthur xvii, 126, 127, 223
The Light of the West xvii, 126
Grant, Kenneth 24, 50, 164
Typhonian Order 50, 164, 165
Graves, Robert xvii
Greek Magical Papyri 50
Green Knight 73
Guinevere, Queen 12, 13, 81, 82, 85, 244
Gwyn ap Nudd 55, 57, 79, 84, 86, 92, 240
Gwythyr ap Greidawl 47, 48, 84

H

Hades 42, 43, 44, 49, 51, 51, 56, 76, 92
hama 116
hamr 116, 117
healing xi, xv, 16, 23, 33, 57, 60, 64, 65, 66, 67, 68, 85, 94, 113, 207, 215, 216, 237
Heb Sed 32, 72, 88, 183
Hecataeus of Abdera 58
Helgakvida Hundingsbana 65
heliolatry xiii, 23, 41
henosis 70, 113, 115
Heraclides Ponticus 43, 116
Hesperides 45
Hieronesos 111, 124, 198, 222
hieros gamos 27, 60, 76, 85
Holy Hill xviii, xix, 12, 92, 112, 113, 130, 133, 146, 148, 150, 151, 152, 175, 176, 178, 182, 186, 188, 190, 192, 193, 195, 196, 198, 203, 204, 205, 215, 230, 257, 262
Holy Thorn 5, 125, 128, 226
Homer 42, 43, 57
Horus 15, 40, 48, 50, 66, 88, 89, 165, 184
hugr 116, 117
Hvergelmir 34
Hygromanteia 40
Hysterema 164

I

Iguvine Tablets 38
Île de Sein 64, 111
imbas 207, 208, 209
immram 198
interoception 119
Iron Age 8, 35, 38, 63, 111

J

jálkr 166
John of Glastonbury 14, 125
Chronica 14
Jörmungandr 24
Joseph of Arimathea xiii, 5, 13, 18, 30, 67, 68, 81, 85, 125, 226, 243, 244

K

ka 87, 116
katabasis 55, 104, 149, 170, 178, 183, 209
Kelley, Edward xiii, 5, 33, 68
kingship 37, 48, 49, 55, 57, 72, 73, 74, 75, 76, 77, 85, 89

L

labyrinth xix, 10, 253
Lady of the Lake 81, 82, 83, 125
Lancelot 31, 81, 85
Lancelot-Grail cycle 31
lapis exilis xiii, 28, 30, 33, 68, 69, 70, 77, 78, 81, 104, 113, 185, 215
Lapis Viridis 115, 118, 121, 151, 178, 181, 186, 190, 195, 204, 211
lares 35, 41, 154
Layamon 86
  Brut 86
Lemegeton 40
Lemnos xiv
ley lines xvi, 17
  St Mary line 25, 27
  St Michael line 24, 25, 26
libations 129, 134, 141, 142, 143, 144, 155, 157, 158, 159, 177, 185, 189, 194
Life of St Collen 54, 55
Lludd and Llefelys 26
Lucifer 67, 68, 69, 79, 99, 188
Lung Mai 25
Lydgate, John 49, 57, 86
  Fall of Princes 57, 86

M

Mabinogion 48, 65
Macrobius 44, 45
Magna Mater xii, xv, 27, 30, 34, 41, 48, 52, 66, 78, 83, 85, 94, 112, 113, 138, 140, 154, 164, 167, 185, 202, 215
Magog 13, 47, 99, 128, 137, 138, 139, 140, 232, 234, 235
Malory, Thomas 11, 86
Maltwood, Katherine xviii, 6, 20, 50, 215
Mary Magdalene 14, 126
Matrona 42, 64, 78, 83, 92, 112, 123, 197, 201, 202, 203, 205, 211, 215
Matronae 92, 97, 134, 140, 141, 154, 155, 157, 158, 159, 168, 177, 185, 189, 194
Matter of Britain 18, 80
Melchizedek 17, 18, 80
Melkin 30, 243
Melwas, King 12
Merlin xiii, 17, 18, 26, 33, 49, 57, 58, 70, 78, 79, 80, 81, 82, 83, 84, 85, 86, 92, 97, 207
metempsychosis xiii, 31, 42, 53, 56, 60, 72, 77, 92, 93, 97, 113, 137, 183, 196, 215, 216
Michell, John xviii, 6, 14, 17, 19, 20, 24
midsummer 37, 39, 44, 47, 87, 98, 99, 160, 207
midwinter 36, 37, 39, 44, 46, 87, 100, 101, 104, 160, 162, 207
mighty dead 128
Milky Way 43, 44, 45, 48, 51, 52, 87, 149, 207
Mímisbrunnr 34
Moon 25, 39, 47, 48, 69, 160, 162, 171
Mor, Barbara xvii, 164
Mordred 82, 86
Morgen 42, 57, 58, 64, 86
Mórrígan xvii
Morrígna 65, 95
Myrddin 26, 79

N

Nāga 25
nekyia 212
Nennius 80, 84
  Historia Brittonum 80
Neolithic xi, xvii, xix, 7, 8, 10, 44, 46, 214
Nephilim 80
New Age movement 6, 15
Newgrange 37, 44
Nigredo 50, 77, 98, 103, 104, 167, 181, 182, 184, 185, 186
Nimue 82, 83
Nine maidens cult 66, 95, 215
Ningišzida 23
Noctifer 69, 101
North Star 30, 48, 49, 50, 69
Nuwa 23, 25, 40, 154

O

Oaken Path 126, 137, 139, 140, 146, 157, 175, 198, 205, 235
Oculi Magicka 115, 120, 123, 124, 125, 128, 129, 130, 133, 134, 135, 139, 140, 146, 149, 152, 175, 176, 178, 190, 191, 192, 193, 195
Óðinn 52, 83, 166
Old Grey Magician 82
ophiolatry xiii, 23

Ophiuchus 47
Orion 47
Orphic egg 23
Orphism 161
Osiris 30, 47, 48, 73, 87, 88, 163, 183, 184
Ouroboros 24

P

Pagan's Hill 8
Paleolithic 7, 72
paresthesia 119
Paris, Matthew 39
  Schema Britanniae (map) 39
Pendragon 19, 30, 48, 49, 50, 81, 82, 83
philosopher's stone 17, 28, 33, 68, 70, 81, 101, 104
Phoenix 28, 51, 92, 101, 184, 195, 215
pilgrimage xiv, xviii, 122, 125, 134, 166, 172, 240, 254
Plato 18, 19, 31, 42, 43, 114, 167
  Critias 19 *Phaedo* 114 *Republic* 42
  Timaeus 42, 114
Pleiades 36, 45, 46, 48, 65
Polaris 30, 48, 51, 204
Polden Hills 126, 147
Pole, Wellesley Tudor 18, 127
Pomponius Mela 53, 60, 72, 74
  Description of the World 60
Pontis Vallum (Ponter's Ball) 8, 125, 147
Porphyry of Tyre 43, 44
Powys, John Cowper 6
  A Glastonbury Romance 6
Preiddeu Annwfn 55, 64
prophesy xv, 30, 57, 65, 66, 80, 86, 103, 243
Pyramid Texts 66, 88

Q

Queens 92, 93, 94, 97, 105, 112, 130, 146, 147, 148, 149, 154, 155, 175, 178, 186, 190, 195, 199, 201, 206, 207, 209, 211
  Aureate Queen 100, 143, 147, 148, 149, 150, 157, 158, 176, 189, 190, 191, 192, 193, 200, 204, 206
  Dark Queen 98, 99, 100, 101, 141, 142, 147, 148, 149, 154, 155, 156, 176, 177, 178, 181, 182, 187, 200, 204, 206, 207
  Pale Queen 99, 101, 126, 142, 148, 149, 150, 156, 157, 176, 185, 186, 187, 188, 201, 204
  Roseate Queen 98, 101, 143, 148, 149, 150, 158, 159, 176, 178, 179, 194, 195, 196, 200, 204, 207
Quotidian Meditations 118, 148, 155, 156, 157, 158, 175, 177, 185, 189, 190, 194, 211

R

Raziel 68
Red Serpent 27, 28, 29, 30, 32, 70, 94, 98, 100, 112, 115, 117, 134, 135, 145, 148, 150, 151, 152, 154, 175, 176, 192, 204
Red Spring 12, 28, 32, 33, 34, 47, 67, 92, 101, 113, 133, 135, 136, 140, 145, 150, 175, 176, 177, 189, 197, 199, 205, 236, 245, 261
resurrection 49, 51, 52, 63, 69, 73, 77, 99, 102, 161, 163, 183
Rich Company 85
Rigel 47
Rites of Lustration 145, 149, 175, 178, 186, 190, 195, 197
Robb, Graham 47
Roman religion 38
Round Table 48, 82, 85
Rubedo 51, 77, 101, 104, 167, 195
Rubeus Lapis 115, 118, 119, 136, 151
Russell, Geoffrey xix, 10

S

Samhain 47, 73, 98
Samo-rriyēn 100
Samothrace xiv, 63, 65
Saturnalia 41
schethiya 68, 69
Scorpius 47
Second Book of Enoch 32, 51
seership 53, 82, 207, 208
seiðrmaðr 166
Set 48, 50, 56, 82, 88, 162, 165, 183, 184
sex magick 37
shamanism xvi, 16, 40, 72, 208
sídh 31

Sido-bremo-rriyėn 101
Sirius 31, 36, 41, 45, 46, 47, 50, 51, 56, 104, 183, 184, 195
Sjöö, Monica xvii, 164
Sokar (Festival) 47, 87, 88
Sol Niger 46, 50, 51, 104, 156, 167, 181, 182, 183, 184, 185, 186
Solomon 31, 68
solstice 37, 38, 39, 41, 43, 44, 45, 46, 47, 48, 52, 65, 72, 87, 88, 89, 91, 96, 98, 99, 100, 101, 122, 127, 137, 147, 149, 162, 166, 169, 206, 207, 225
Sororitas Avalonis 57, 64, 65, 86, 95, 102, 138, 139, 202, 211, 215
spïrïd-karant 131
spïrïd-tud 122, 128
St John's Church 30, 31, 243
St Michael 10, 24, 25, 26, 147, 245, 262
Stobaeus, Joannes 48
Strabo 39, 61, 63, 64
Stukeley, William 58
synkatathesis 129

T
Tacitus 61, 74
Taliesin 12, 55, 64, 65, 70, 80, 98, 102
terma xiii, 178
terra Adamica 77, 117
Terra Mater xvi, 37, 73, 74, 76, 78, 85, 92, 95, 101, 214
theandry xi, xv, xix, 152, 191, 192
The Book of Dunstan 33
Theodosius, Emperor 10
theomania 102, 103
Theosophy xiii, 53
Thuban 30, 48, 50, 69, 165
Tír fo Thoinn 53
Tír na nÓg 53, 57
Tír Shorcha 53
Tolkien, J. R. R. 56
Tuatha Dé Danann 37, 102
tutelary spirits 33, 35, 40, 41, 128, 154, 169, 178
Twelve Hides 13, 14
tylwyth teg 51, 56, 83, 137, 171, 182
tzohar 68, 69

U
úlfhéðnar xix
Umbra Animae 53, 114, 117, 118, 119, 120, 121, 123, 124, 129, 130, 139, 152, 168, 172, 173, 178, 179, 181, 186, 187, 188, 191, 192, 195, 197, 199
Urðarbrunnr 34
Ursa Major 14, 48, 49, 51, 204
Ursa Minor 30, 48, 51, 204

V
vættir 35
valkyrja 65
vama marg 165
Venus 69
Vortigern, King 26, 80, 81
Vulgate Cycle 31, 79, 86

W
Wearyall Hill 14, 46, 47, 101, 125, 126, 147, 224, 226, 227
Wellhouse Lane 133, 135
Well Maidens 33, 34, 74, 78, 83, 85, 136, 164
Well of Souls 68, 69
White River of Tears 31
White Serpent 27, 28, 29, 30, 32, 70, 78, 94, 99, 101, 112, 115, 117, 135, 145, 148, 150, 151, 152, 154, 175, 176, 192, 204
White Spring 12, 28, 32, 33, 34, 67, 78, 92, 101, 113, 133, 134, 135, 136, 140, 145, 150, 175, 176, 177, 185, 194, 197, 199, 205, 239, 240, 243, 245, 261
Wicca xvi, xvii
Wild Hunt 47, 51, 55, 133, 207
William of Malmesbury 5, 12
Witches' Sabbat xix, 207

Y
Yggdrasil 34, 35
Yngvi-freyr 55, 57

AVALON WORKING

Published by Scarlet Imprint in May 2024 in a limited hardback edition comprising 900 copies bound in verdant green cloth, and 30 slipcased copies hand-bound in full green goatskin.